# **OUT** SPOKEN

# OUT SPOKEN

## PERSPECTIVES ON
## QUEER IDENTITIES

edited by
WES D. PEARCE and JEAN HILLABOLD

U OF R PRESS

Printed and bound in Canada at Friesens.
The text of this book is printed on 100% post-consumer recycled paper with earth-friendly vegetable-based inks.

COVER AND TEXT DESIGN: Duncan Campbell, University of Regina Press.

COVER PHOTOS: ( l to r) *Untitled* (detail), Ariwasabi/Veer; *Portrait of Confident Young Man* (detail), stocklite/Veer; *Woman with Pensive Expression* (detail), Ocean Photography/Veer; *Headshot of a Serious Young Man* (detail), Ocean Photography/Veer; *Grandmother* (detail), kuzma/Veer; *Native American Male Model* (detail), Juanmonino/iStockphoto.

**Library and Archives Canada Cataloguing in Publication**

Out spoken : perspectives on queer identities / edited by Wes D. Pearce and Jean Hillabold.

(University of Regina publications, ISSN 1480-0004 ; 30)
Includes bibliographical references.
Issued also in electronic format.
ISBN 978-0-88977-280-9

1. Queer theory. 2. Gays--Identity. 3. Homosexuality—Social aspects.
4. Homosexuality—Psychological aspects. I. Pearce, Wes D., 1965–
II. Hillabold, Jean Roberta, 1951– III. Series: University of Regina publications ; 30

HQ76.25.O98 2013          306.76'6          C2013-901814-X

10  9  8  7  6  5  4  3  2  1

**U OF R PRESS**

University of Regina Press
University of Regina
Regina, Saskatchewan, Canada, S4S 0A2
tel: (306) 585-4758  fax: (306) 585-4699
e-mail: canadian.plains@uregina.ca  web: www.uofrpress.ca

This book has been published with the aid of a grant from the University of Regina President's Fund.

The University of Regina Press acknowledges the support of the Creative Industry Growth and Sustainability program, made possible through funding provided to the Saskatchewan Arts Board by the Government of Saskatchewan through the Ministry of Parks, Culture, and Sport.

We also acknowledge the financial support of the Government of Canada through the Canada Book Fund for our publishing activities.

 Canadian Heritage  Patrimoine canadien   Government of Saskatchewan   University of Regina   FSC  Mixed Sources  Cert no. SW-COC-001271  © 1996 FSC

# CONTENTS

# Foreword

MADELEINE MORRIS

Writings like the ones contained in this book present us with the dilemma of historicity. Heidegger and many philosophers that came after him argued that we haven't a hope in hell of understanding the experience of others: time, space and the lack of an embodied experience precludes it. The bridge of language is, admittedly, a rickety one.

As a writer, I have to trust in language, no matter how flawed a tool it might be. It has been fashionable in the last few decades to be suspicious of language, and rightly so. We have interrogated the baggage that it carries with it, the hegemonies it communicates, perpetuates and seeks to legitimize. Yet language still remains the most reliable, most accessible pathway into realities other than our own. So, as suspect as it might be, it still serves us admirably as a vehicle by which we can delve into the myriad spaces offered in the essays in this book.

This is a collection of artifacts: fragments of Queer spaces in time, culture, and gender. Since I belong to the approximately white and approximately straight camp, and my field is creative writing, it's fair to say I'm a tourist in the worlds offered up in this book. But these worlds are stories, the intensely personal narratives of either the writers, or the subjects, or both. So it's important to point out that, straight or queer, female or male, no matter what ethnicity we spring from, we are all tourists in the lived experiences of others.

In their 1996 introduction to *Queer Studies: A Lesbian, Gay, Bisexual, & Transgender Anthology*, Brett Beemyn and Mickey Eliason warned that "lesbian, gay, bisexual and transgendered people are so diverse that no one anthology could hope to include all possible perspectives."[1] Today, a statement like that seems ridiculous. And yet, in mainstream culture, non-normative sexualities are still represented as stereotypical or archetypal figures.

We live in a world made sticky with generalities. The news, television, movies offer us up a gray, sludgy stream of exemplars for easy consumption. We are faced with a quandary: information chunking makes cognition possible. Races, genders, and groups joined together by common interests have clawed back considerable power from the dominant players in our society—inarguably, to their benefit. But this solidarity is a double-edged sword, because it also often serves to erase the individual in favour of the group.

These days, we have an appetite for extremes. We demand that all our stories either end well and happily or, failing this, end catastrophically. We want a wedding—or we want someone to die tragically. Our ability to tolerate anything in between seems to have eroded. This is especially true for Queer stories.

A number of the chapters in this anthology explore individuals in their historical context, bringing singular experiences to the fore. They illustrate the struggles and strategies to survive intact, both physically and psychologically, in what to us, now, must seem incredibly hostile environments. They move us beyond simply pitying the poor gay actor trying to make his way during the Spanish Inquisition to a sincere admiration for the splendid creativity inherent in that act of survival.

With the recent rise in popularity of gay and lesbian historical fiction, it might be easy to look on these real lived experiences and wish for less compromised outcomes. Wouldn't it have been nicer if Radclyffe Hall's heroine could have shrugged off her Judeo-Christian baggage and just come out? Wouldn't it be grand if Chinese students were all willing to actively and strenuously confront prejudice against non-heteronormative sexualities? If Shakespeare could have married the man he loved and Whitman had celebrated the wedding with a different poem? Wouldn't it be fairer if the gay high school teacher didn't have a moment of sleeplessness, wondering how his gayness is perceived by students and colleagues?

And yet most of the writings in this book present and, at times, revel in the compromises that people make in order to negotiate their way through the world, while still retaining a sense of self. That, in my view, makes this collection of essays not only valuable, but also useful. They serve to remind us of what real outcomes look like. They challenge our rather pathetic need to "Hollywood-ize" all our stories.

In the last 30 years, mainstream media slowly stopped casting every queer character as suspect or villainous. Political correctness has taken over and insists that every gay or lesbian character be, somehow, heroic. They have, with few exceptions, gone from stand-ins for the dangers that lie beyond the pale to the poster children for an age of tolerance. Neither extreme is even vaguely representative of the lived experiences of most gay, lesbian, bi or transgendered individuals.

Whether faced with physical threat, social vilification or professional alienation, the individuals in these pages have taken existing social matrixes and shaped them to the purpose of cementing their own identities—this is what is at the heart of these stories for me. In reality, for most of us, there are and always have been imperfect, middle ways. Although they are regularly despised, I would argue that inherent in these compromises, these negotiations, lurks a vast art form: this is how we make it through.

**NOTE**

1    Beemyn, B., and M. Eliason (eds.). 1996. *Queer Studies: A Lesbian, Gay, Bisexual, and Transgender Anthology.* New York: New York University Press.

# Acknowledgements

This volume would not have been possible were it not for the University of Regina Press (formerly Canadian Plains Research Center Press) and in particular then publications manager Brian Mlazgar, who approached us with the idea of celebrating five years of the University of Regina Queer Initiative Speakers Series, who demonstrated amazing patience as we unilaterally shifted deadlines and in all matter of attention and detail helped shepherd the book along. Much thanks as well to Donna Grant and the rest of the incredible University of Regina Press team who have made the process quite painless.

Further thanks to the vision and foresight of Dr. Alan Cahoon and Dr. Stephen McClatchie who spearheaded the formation of the University of Regina Queer Initiative. This volume is evidence of the good that can happen when people see a need and act accordingly.

Much thanks to all of the contributors to this anthology—your scholarship, creativity and commitment is much appreciated and a huge thank-you as well for having agreed to participate in the Speakers Series in the first place. A special mention as well to those who, for a variety of reasons, presented as part of the series but who are not represented in the volume; over the years the contributions of Charity Marsh, Darci Anderson, Troni Grande, Krista Baliko, Carla Blakley, Laurie Sykes Tottenham, and Gary Varro greatly enriched the series.

Finally, a special thanks to Mirtha and Brett, who have been incredibly supportive during this entire process.

# Introduction

WES D. PEARCE AND JEAN HILLABOLD

In 2007, the University of Regina Queer Initiative (URQI) developed the In and Out Speakers Series with the goal of providing a platform for the presentation of gay, lesbian, bisexual, transgender, queer (GLBTQ) research and creative work. Participants in the series have been faculty members, graduate students and guests from local, provincial and national communities. Some of the material presented has been based on the subjective reality of lives lived outside the cultural norm, while some has been more research-based. The inclusive approach of the series has provided speakers with a safe and welcoming place to air exciting new research, to work through ideas for articles that were "almost there" but needed supportive feedback, or to introduce already-published work to a wider audience.

The work explored in the series has covered an astonishingly diverse range of ideas, positions and subject areas: biology, popular culture (including analyses of Madonna, music videos, and the television programs *The L Word* and *Dexter*), history, literary theory, textual analysis, curriculum development and personal growth. Styles of presentation have been as diverse as the titles and topics themselves: readings from new plays, illustrated lectures, personal narratives, performances and a song or two!

We were thrilled when Brian Mlazgar, representing the Canadian Plains Research Center Press (now the University of Regina Press), invited us to edit a set of articles to celebrate the fifth anniversary of the Speakers Series. This collection of printed words can't capture the excitement of live presentations, but it enables readers who couldn't be there to get a taste of the ideas and works presented as part of the series.

*Out Spoken: Perspectives on the Creation and Reception of Queer Identities* is not a "best of" collection, nor is it the "complete (but abridged) collection." It is a compilation of favourite pieces, chosen by authors who have been speakers in the series. When our call first went out, we weren't sure what, if anything, we would receive from our colleagues, but we have been extremely pleased with their generous response. This collection represents the spirit of the series: the pieces are diverse, multi/interdisciplinary, provocative and passionate. Our one regret is that, for a variety of reasons (including time and the ephemeral nature of some presentations), not everyone who has made a valuable contribution to the series has been included in the collection.

That being said, as we reread and considered the articles before us, we were surprised to discover a common theme. Every article, regardless of the primary disciplinary lens or topic at hand, eventually explores the complex, ongoing negotiation of public and private identity(ies). Not every piece in this collection deals explicitly with "queer" identities (or "unqueer" disguises), but the formation of individual and collective identity has emerged as an important subtext of the anthology.

As a result of this revelation, the anthology has been organized into four sections. The discussion of identity moves from the, at times, very conscious creation and awareness of public identities in Part I to essays focused on discovering (and at times refining or even redefining) one's own identity in Part II to writings focussed on the creation of the identity in and of the public sphere in Part III. The book closes in Part IV with two essays examining the private act of writing and the author's negotiation of this personal act with the reading public. While we have chosen to organize this collection around these issues of identity, we hope that readers will understand that the essays in this anthology are about so much more than identity and identity politics in our contemporary world.

We are not only editors of the collection. We have also been speakers in the series, and since we have included our own pieces in the collection, we agreed that a Foreword should be written by an "outside reader": someone who is not a contributor and has not been involved in the Speakers Series. Jean first discovered the work of Madeleine Morris in an online writers' forum more than a decade ago, and first met her in person at a conference in 2011. We invited her to read the articles (we had to date) as a work-in-progress and write a response. Madeleine accepted this somewhat daunting challenge, and we are proud to include her Foreword, which speaks for itself.

### NEGOTIATING PUBLIC PERSONA(S)

The essays in this section reflect and comment upon historic and, unfortunately, contemporary efforts of "deviant" individuals to negotiate a complex and (at times) dangerous truce between a public and a private identity. Inevitably, this compartmentalization of public life and private life, whether imposed by oneself or by others, leads to a duality in which some part of the self (usually the queer part) remains hidden while the public (usually the non-queer, "socially-acceptable part") is offered for public consumption.

In his essay, "Being Green: Sex and Tadpoles in the Drama of Juan Rana," Jes Battis examines the overlooked but fascinating history of Cosmo Pérez, the acclaimed actor in seventeenth-century Spain who (along with his stage persona Juan Rana) negotiated a complex but surprisingly open life as a sexual deviant. Royal patronage helped to protect the actor from church and state law, but Pérez, quite consciously, manipulates his own persona. By adopting the stage name "Rana," Pérez creates "markers of self," which situates Juan Rana outside cultural and societal norms but allows for the relatively peaceful life of Cosmo Pérez.

In her essay, "The Christian Martyr and the Pagan Witness in *The Well of Loneliness*," Jean Hillabold provides a close reading of Radclyffe Hall's seminal work, highlighting the moments of personal and public tragedy borne by Hall's protagonist, Stephen Gordon. Most, if not all, of Stephen's personal anguish and deepening crises are brought about by the conflict between her sense of self and the only public role available to her as a member of a "deviant" community. Valerie Seymour, the "pagan witness" of the title, seems perplexed by Stephen's inability to function as a healthy, whole individual, and suggests that Stephen could become more like herself: "supposing you could bring the two sides of your nature into some sort of friendly amalgamation." Ultimately, Stephen is unable to reconcile her private self with the public self expected of her. Her resulting isolation strengthens her belief that martyrdom is her fate.

In their essay, "Chinese University Students' Commitment to Social Justice and Their Willingness to Confront Sexual Orientation Prejudice," Don Cochrane and Jinjie Wang explore this idea of private/public identity in relation to their study of social policy issues and sexual minorities. In a brief historical overview, they explain that until the fall of the Qing Dynasty in 1911, Chinese society "tolerated and, at times, even encouraged same-sex eroticism," but, since then, homosexuality in China has been viewed as immoral and homosexual acts criminalized. Within this cultural context, both authors hypothesized that the Chinese students who participated in the study would be considerably less liberal in their views towards sexual minorities than participants in similar studies in North America/Western Europe.

However, the opposite proved to be the case: participants indicated strong sympathy (if not empathy) for sexual minorities. This private identity/moral position became less stable and more subjective when participants were asked about their willingness to intervene in the presence of homophobic actions. There are numerous reasons for participants to become less liberal, at least in public, as their constructed identities and those of others become more exposed, and when a public statement makes public conflict more likely. It should be noted that many people, and not just the students in this survey, have expressed fear of intervening in public bullying or abuse in various forms and that many students in the study may well fear being considered social dissidents if this intervention become public knowledge.

In "'I Won't Discuss Who I'm Dating:' Same-Sex Celebrity Gossip as Social Control," Wes D. Pearce presents the "birth" of nineteenth-century tabloid journalism as a product of a puritanical American middle class, which was growing increasingly repulsed and yet fascinated with the notion of celebrity. As the cult of American celebrity grew, so too did the notions that American celebrity, and American culture, should align with the values of "middle America." As a result, gossip around celebrity sexuality (and, more often than not, same-sex celebrity gossip) emerged and continues to be understood as a very effective means by which gossipmongers are able to manipulate the public (non-queer) and private (queer) personas of celebrities, regardless of actual sexual orientation. Same-sex celebrity gossip is typically associated with major Hollywood stars, but Pearce further suggests that same-sex celebrity gossip has also been effective in marginalizing and ghettoizing Broadway actors.

### NEGOTIATING SELF (SELVES)

The essays that appear in this section are the most personal, and in many ways, the most private of the essays in the anthology. Each of the authors shares with the reader powerful glimpses into the challenges and the celebrations that they have experienced as they work, or help others work, through this complex navigation of self. These essays vividly highlight Eve Sedgwick's argument that "coming out" is not a one-time event and that negotiating and constructing the self is an ongoing, challenging process.

The poetic writing found in Kelly Handerek's play "Small Boy DREAMS" is just one of the highly theatrical devices that he uses to lure the reader into his emotionally powerful scenes of blossoming love and self-knowledge. Handerek's play, which so eloquently captures the joy, the fear and, at times, the awkward pain of discovering another "just like you," is not simply a "boy meets boy" story. Rather, glimpses and flashes of both discreetly private and brazenly public moments are (re)presented in various forms, plot lines, characters and outcomes. Handerek deconstructs a version of his own journey, and his past, with the hope of contributing to a culture in which "each young man in a small world will know that the future can be good."

Many of the themes addressed by various writers in this anthology are woven together in James McNinch's essay, "Eros and the Erotic in the Construction of Queer Teacher Identity." This essay chronicles the construction and understanding of his own "conflicted but privileged identity as a gay man" within the halls of academia. McNinch problematizes concepts from recent popular culture of both hetero-normative teaching identities and idealized pedagogies, repeatedly disquieting the "mythological media construct that defines us." Holistic, and therefore successful, pedagogy is that which embraces the essential notion of teaching as a seductive act.

Finally, this section closes with "Camp fYrefly: Linking Research to Advocacy in Community Work with Sexual and Gender Minority Youth," in which André Grace passionately articulates the desperate need of Camp fYrefly in providing a safe space for sexual and gender minority (SGM) youth. Sanctioned heterosexist/sexist systems that define contemporary North American society purposefully exclude

SGM youth and this isolation is reinforced by tacitly accepted bully- ing and other forms of violence in most, if not all, aspects of their lives. Established in 2004, Camp fYrefly is a unique leadership program for SGM youth, giving them the tools to "learn about coming out, coming to terms, and growing into resilience in the face of the traumas they experience." Grace situates the conception of this alternative to a con- ventional summer camp for youth within the "current spate of gay-male youth suicides" and the "it gets better" campaign, which he argues is an oversimplified response to the abuse and isolation that lead to suicide. Camp fYrefly is shown to provide a hopeful refuge for SGM youth as they navigate the difficult path to establishing a strong, healthy, posi- tive self.

### NEGOTIATING PUBLIC SPHERE(S)

The essays in this section help to situate ideas and concepts of identity within public cultural spheres; each essay destabilizes various read- ings of the public sphere from its assumed hetero-normative identity. These essays each approach "the public sphere" quite differently but each essay gives the reader a sense of this sphere as a site of instability. Identity within the public sphere is never fixed and, inevitably, is at risk of fracture. Yet, paradoxically, it is this public sphere which allows for multiple and simultaneous readings of identity(ies).

Based on a recent summer spent exploring various urban environ- ments, Caitlyn Jean McMillan's essay, "Repressed Identities: A Traveling Exploration of Sexuality, Gender and Place," situates the author/artist within four disparate urban landscapes. Framing her interactions and experiences of these urban spaces through Doreen Massey's reflective/ affective theoretical framework of gendered space and place, McMillan questions "how each city forms an identity by the experiences it provides."

Reflecting and analyzing upon the radically different urban sur- roundings and subsequent experiences found in Saskatoon (Saskatch- ewan), New York City, Thunder Bay (Ontario) and Banff (Alberta), McMillan discovers that each city has its own unique gendered and sexual identity, and she produced a stunning series of artworks based on her experiences in each place.

Terry Goldie's essay, "Gay, Straight and In-Between: John Money on Homosexuality," is a biographical sketch of controversial physiolo- gist and sexologist John Money. Including an essay on an individual in the section dealing with "public" as opposed to "private" identity might seem curious, yet this decision is logical if one considers the enormous effect that Money had on the public understanding of gender and gender identity, and nowhere is this more evident than in Money's involvement in the infamous Reimer case. In many ways Money's writings in the 1960s and 1970s created the foundational groundwork for a contemporary, if no longer "in vogue" understanding of gender, and in this respect he had an enormous impact on the creation and reception of identity in the public sphere.

Goldie's essay highlights a number of Money's essential arguments and writings while exploring the development of Money's evolving and controversial theories of gender. Goldie does not attempt to respond to all the tangents nor does he shy away from discussing the seemingly contradictory arguments put forward in Money's numerous publications. Some, if not most, of these contradictions stem from Money's clinical and theoretical attempts to "overcome the simplicity of the gay/straight divide, to present sexual orientation as one more of the many aspects of gender and sexuality," as Goldie explains. He neither exonerates nor vilifies John Money but asks us to reconsider Money's pioneering work while demonstrating the seeming impossibilities of truly understanding gender, identity and the public sphere.

This section on identity and the public sphere closes with Randal Rogers' provocative essay "Thinking through Blood in Post-9/11 Visual Culture: *The Passion of the Christ* and *Bobby*." Certainly, no event has so shaped our contemporary lives and our identity within the public sphere more than the events of 9/11; this essay "looks back at the haunting generated by the events of 9/11/01 and considers the manners in which the ghosts of 9/11 have appeared in popular culture forms during this time." Rogers is most interested in blood, both metaphorical and literal, and more specifically, in the concept of bloodletting/blood spillage as one of the central "ghosts" that has become standard in political and popular cultures. In a comparison of Mel Gibson's *The Passion of the Christ* and Emilio Esteves' *Bobby*, Rogers argues that while the presence, or the absence, of blood is remarkably different in the two films, blood (inherently encoded with multiple meanings) is, above all else, a recurrent trope of crisis. We have become, he argues, "saturated by the blood of recent red events," and our understanding of them has forever changed how we negotiate the spheres of public and popular culture.

### NEGOTIATING PRIVATE REALM(S)

It is perhaps fitting that this collection closes with two selections that are more contemplative. These pieces address issues of identity within a private (or semi-private) world of the writer and yet, somewhat ironically, in both essays this private identity eventually manifests itself in a more public discussion. There are substantial differences between Nils Clausson's reading of Whitman's poem and Liz Bugg's autobiographical essay, but both Whitman and Bugg inevitably negotiate that cultural/personal/public sphere that authors occupy when the private becomes public.

In "'Hours Continuing Long' as Whitman's Rewriting of Shakespeare's Sonnet 29," which originally appeared in the *Walt Whitman Quarterly Review*, Nils Clausson deftly analyzes Whitman's poem and directly connects it to Shakespeare's well-known sonnet. Clausson suggests that there is more than homoerotic tension linking both poems, arguing that "Whitman clearly modeled both the form and the content of his 'sonnet' on Shakespeare's 'Sonnet 29'" and that Whitman also expected his readers to be aware of the similarities and differences in the two poems. Clausson demonstrates through his careful analysis that Whitman's "sonnet" does more than simply respond to Shakespeare's work but reshapes his personal poem about same-sex love into a "political protest against having to suffer, like countless others, in silence."

Although Liz Bugg did not actually present "*Red Rover* Revisited: The Making of a Lesbian Mystery Novel" as part of the URQI Speakers Series, it is contained within this collection for various reasons. The most important is that the Speakers Series (and the school year) had ended before Liz spoke at the University of Regina as part of Pride Week Celebrations 2011. It is safe to say that if Liz's visit had coincided with the academic year she would, most definitely, have been part of the series and therefore her essay seems a fitting way to end this collection.

Bugg's autobiographical essay charts the ups and downs of composition as Bugg developed the first novel in her Calli Barnow Mystery Series. Bugg's essay is not a "how to" guide. In fact, she comments, "my writing process is not necessarily one I would recommend." Bugg takes a humourous look at the years of ignoring "that little voice in my head" and the five summers it took her to write, in longhand, the first draft of the novel. Bugg's colourful essay chronicles a private process/identity that, with publication, becomes quite public; while mentioning that her goal is not necessarily to "write queer novels," she certainly demonstrates how private concerns and commitments become central for both character and author.

And so with these introductory words, we invite you to discover for yourself the range of topics, the enthusiasm for the subject matter and the stimulating ideas first put forth by the contributors in public presentations. These qualities are hallmarks of both the University of Regina Queer Initiative Speakers Series and this collection of essays.

PART I

# NEGOTIATING
# **PUBLIC PERSONA(S)**

"Resolve to be thyself; and know that he
Who finds himself loses his misery!"
—MATTHEW ARNOLD, FROM "SELF-DEPENDENCE,"
*Empedocles on Etna, and Other Poems* (1852)

## Being Green: Sex and Tadpoles in the Drama of Juan Rana

JES BATTIS

The year is 1672, and Cosmo Pérez is about to give his last performance in the entremes[1] entitled *El triunfo de Juan Rana* (*Juan
Rana's Triumph*), written by Calderón de la Barca. At this point,
the celebrated actor is so frail that he has to be carried on stage, which is
accomplished through the use of a kind of float, or "carro triunfal." He
floats onto the stage, accompanied by a great deal of fanfare, and the
audience cheers because they love him. Pérez is known to have acted
in over forty interludes, many of which were written expressly for him,
or rather, for his stage presence, Juan Rana. Calderón designed this
particular interlude to break up the heavy mythological drama of his
court play, *Fieras afemina amor* (*Wild Beasts Are Tamed by Love*), which
ends with the character Hercules being forced into drag so that he will
lose the respect of his soldiers. Compared to the sly cross-dressing that
goes on in Calderón's earlier works, this seems more like a cruel prank.
Unlike Juan Rana, who often finds himself wearing women's clothes,
Hercules is not happy to wake up wearing blush and a wig.

Thirty-six years earlier, a much younger and possibly less-cautious
Pérez was arrested for committing the *pecado nefando* (the nefarious
sin) with a page. One of the only indications that we have of this event
is a note written much later by Antonio Rodriguez Villa. Lamenting the

3

laxity of punishment meted out for this particular crime, he observes that "a don Nicolas, el paje del Conde de Castrillo, vemos que anda por la calle, y a Juan Rana, famoso representante, han soltado/ *Now we see Nicolas, the page of the Conde de Castrillo, out on the street, along with the famous Juan Rana, whom they've let go*" (quoted in Thompson, "Triumphant," 6–7). Interestingly, it is not Cosmo Pérez, the actor, who is "seen" on the streets, but rather, Juan Rana, the character. One could argue that Pérez spends the rest of his career defining this life-or-death distinction between the fool that he plays on stage and the actor who is a friend of the royal family. It was Juan Rana who committed the *pecado nefando*, not Cosmo Pérez. Maybe Pérez was seen going to jail, but after a short time, it is Juan Rana who emerges, walking, we assume, a safe distance apart from Nicolas.

The Baroque era, which stretched roughly from 1580 to 1680, was known for its intense focus on secrecy and "positionality." It was governed by what Fernando de la Flor calls "techniques of deception," which manifested themselves in structures that trembled between defense and melancholy (16). Drama was seen as a market of replicable surfaces without any original, encouraging "deceptive spectacles" (17), and court life depended upon calculating one's coordinates in relation to everyone else. This game of subjectivity encouraged what de la Flor describes as a "culture of interiority" and a "profundity of self-immersion" (33, 43). The Inquisition kept Spain's borders closed to foreign influence, which meant that while the rest of Europe was making scientific and cultural strides, Spain lagged behind. Despite the brilliance of its writers and artists during this period, Spanish universities remained profoundly outdated, and illiteracy was high.

In *Juan Rana's Triumph*, the beloved fool becomes a living statue. The audience is told that a statue of Juan Rana is being transported to the "Hall of Fools" in the royal palace; only the statue turns out to be Rana himself (who marvels at how 'life-like' his body is). Just as characters have convinced him in the past that he was pregnant, or that he was a corpse, this time they convince him that he is a sculpture. He even urges everyone not to break him. As the scene draws to a close, nymphs rise from the fountain where Rana has been "placed" as a statue, and sing about his life. He wonders what it would be like to have a voice, even though he's been talking the whole time:

JUAN RANA: Si yo tuviera aqui mi habla,
    les dijera a los Reyes.
CANTA PRIMERA: Esten con el gozo
    de ver que les cuenten
    los diciembres locos
    los siglos perennes (Thompson 290).
JUAN RANA: *If only I could speak,*
    *I'd talk to the royal family.*
FIRST SINGER: *They are always eager to enjoy*
    *all of those stories*
    *during the endless Decembers,*
    *the interminable years.*

It is the heat of these stories—told by Cosmo Pérez, not Juan Rana—that melts the tedium of long winters at court. The audience would have understood that these stories pertained to the actor's love life, and that it was largely the queen's patronage that allowed him to escape the gruesome punishments of the Inquisition.

Various trials that took place during the seventeenth and eighteenth centuries—not only in Spain and Portugal, but as well in England and the Netherlands—give us an idea of what queer subcultures might have sounded like at this time. In her book *Lesbians in Early Modern Spain*, Sherry Velasco cites ten slang words for female homosexuals alone, including *marimacho* (butch lesbian), *entre hombre y mujer* (man/woman), and *bellaca baldresera* (dildo-wearing scoundrel).[2] In fact, the term *bellaca* can still refer to a prostitute, or to a fashionable woman who simply doesn't care what others think of her. Although we cannot confirm the existence of spaces designed exclusively for women seeking same-sex contacts during this period, writing circles—*las tertulias*—frequented by upper-class women were sometimes criticized for their Sapphic undertones. These gatherings often occurred in proximity to the outdoor Spanish playhouses known as *corrales*, and a few wealthy women had the luxury of viewing sexually-charged comedies from their own private *aposentos*, or boxes (Arroñiz 79). Theatre historian Othon Arroñiz notes that Doña Luisa de Carmona had an *aposento* located beneath the women's balcony in the Corral de Príncipe, accessible like the others by a warren of obscure passages.

Queer double-entendres were a staple of comedic theatre. While Lope de Vega explored the dignity of same-sex friendship in plays like *The Marriage of Two Husbands* and *The Proof of the Wits*, entremes authors preferred scatological humour. In *Los muertos vivos* (*The Living Dead*), an entremes written by Luis Quiñones de Benavente, Juan Rana tries to prevent a young gallant from marrying his sister. Their duel becomes a long gay joke, full of coded language, and the punch-line arrives when Juan Rana is convinced that he has actually died. Prior to this, he spars both verbally and physically with the gallant:

> GALAN: Yo os quiero hablar sin colera.
> JUAN RANA: Y yo quiero
> recule un poco atras, como cochero.
> GALAN: Juan Rana, el mas bonito que yo he visto!
> JUAN RANA: Esto es mucho peor, por Jesuchristo!
> (Thompson, 67–68).
> GALLANT: *I only want to talk to you peacefully.*
> JUAN RANA: *And what I want*
> *is to back up a bit, like a coachman.*
> GALLANT: *Juan Rana, the most beautiful man I've ever seen!*
> JUAN RANA: *This is much worse, by Jesus!*

The word "rana" means frog. Cosmo Pérez adopted this stage name long before starring in a 1675 entremes written by Luis Belmonte Bermudez, entitled *Una rana hace un ciento* (*One Frog Makes a Hundred*). Nobody is certain why he chose this particular surname for his persona, but the notion of the frog as a distasteful hybrid was already longstanding. Frogs were known to be neither fish nor fowl, which gave them a murky spot on the great chain of being. Even illiterate theatregoers would have been familiar with the role of the frog in Aesop's fables, a tragicomic creature, arrogant, loud, and curiously evil. A mother frog, thinking herself as broad as the ox, puffs up her body—much to the dismay of her son—until she bursts. The bachelor frog makes friends with a mouse, only to drown him for no reason. In his study of the frog and mouse fable as it appears in Canto XXIII of Dante's *Inferno*, Larkin reminds us that: "there must be no hint of revenge or of just retribution behind the frog's actions; the gratuitousness of the treachery must be complete" (98). The frog ties himself to the mouse, claiming that he's going to teach him how to swim, but instead drowns him. Unfortunately for the frog, a passing eagle spies the floating body of the poor mouse, and snatches up both of them.

Dante's citation of this fable is odd. A group of demons are pursuing the character Ciampolo, and both the poet and Virgil find themselves caught in the middle. Virgil grabs the poet and carries him protectively, like a mother rescuing her child from a burning building:

> ch'al romore è desta
> e vede presso a sé le fiamme accese
> avendo più di lui che di sé cura
> tanto che solo una camiscia vesta
> *My guide wasted no time at all in snatching*
> *Me—as a mother wakened by a roar*
> *Of burning, and observing flames approaching,*
> *Snatches her son and runs and does not pause* (Nichols, 235)[3]

As the poet watches the demons fall into a lake of burning pitch, he likens them to Aesop's frog, even if, as Larkin illustrates, this syllogism is a tad unclear. The point of the fable is that the mouse is an innocent victim, and the frog is a killer without motive. During the Baroque era, the amphibian comes to represent one of two popular metaphors for addressing homosexuality. The other metaphor is that of the *mariposa*, or butterfly, regarded as a kind of Chatty Cathy whose pointless peregrinations were the opposite of masculine discourse. Only a few decades later, Alexander Pope would take to calling John Hervey both a frog and a butterfly, a placeless thing, neither fish nor fowl. The name of butterfly, in point of fact, was used to designate homosexuals who were arrested during the Inquisition, which explains the title of a monograph written recently by Federico Garza Carvajal: *Quemando Mariposas/Burning Butterflies*.

Homosexuality was nothing new to a Baroque audience. The Inquisition exposed a whole series of overlapping queer communities, and the trials for the *pecado nefando* were infamous. In his detailed study of arrests during this period, which stretched from 1540 to the middle of the eighteenth century, Cristian Berco notes an impressive variety of spaces where queer sex was elicited: public washrooms in fish markets, ships in port, stables, hospitals, and even a "ravine" where six men were arrested, although I am not sure if they were apprehended at the same time. It was understood that these encounters depended on communication, and that certain spaces needed to be monitored in order to eliminate the unruly speech-acts that led to unruly sex-acts. Monks were seen as being particularly likely to indulge in this sort of behaviour, and in his fifteenth-century text, *Espejo de disciplina regular/The Mirror of Common Discipline* (1458) Bonvantura issues a warning to the various orders: "Si al alguna le parece cosa torpe hablar en el lugar de la secreta necesidad, entienda cuanto mas torpe y fea cosa es cometer en aquel lugar alguna cosa ajena a la honestidad/*If someone thinks it an unseemly thing to speak in the latrines, imagine how more unseemly and ugly it is to commit there something against chastity*" (Berco, 152/46). The latrine remains a place of *secreta necesidad*, of secret necessity, which is especially vulnerable to acts that are *ajena a la honestidad*.

Scholarly articles by Frederic Serralta and Peter Thompson have analyzed how Cosmo Pérez managed to separate his sex-life from his stage-life, a separation that was nearly impossible given the bawdy language and prurient double-entendres that were a staple of his performances in particular. Juan Rana dresses in women's clothes. Juan Rana gives birth (this was an entertaining trope in Spanish theatre, and has been studied in great detail by Velasco). Juan Rana cries after being challenged to a duel. All these plots, amplified by the actor's own *gestus*, or comportment, slyly referenced his personal life while maintaining that he was a *gracioso*, a fool, whose actions needn't be taken too seriously. Calderón, in fact, names Juan Rana *el maximo gracioso*, "the greatest fool," in Spanish theatre. But Pérez himself was no fool. He depended upon the goodwill of his fans, and read every one of his lines as they were written, including oafish soliloquies that have been interpreted by both Thompson and Serralta as winking apologies for his arrest in 1636. Rather than trying to figure out how he accomplished this feat, or whether Pérez himself was indeed homosexual, I am more interested in the idea of queer comedy in general.

Being a *gracioso*, a fool, is a performance that remains popular in both mainstream and avant-garde drama. To step into the role of the fool is to say, "I'm no longer bound by public convention." One's words become senseless. One is able to say anything, because anything one says will be reduced to a punchline. But the space of the *gracioso*, if manoeuvred correctly, can yield a certain political freedom. In Maria de Zayas y Sotomayor's drama *Betrayal in Friendship*, León, the fool, has no dialogic boundaries. Both Ana Caro de Mallén and Maria de Zayas employ fools in their drama to great effect, allowing them to criticize a variety of issues pertaining to women's lives through the sarcastic voice of a male character. León takes aim at duplicitous men who "pretend to be well-bred and spit like machos" as well as women who insist on carrying around their "mirrors and makeup-kits" (37). In the hands of female playwrights, fools become more visibly political. León's bawdy nature allows him to express what Maria de Zayas herself is supposedly too modest to endorse. The fools of these women perform a daring travesty act, because the license traditionally allowed to these characters permits them to be wildly transgressive without fear of dramatic censorship.

Buffoons like León and Juan Rana have paved the way for contemporary queer characters, like Jack McFarland in *Will and Grace*, Emmet Honneycut in *Queer as Folk*, and Mauri Hidalgo in the popular Spanish series *Aquí, no hay quien viva/Nobody Can Live Here*, which ran from 2003–08. I will return to Mauri in a moment. The point is that queer comedy, from the seventeenth century to the present day, depends on the same style of comportment, the same *gestus* or mannerisms, which can be instantly read by the audience as "queer." In order for Juan Rana's fans to laugh at his performance, they needed to possess a kind of primeval "gaydar," an awareness of queer aesthetics, whose legibility was based on behavioural pseudo-science.[4] The idea that a queer person is recognizable, that he or she can be picked out of a crowd, is not new.

In the entremes *Una rana hace un ciento*, Juan Rana emerges from an imaginary pond, or *charco*, in the guise of a frog. The entremes opens with six women, "two squadrons of beauties," who are fishing for men. They cast their lines at the audience, remarking: "Pece o rana a la capacha/*Fish or frog, it doesn't matter, into the basket*." One of the women sees a figure emerge from the pond, described as "una rana verdinegra, ni bien pescado ni carne/*A black and green striped frog, neither fish nor flesh*." Juan Rana mounts the stage wearing a smock and a pointed green hood, meant, we assume, to accentuate his appearance as an amphibian. We discover that Rana has been fishing for men as well, and he offers to give the women a doubloon for each one that they catch. Still, the women are skeptical. They tell him that he doesn't belong, despite the fact that he's proclaimed himself to be "Orfeo de los aguas," "the Orfeus of the waters." Rana encourages them to keep fishing, and points out the amphibious men who are just waiting to be caught:

Pues en buena parte
estan. Miren como bullen
en las olas del estanque.
Anzuelos al aqua, anzuelos!
y por uno que me saquen
dare un doblon (Thomspon 150).
*But they're everywhere.*
*See how their bubbles stir*
*the stagnant pond.*
*Hooks, hooks in the water!*
*For each that you catch me,*
*I'll pay you a doubloon*

The introduction of currency to this scene only further under-scores the relationship between homosexuality and capital in the seventeenth century. Queer sex was available, if you were willing to pay for it, and it was the act of paying that so often attracted the unwanted attention of the authorities. It was the act of paying that was gossiped about, told and retold, until eventually it reached the ears of someone who refused to tolerate it. This nexus of cash, sex, and secrecy paints what many critics have called a bleak picture of same-sex erotic relations during this period. But this bleakness only holds if you believe that having sex in a bathroom, or on a docked ship, or in a ravine, is an unhappy affair. The records of the Inquisition give us detailed accounts of where and how the *pecado nefando* occurred, but there is no trace left of the pleasure taken by both parties. A variety of outlawed activities fell beneath the Latin category of *molicies*, which I translate as "soft acts."

In the case of Spain, the most powerful manifestations of women's desire were realized in the writing of Maria de Zayas y Sotomayor, who was as popular as Cervantes during the height of her career. In her series of frame tales, entitled *Novelas amorosas y ejemplares* (*The Enchantments of Love*), de Zayas includes a conspicuous moment of same-sex desire between women. The character Flora, who dresses in men's clothing to attend scandalous parties, is employed by her brother to ensnare the virtuous Aminta within an *engaño*, or deceptive intrigue. Flora admits, quite clearly, that she is attracted to Aminta:

Aguarda, hermano, no pasemos de aqui, que ya sabes
que tengo el gusto y deseos mas de galan que de dama,
y donde las veo y mas tan bellas, como esta hermosa
señora, se me van los ojos tras ellas y se me enternece
el Corazon. (223)

*Take care, brother, that we pass no further, for you know
that my taste for women is more than courtly, and whenever I see such beauties as this lovely lady, my eyes traverse
them, and my heart skips a beat.*

My copy of *Novelas amorosas y ejemplares* is used, and the previous
owner has written a helpful note in the margin next to this passage:
"Flora is a lesbo." This is the only English notation, which makes me
think that the writer couldn't think of a word in Spanish for "lesbian,"
or maybe "lesbo" just felt right. What I like about this note is its bare
and insulting veracity. Flora is a lesbo. In Golden Age Spanish literature,
the cipher that exists for understanding desire between women is the
exquisitely complex notion of *amistad*, or friendship, whose betrayal is
often seen as a crime worse than infidelity.

In popular theatre, the fool's job is play with error. Juan Rana's dialogue depends on a mixture of grammatical errors, misapprehensions,
and folk sayings, similar to the mixed-up idioms of Sancho Panza that
so annoy Don Quixote. The character of Sancho, who dreams of food,
beer, and an *insula* of his own to rule, rather than about chivalry, has
many contemporary manifestations in Spanish literature and culture.
He appears in the program *Aqui, no hay quien viva* as Emilio the porter,
who popularizes such phrases as "un poquito de por favor, señor," meaning, "a little bit of please, sir." Every character on the show represents
a cultural type—the gossiping older woman, the horny bachelor, the
child who doesn't respect his parents—but the most interesting character, to me, is Mauri Hidalgo, who lives with his partner, Fernando.

Mauri is the opposite of a *gracioso*. He is clean-cut and well-dressed,
a photo journalist with unimpeachable taste. But despite his outward
confidence, Mauri's relationship with Fernando constantly pushes
him into the space of the *gracioso*, since he is so consumed by neurotic
anxiety. Every one of their fights escalates into a screaming match. The
running joke among their neighbours is that both men often identify

themselves as "amigos," when everyone has already read their queerness. Once again, the neighbours depend upon a queer *gestus*, a comportment that includes posture, movement, and vocal intonation. Fernando, who wears track pants and flirts with bisexuality, is always being hit on by women. Mauri is not, because everyone in the building knows that he is gay; even strangers know it. His antics are funny, like those of Jack MacFarland, because everything that he does seems to be exaggerated. But what looks like a dramatic amplification is actually who he is. Mauri sees Fernando's pseudo-straight posturing as the true exaggeration, which annoys him.

The reason that I'm ending this analysis with a digression about a contemporary Spanish television show is that Mauri and Fernando, at least to me, are an intriguing couple. They fight; they make up; they kiss in every episode, which is a lot more than we got from eight seasons of *Will and Grace*. In an episode involving health insurance, Mauri becomes hysterical, demanding that Fernando stay home to avoid injuring himself. "Where's your medic-alert bracelet?" he asks. "What if you slip? Anything could happen out there." He keeps kissing Fernando, first on the lips, then all over his face, as if bestowing a kind of talismanic protection, all the time saying, "te quiero mucho, te quiero mucho."[5] The scene is funny, but because it is funny, we're allowed to witness a moment of profound love shaded through the lens of Mauri's paranoia. His question—"what if I lost you?"—echoes the question that Judith Butler asks in *Precarious Lives*: "Who am I, without you?"

In an era punctuated by plague, famine, and extreme economic instability—the result of interminable wars, both civil and foreign— the comedy of Juan Rana provided a necessary outlet for public frustration. But *teatro breve* also offered a space for dark humour and subversion. I am drawn to both Juan Rana and Cosmo Pérez because, like them, I often consider myself to be a frog, neither fish nor flesh. Since the very meaning of the word *barroco* points to an unsolvable complexity, it seems only fitting that the Baroque period would produce double-voiced drama with a deep end full of singing frogs and murmuring mariposas.[6] As Rana tells the squadron of beauties in *Una rana hace un ciento*:

> Si soy rana o no soy rana,
> eso, no dire a nadie.

Que cosa soy me mando,
que lo rece y no lo cante. (148)


*Whether I'm a frog or not,*
*I won't tell anyone.*
*I am what I am,*
*for which I must pray, but not sing.*


## NOTES

1   A brief, between-the-acts farce.
2   In his edited volume *Queer Sites*, David Higgs discusses a variety of terms used for male homosexuals in Baroque Lisbon, including *bobija* (bugger), *fanchono* (fairy), and *fanchonices* (fairy-stuff). In England, *molly* became a specific term for cross-dressing men, as discussed at length by Alan Bray and Rictor Norton, while *Anandrine* (i.e., to be of the Anandrine Sect) was a familiar term in France for lesbians.
3   Nichols supplies this translation in his 2010 edition of Dante's work.
4   In her book *Embodying Enlightenment*, Rebecca Haidt discusses the role of physiognomy in the detection of *lindos* (lovelies) and *petimetres* (fops) in Baroque and eighteenth-century Spain: "The *petimetre* as embodiment of the limits of masculinity is an eighteenth-century continuation of an ancient figuring of deviance assessable by the interpretation of physiognomic evidence ... physiognomics divines one's interior disposition, fate, or characteristics through examination of the body's external appearance" (123).
5   "I love you so much."
6   It may be worth noting that *barroco* is a Spanish derivation of a Portuguese word, meaning "rough pearl."

## REFERENCES

Aesop. 1998. *The Complete Fables,* edited by Robert and Olivia Temple. London: Penguin Classics.

Alighieri, Dante. 2010. *The Divine Comedy: Inferno,* edited and translated by J.G. Nichols. Surrey: Oneworld Classics.

Arroñiz, Othon. 1977. *Teatros y Escenarios del Siglo de Oro.* Madrid: Editorial Gredos.

Bellini, Ligia. 1989. *A coisa obscura: mulher, sodomía, e inquisicão no Brasil colonial.* São Paulo: Editora Brasiliense.

Berco, Cristian. 2007. *Sexual Hierarchies, Public Status: Men, Sodomy, and Society in Spain's Golden Age.* Toronto: University of Toronto Press.

Butler, Judith. 2004. *Precarious Lives.* London and New York: Verso Books.

Calderón de la Barca, Pedro. 1984. *Fieras afemina amor,* edited by Edward Wilson. Kassel: Reichenberger.

Carvajal, Federico Garza. 2002. *Quemando mariposas: sodomía y imperio en Andalucía y México*. Barcelona: Laertes.

de la Flor, Fernando. 2005. *Pasiones frías: secreto y disimulación en el Barroco Hispano*. Madrid: Marcial Pons.

Haidt, Rebecca. 1998. *Embodying Enlightenment: Knowing the Body in Eighteenth-Century Spanish Literature and Culture*. London: Palgrave.

Higgs, David (ed.). 1999. *Queer Sites: Gay Urban Histories Since 1600*. New York: Routledge.

Larkin, Philip. 1962. "Another Look at Dante's Frog and Mouse," MLN 77, no. 1 (January): 94–99.

Serralta, Frederic. 1990. "Juan Rana homosexual," *Criticon* 50: 81–92.

Thompson, Peter E. 2006. *The Trumphant Juan Rana: A Gay Actor of the Spanish Golden Age*. Toronto: University of Toronto Press.

——. 2009. *The Outrageous Juan Rana Entremeses: A Bilingual and Annotated Selection of Plays Written for This Spanish Age*. Toronto: University of Toronto Press.

Velasco, Sherry. 2011. *Lesbians in Early Modern Spain*. Nashville: Vanderbilt University.

de Zayas y Sotomayor, Maria. 2000. *Novelas amorosas y ejemplares*. Madrid: Ediciones Catedra.

——. 2007. *La traición en la Amistad,* edited by Michael McGrath. Newark: European Masterpieces.

# The Christian Martyr and the Pagan Witness in *The Well of Loneliness*

T*he Well of Loneliness* is the novel that most lesbians think they know; in some sense, it has become a part of folk culture. As the tragic story of a female "invert," the novel itself has been dramatically persecuted: attacked in a courtroom in 1928 as a corrupting influence on the young, it has been attacked since 1970 by feminist critics for its essentialist and conservative world view. Like the works and (especially) the image of the martyred writer Oscar Wilde, however, Radclyffe Hall's lesbian novel has had so much influence on an evolving gay/lesbian culture that to dismiss it simply as a relic of the past is to distort the cultural history that has led to the development of the modern lesbian/gay/bisexual/transgendered (or "queer") community, complete with flag and national holiday.[1]

Hall's central character, Stephen Gordon, has moved generations of young readers who have secretly feared (and hoped) that they were/are fundamentally different from everyone else they know. Her neckties have influenced a masculinizing trend in women's fashion as her chivalry has influenced a certain school of lesbian ethics. Her image as an archetypal female "butch" has obscured the textual evidence that her social isolation is not simply a result of persecution by the prejudiced human majority.

The brief but significant appearance of the "pagan" lesbian character Valerie Seymour serves to show that Stephen is not doomed simply
because she loves women but because her masculine, genetically-deter-
mined nature, combined with her traditional Christian value system
(endorsed by the narrator), leaves her no room for the ethical fulfill-
ment of her emotional needs. According to God's laws as Stephen
understands them, wholesome joy in the lives of her "people" can only
be an illusion.

Stephen's life story, like that of a saint or a hero of legend, seems to
be largely predetermined by forces beyond her control. It begins, appro-
priately enough, with the courtship of her Irish mother and her English
father, who recognizes his true mate when he meets the fair Anna, "all
chastity," in Ireland. Sir Philip Gordon brings his bride to his ancestral
home, which seems like a structural expression of her personality:

> It is indeed like certain lovely women who, now old,
> belong to a bygone generation—women who in youth
> were passionate but seemly; difficult to win but when
> won, all-fulfilling. They are passing away, but their
> homesteads remain, and such an homestead is Morton.[2]

Sir Philip and Lady Anna seem complementary in every way, and eventually they complete their union by having a child:

> Sir Philip never knew how much he longed for a son
> until, some ten years after marriage, his wife conceived
> a child; then he knew that this thing meant complete
> fulfilment, the fulfilment for which they had both
> been waiting.[3]

The unborn baby, whom both parents presume to be a son, is named Stephen. When the baby is born female on Christmas Eve, her father insists
on keeping the name he has chosen, that of the first Christian saint.

Stephen's mother is instinctively repelled by the changeling at her
breast: something not recognizable as a daughter, even in infancy. Lady
Anna tries to be a good mother, but she must continually wrestle with
her anger at something amiss when she notices the growing child's
resemblance to her father. The "lady of Morton," who reminds the

village peasants of the Virgin Mary, does not understand her own child, who seems cursed or blessed beyond ordinary parental expectations.

Ironically, Anna has passed a certain "Celtic" sensitivity to Stephen, who is in some sense a half-breed as well as a bundle of sexual contradictions:

> ... her mother had looked at her curiously, gravely, puzzled by this creature who seemed all contradictions—at one moment so hard, at another so gentle ... even Anna had been stirred, as her child had been stirred, by the breath of the meadowsweet under the hedges; for in this they were one, the mother and daughter, having each in her veins the warm Celtic blood that takes note of such things.[4]

Stephen can no more ignore the "Celtic blood" which makes her emotionally receptive to the natural world than she could choose to become feminine. When Stephen, an excellent rider, is given her own horse, the animal and the owner form a feudal bond partly because of their shared Irish "wildness":

> ... his eyes were as soft as an Irish morning, and his courage was as bright as an Irish sunrise, and his heart was as young as the wild heart of Ireland, but devoted and loyal and eager for service, and his name was sweet on the tongue as you spoke it—being Raftery, after the poet. Stephen loved Raftery and Raftery loved Stephen.[5]

The devotion of Raftery, the good animal servant, is matched by the devotion of the human servants of Morton to their master and mistress. Stephen also shows an instinct for service and self-sacrifice for those she loves, which seems both feudal and Christian. (It also seems to foreshadow the revival of this idealized concept of loyalty in "leatherdyke" literature.)[6]

When the housemaid Collins, on whom the seven-year-old Stephen has a crush, complains of pain in her knees, Stephen tells her that she would like to suffer for her sake:

> Stephen said gravely: "I do wish I'd got it—I wish I'd
> got your housemaid's knee, Collins, 'cause that way I
> could bear it instead of you. I'd like to be awfully hurt
> for you, Collins, the way that Jesus was hurt for sinners.
> Suppose I pray hard, don't you think I might catch it?"[7]

The child is bitterly disappointed when God seems to ignore her request for an affliction which would unite her with her beloved.

The God to whom young Stephen prays for suffering (and Who eventually seems to answer her prayers abundantly) is strangely non-denominational, especially considering the probable religious difference between a typically English father and an Irish mother. The "God of creation" whom Stephen later seeks in a church in France, land of her exile, seems to transcend specific details of doctrine and ritual. As a convert to Catholicism,[8] the author seems to place her hero in a universe for which the traditional, hierarchical doctrines of "the Church universal" serve as a reliable guide. This fictional world is not, however, seamless enough to prevent radically different world views from being glimpsed through the comments of minor characters, notably Valerie Seymour and the faintly decadent novelist Jonathan Brockett.

Much of the narrative, in hagiographic style, recounts Stephen's struggles to understand God's inscrutable will. As a young adult, she is betrayed by each of her earthly parents as she feels she has been betrayed from birth by her heavenly Father. Like Adam, Stephen feels abandoned by the loving father who modeled gentlemanly honour in her life, as well as by the mother who drives her into exile for surrendering to erotic temptation.

Stephen's father reads and rereads a "slim volume" by a German author, Karl Heinrich Ulrichs, which explains Stephen's "nature." Sir Philip does not want to tell his wife or daughter what he has learned—until it is too late. He is killed unexpectedly when a tree falls on him, as though to punish him for "the sin of his anxious and pitiful heart."[9] Ironically, Sir Philip succumbs while pruning a beloved old cedar tree because it is overburdened with snow. Like Stephen's friend and spiritual brother, Martin, Sir Philip cares about trees as part of God's creation.

Deprived of her father's protection and watched anxiously by her lesbian tutor, Puddle, who dares not reveal what she knows, Stephen falls passionately in love with another outsider in the village, Angela Crossby. Like her father before her, Stephen tries to offer her beloved a home: "'all this beauty and peace is for you, because now you're a part of Morton'."[10]

Trapped in a sordid marriage into which she sold herself, Angela encourages Stephen to court her. Like Jezebel or Delilah, however, she is wily and incapable of loyalty. Pressed to make a commitment, Angela taunts her lover: "'Could you marry me, Stephen?'"[11] Tormented by her inability to offer her own and God's protection in an honourable marriage to the woman she loves, Stephen buys her an expensive ring set with a "pure" pearl, in a kind of parody of her parents' engagement.

Angela predictably exposes Stephen to the scorn of her enemies after Stephen finds her *in flagrante* with a bullying male who is Stephen's oldest rival: an unworthy man who appeals to an unworthy woman. Stephen describes herself as "God's mistake" in an anguished love letter to Angela, who hands it to her husband to protect herself from the consequences of her infidelity. Angela's husband completes the betrayal by forwarding Stephen's letter to Stephen's mother, who refuses to continue living under the same roof with her. Stephen chooses to leave Morton, taking the loyal Puddle with her, and enters the purgatory of a world in which she feels rootless.

Although she has inherited wealth, Stephen wants to distinguish herself in a respectable profession so as to justify her existence to a hostile world. She becomes a novelist with the intention of eventually writing the story of her life: a novel such as *The Well of Loneliness*.

Stephen is approached by Brockett,[12] a male novelist whom she finds offensive and unmanly but who serves as her Beatrice: a guide to the hidden world of fellow "inverts" in Paris, Stephen's home in exile. Brockett introduces her to Valerie Seymour, a noted hostess of the demi-monde. Stephen initially resents Valerie's interest in her because she assumes it is as "morbid" as Brockett's: "she was seeing before her all the outward stigmata of the abnormal—verily the wounds of One nailed to a cross—that was why Valerie sat there approving."[13] Valerie seems to sense Stephen's resentment and charms her out of it by talking to her "gravely about her work, about books in general; about life in general."[14]

Valerie Seymour seems to be clearly based on an actual person, the bilingual American heiress and "Amazon of letters" Natalie Barney, whose Friday salons were legendary in early twentieth-century Paris.[15] Possibly because the character is drawn from life, she seems out of place among the stock characters of the novel. Valerie is described from Stephen's viewpoint as giving an impression of feminine grace, yet she shows a degree of iconoclastic independence which seems incompatible with femininity as Stephen conceives of it.

By Stephen's conservative standards, Valerie's home and her life are chaotic: "The first thing that struck Stephen about Valerie's flat was its large and rather splendid disorder."[16] Stephen comes to learn that Valerie's large circle of friends is also "disordered" in the sense of being diverse and not highly respectable; several of her other lesbian friends are dissolute by Stephen's standards, yet their alcoholism and maudlin despair do not seem to affect Valerie, who does not indulge in alcohol or self-pity.

Valerie's world view, as well as her coterie, clearly upsets Stephen's sense of order, and Stephen is at pains to understand Valerie's apparently effortless success in surviving on her own terms. She attempts to explain this phenomenon to herself as well as to the reader:

> Stephen began to understand better the charm that many had found in this woman; a charm that lay less in physical attraction than in a great courtesy and understanding, a will to please, a great impulse toward beauty in all its forms… And as they talked on it dawned upon Stephen that here was no mere libertine in love's garden, but rather a creature born out of her epoch, a pagan chained to an age that was Christian, one who would surely say with Pierre Louys: "Le monde moderne succombe sous un envahissement de laideur." [The modern world has succumbed to an invasion of ugliness.] And she thought that she discerned in those luminous eyes, the pale yet ardent light of the fanatic.[17]

Valerie's perceived "fanaticism" seems to be her determination to create, as far as possible, an alternative culture for herself and all those who seem "out of place" in a society which does not accept them. She seems "pagan" in the sense of resembling a Lesbian of old, a follower of the poet Sappho on the island of Lesbos, where Natalie Barney seriously proposed to establish an all-female colony.[18] Valerie seems both behind and ahead of her time, as a forerunner of the lesbian-separatists of the 1970s who denounced patriarchal "order," valued an androgynous combination of qualities, and rediscovered the goddesses of pre-Christian religion.

Valerie recommends an old house to Stephen, which she agrees to buy. Like Valerie's flat, the house and its neglected garden seem characteristic of her: "A marble fountain long since choked with weeds, stood in the center of what had been a lawn. In the farthest corner of the garden some hand had erected a semi-circular temple."[19] However, neither the pseudo-pagan ruins of her new home nor Valerie's feminist and woman-centred viewpoint[20] affect Stephen's sense of herself as marked by "stigmata" in a Christian universe.

Valerie tactfully offers her friendship to Stephen, saying: "'I'm not going to bother you until you evince.'"[21] In the language of the 1970s counterculture, however, Stephen does not find Valerie "relevant" until Stephen reluctantly joins her community of outcasts to relieve the loneliness of the woman for whom Stephen feels responsible. Although Valerie eventually becomes a kind of mother-confessor for Stephen, Valerie cannot change Stephen's world view, and wisely refrains from  rying.

When war breaks out, Stephen feels morally compelled to serve England. Rejected for combat, she is forced to settle for being an ambulance driver in an all-female unit, where she meets a young, feminine orphan with whom she falls protectively in love. After the war, Stephen tries to spare her beloved Mary from the degradation of a life with herself.

As her name suggests, however, Mary is pure-hearted and brave enough to accept a hard fate; her passionate nature seems to arise from her own "Celtic blood" (in her case, Welsh). Mary asks Stephen: "'Can't you understand that all that I am belongs to you?'"[22] Stephen accepts the gift of Mary's virginity, despite her misgivings. Her "bride" has none: "Mary, because she was perfect woman, would rest without thought, without exultation, without question; finding no need to question since for her there was now only one thing—Stephen."[23]

Although Mary is the mate for whom Stephen has longed, her acceptance of masculine responsibility for Mary's "unthinking" feminine nature eventually prompts Stephen to make the ultimate sacrifice by driving Mary into the arms of her old friend Martin, an honourable and "natural" man who can be trusted to take care of her. By this time, Stephen's inability to protect Mary from isolation and insult has convinced her that "giving" her to Martin is the only morally acceptable course of action left to her.

Stephen, as feudal protector, is devastated when Lady Anna refuses to invite Mary to Morton or to acknowledge her role in Stephen's life. Stephen is forced to watch helplessly as Mary is ostracized by "normal" people like herself because of her loyalty to Stephen. Even Mary's desire to be indispensable to Stephen as a housekeeper and secretary is thwarted because Stephen's household is run by paid staff.

Ironically, Mary languishes in isolation while Stephen is hard at work, presumably to justify Mary's faith in her, on an *apologia pro vita sua* like the novel in which both women appear as characters. Recognizing her lover's need for other human companionship, Stephen descends with her into the night world that Valerie inhabits, where Stephen and Mary meet other outcasts who resemble damned souls.

Stephen unburdens herself to Valerie, whom Mary begins to resent as a rival. Valerie points out the contradictions in Stephen's personality:

> You're rather a terrible combination: you've the nerves of the abnormal ... you're appallingly over-sensitive, Stephen—well, and then ... you've all the respectable county instincts of the man who cultivates children and acres ... one side of your mind is so aggressively tidy ... supposing you could bring the two sides of your nature into some sort of friendly amalgamation and compel them to serve you and through you your work—well then I really don't see what's to stop you.[24]

Stephen thanks Valerie for her kindness, apparently without understanding her assessment of the "contradictions" in Stephen which lead her to martyrdom.

To her consternation, Valerie proves most useful to Stephen as a means of driving Mary away. Valerie responds with concern to Stephen's request: "If you want to pretend that you're my lover, well, my dear ... I wish it were true.... All the same.... Aren't you being absurdly self-sacrificing?"[25] Stephen explains grimly that her strategy is necessary. It succeeds.

'St Stephen' by Beresford Egan: caricature of Radclyffe Hall as a crucified martyr in anonymous mock-heroic poem, *The Sink of Solitude* (Hermes Press, 1928), one of the earliest of several parodies of *The Well of Loneliness*. Reproduced in Michael Baker's biography of Radclyffe Hall, *Our Three Selves*. Used with permission of the Estate of Beresford Egan.

Alone in her Calvary, Stephen has a vision of her "children," the "inverts" of the future who pray for salvation through her, their spokesperson:

> They would turn first to God, and then to the world, and then to her. They would cry out accusing: "We have asked for bread; will you give us a stone? You, God, in Whom we, the outcast, believe; you, world, into which we are pitilessly born; you, Stephen, who have drained our cup to the dregs—we have asked for bread; will you give us a stone?"[26]

The novel concludes, in Biblical-epic style, with Stephen's anguished prayer:

> "God," she gasped, "we believe; we have told You we believe... . We have not denied You, then rise up and defend us. Acknowledge us, oh God, before the whole world. Give us also the right to our existence!"[27]

Unfortunately, the influence of this cry on generations of readers who have identified with Hall's martyr has almost drowned out Valerie's gentle admonishment to Stephen: "'even the world's not as black as it's painted'."[28] Or (to flirt further with essentialist notions of race) as white.

**NOTES**

1   The rainbow flag, now widely recognized as a symbol of "gay (GLBT) pride," was designed in San Francisco in 1978. It is usually flown, like a national flag, during celebrations on the anniversary of the Stonewall Riots of June 1969. This annual event has increasingly come to be regarded as the "queer" equivalent of a national holiday (various sources).

2   Radclyffe Hall, *The Well of Loneliness* (New York: Permabooks, 1954), 11.

3   Ibid., 12.

4   Ibid., 39.

5   Ibid., 59.

6   Works of erotic fiction and theory on lesbian sado-masochism (or Dominance/submission) are now too numerous to be listed here. The anthology *Coming to Power* (Alyson Publications, 1982), edited by an early lesbian s/m

organization, Samois, was probably the first to have widespread cultural influence.

7    Hall, *The Well of Loneliness*, 21.

8    Radclyffe Hall was officially accepted into the Catholic Church on February 5, 1912 (Michael Baker, *Our Three Selves: A Life of Radclyffe Hall*, London: Hamish Hamilton, 1985), 44.

9    Hall, *The Well of Loneliness*, 118.

10   Ibid., 145.

11   Ibid., 148.

12   One literary historian, Terry Castle, provides extensive evidence that Jonathan Brockett is based on the playwright Noel Coward, whom Radclyffe Hall knew fairly well. Terry Castle, *Noel Coward and Radclyffe Hall: Kindred Spirits* (New York: Columbia University Press, 1996), 38–55).

13   Hall, *The Well of Loneliness*, 246.

14   Ibid.

15   Barney's status as a salon hostess is mentioned by Hall's biographer, Michael Baker (p. 142 in *Our Three Selves*) and by critic Karla Jay in *The Amazon and the Page: Natalie Clifford Barney and Renee Vivien* (Bloomington and Indianapolis: Indiana University Press, 1988), passim. Baker, Castle, Jay and other critics have followed the lead of Hall's lover and first biographer, Lady Una Troubridge, who states that the character Valerie Seymour is based on Natalie Barney in *The Life and Death of Radclyffe Hall*, Hammond and Hammond, 1961), 83–84).

16   Hall, *The Well of Loneliness*, 244.

17   Ibid., 246.

18   Barney proposed this plan as early as 1901, during a visit to Lesbos with her lover Renee Vivien (Jay, *The Amazon and the Page*, 15).

19   Hall, *The Well of* Loneliness, 249. Michael Baker refers to Natalie Barney's seventeenth-century home at No. 20, Rue Jacob, Paris, which included a courtyard "with an enchanting enclosed garden containing a Doric 'Temple d'Amitié' [Temple of Friendship]." (Baker, *Our Three Selves*, 142).

20   For an historical account of the feminist movement which was gathering strength from before Hall's birth in 1880 to the end of the Great War, when British women gained the right to vote in 1918, see Midge Mackenzie, *Shoulder to Shoulder: A Documentary* (Harmondsworth, Middlesex: Penguin Books, 1975) and Rose Tremain, *The Fight for Freedom for Women* (New York: Ballantine Books, 1973).
     For an account of the intimate "smashes" among women which flourished without social censure in the era in which *The Well of Loneliness* was written, see Lillian Faderman, *Surpassing the Love of Men: Romantic Friendship and Love Between Women from the Renaissance to the Present* (New York: Junction Books, 1981).

21   Hall, *The Well of Loneliness*, 249.

22   Ibid., 313.

23    Ibid., 314.
24    Ibid., 407–8.
25    Ibid., 433.
26    Ibid., 437.
27    Ibid.
28    Ibid., 408.

## A BRIEF PUBLICATION HISTORY OF
### *THE WELL OF LONELINESS*

AUGUST 12, 1880—Author, Marguerite Radclyffe Hall, born at Bournemouth, England. Coming of age at 21, she asks friends to call her "Radclyffe." Later, she asks them to call her "John."

JUNE 1928—Publication of *The Well of Loneliness* by Jonathan Cape, Ltd., in London.
"John's" fiction writing is encouraged by her lover, Una Troubridge.

AUGUST 19, 1928—"A Book That Must Be Suppressed" by James Douglas appears in *The Sunday Express*. Douglas claims that the novel could "devastate young souls" with its themes of "sexual inversion and perversion."

AUGUST 20, 1928—Jonathan Cape sends a copy of the book to the Home Office and the Director of Public Prosecutions, asking whether they believe that the book should be withdrawn from circulation.

AUGUST 22, 1928—A letter from the Home Secretary to Jonathan Cape says that the book must be withdrawn from circulation because it is obscene. Proceedings are brought against Cape and Pegasus Press in Paris.

NOVEMBER 1928—Case heard at Bow Street Police Court. Despite supporting testimony from forty witnesses, Judge Sir Chartres Biron orders the book destroyed on grounds that it is an "obscene libel" under the terms of the Obscene Publications Act of 1857. He claims, in part: "Unfortunately these women exist, and the book asks that their existence and vices should be recognised and tolerated, and not treated with condemnation, as they are at present by all decent people."[1]

DECEMBER 1928—An appeal is heard in the Court of Quarter Sessions. The publisher's solicitors ask that the twenty-four attending Justices be allowed to read the book before the hearing, but Sir Robert Wallace, Chairman of the Court, claims that this would not be appropriate. Sir Robert dismisses the appeal.

1929—A U.S. publisher, Alfred Knopf, backs out of publishing the book for fear of legal consequences. Covici Friede publishes the book.

1929—In a New York court, the judge rules that the novel "tends to debauch public morals," and that the U.S. edition must be judged obscene according to the Hicklin Rule (if any part of a work is found obscene, the whole work must be found obscene). This ruling is overturned on appeal.

*The Well of Loneliness* is eventually translated into fourteen languages and continues to sell briskly in the U.S. and France. It is republished in Britain in 1949.

**NOTE**

1    H. Montgomery Hyde, *A History of Pornography* (New York: Farrar, Straus and Giroux, 1965), p. 75.

# Chinese University Students' Commitment to Social Justice and Their Willingness to Confront Sexual Orientation Prejudice[1]

DONALD COCHRANE AND JINJIE WANG

## HISTORICAL CONTEXT

From ancient times through many dynasties, Chinese society tolerated and, at times, even encouraged same-sex eroticism.[2] In texts that have survived millennia, most recorded encounters involve members of the male ruling classes. While accounts of "amours among commoners" are understandably rare,[3] Crompton notes that the sexual attitudes in many stories "tacitly assume bisexuality as the human norm."[4] All of this changed dramatically in 1911 with the fall of the Qing Dynasty. China experienced its first "opening to the West" and welcomed Western science,[5] Christianity, sex education, and psychology[6]—including their negative views about same-sex relations. When their own traditions and values conflicted with those of the West, Chinese reformers judged their own to be signs of the weaknesses that had contributed to the collapse of the dynasty.

Hinch claims that within a few generations "China shifted from a relative tolerance of homosexuality to open hostility,"[7] but cautions that "the reasons for this change are complex and not yet fully understood."[8] When the People's Republic of China (PRC) was established in 1949, the Communist Party banished Christian agencies but retained their abhorrence of homosexuality, declaring it a sign of bourgeois decadence. In good Marxist fashion, it substituted economic and cultural factors for biological determinism and predicted that homosexuality would evaporate as the new proletarian society emerged. Same-sex relations were never explicitly criminalized in post-1949 China. However, the charge of "hooliganism" has been applied to many forms of deviation and thus undesirable behaviour,[9] and has been used as a convenient tool to assist authorities in their attempts to hasten the process of "evaporation." Treatment of suspected homosexuals during the Cultural Revolution (1966–76) was particularly harsh.[10]

With the second "opening to the West" initiated by Deng Xiaoping in 1978, Western influences once again penetrated the Bamboo Curtain and with them came new ideas about social and sexual relations. At the same time, China experienced a resurgence of Confucian priorities, particularly the emphasis on maintaining social order and the obligation of all children to maintain the paternal family line. The value placed on preserving social harmony does give "tongzhi"—the most popular contemporary word for gays, lesbians, and bisexuals—some protection from the intrusion by the state into their private lives. At the same time, "les-bi-gay" people are under enormous pressure from parents to marry and produce offspring, especially since the "one-child policy" was introduced in 1978.

Thus far, research on how tolerant contemporary Chinese society is of its sexual minorities has been inconclusive. Commenting on a 2007 national telephone survey, Li concluded that "Chinese society, on the whole, is tolerant,"[11] yet only about 20 percent of the respondents were prepared to say that there was nothing wrong with being homosexual. She reports that "30 percent said there was something wrong with homosexuality, and nearly 40 percent said it was wrong."[12] The view of our own participants was less charitable. When asked whether they thought the attitude of most Chinese toward gays and lesbians was positive or negative, their response was overwhelmingly negative (F=93%, no.=70; M=86%, no.=101).[13]

Research among university students on sexual orientation issues has grown steadily in the last twenty years and, by and large, reveals a trend toward greater tolerance. In their early groundbreaking 1992 study, Dalin Liu et al. found that 79% of his large student sample regarded homosexuality as a form of "sexual deviancy" and an illness that doctors might solve or alleviate."[14] Almost a decade later in 2001, Cui and Liang reported similar numbers: almost 80% of male and female students considered homosexuality to be abnormal and half of them also believed it to be immoral. The majority would recommend that a friend who was attracted to members of the same sex should visit a doctor.[15] In 2002, Higgins et al. concluded that "Intolerance of homosexuality … was pervasive among our Chinese student sample with 78.6% of men and 66.4% of women disapproving of the statement 'homosexuality should be allowed'."[16] However in the same year, a survey conducted at three universities in Shanghai reported a very different view in which "about 60 percent of the students hold a tolerant view about homosexuality, thinking it should be permitted openly."[17]

By 2005, Cen Guozhen, a professor of psychology at Shanghai Normal University, was able to report that a recent survey "indicate[d] young people are more broad-minded about homosexuals as a group, with 75 percent of those polled accepting homosexual acquaintances, 37 percent among their friends, and 21 percent among their relatives."[18] Finally, a loosely conducted survey of students in "around ten universities in Beijing" conducted by Jiang Qiuyu and five classmates at Beijing's China University of Nationalities in 2006 concluded that "universities are becoming much more liberal."[19]

## PURPOSE OF THE RESEARCH

This research explores Chinese university students' commitment to social justice on public policy issues and their perceptions of sexual orientation prejudice on their campus. In a 2006 survey, 200 students (M=117; F=82) from a large university in southeastern China were asked about their stance on seven social policy issues and then how often they heard homophobic comments from their peers, when they did hear them whether they intervened and, importantly, if they did intervene, why they would have done so.

## PROCEDURE

Our survey instrument was developed in English at the University of Saskatchewan. Two Chinese social science professors—one in China and one in Canada—were consulted about the cultural appropriateness of the questions as well as the Chinese slang equivalents for words such as "fag," "faggot," "dyke," "homo," "queer," "lezzie," and "gay." The following substitutions were used: "tongxinglian" ("same-sex relations/love"), "tongzhi" ("comrade"), "boli" ("from 'BL', "Boy Love" and so a boy who loves another boy and refers to gay men), "niangniangqiang" ("men who speak with a womanish accent," and so, effeminate), "lala" (transliteration of the English "lesbian"), and "biantai" ("perverted"). The survey was then translated into Mandarin, back-translated into English, and field tested on eight Chinese graduate students at the University of Saskatchewan.

To gauge the liberalness of our participants, we placed our questions in the context of social policy issues. This, we believed, would sharpen their perception and move responses beyond simple attitudes. Thus, we selected seven "hot-button" issues for their consideration: same-sex marriage, adoption, child custody in the event of divorce, housing, jobs, police harassment, and immigration.

## PARTICIPANTS

Of the 200 students who were surveyed, 82 were females, 117 were males (one was undeclared). Participants were chosen randomly by contacts made over a four-day period in dormitories, cafeterias, and around recreational centres. When invited to complete the survey, they were informed immediately about the nature of the research and were offered ten yuan (about $1.32 US)—the cost of a good lunch—to participate.

Nearly 80% of our female (65/82) and more than 90% of our male (107/117) participants were 21 years or younger. Because we were visiting the university in June, most third- and fourth-year students had completed their examinations and had left campus. As a result, almost 80% of the females (63/81) and more than 90% of our males (108/117) were in their first two years of university. Less than 25% of them (45/200) had chosen the humanities as their major field of study. Students were not asked to reveal their own sexual orientation.

Participants were asked about three conditions that in the West are thought to influence attitudes towards gays and lesbians. A high degree of religious belief (sometimes referred to as "religiosity") is often associated with higher levels of homo-negativity.[20] So few of our participants—particularly males in the sample—claimed to be religious to any significant degree that it was safe to conclude that religion would not be a significant factor:

| | Very religious | Somewhat religious | Not at all religious |
| --- | --- | --- | --- |
| Females | 2% (no.=2) | 16% (no.=13) | 82% (no.=66) |
| Males | 0% (no.=0) | 5% (no.=6) | 95% (no.=109) |

We concur with Pan Suiming's observation that "homosexuals in China do not ... have to deal with the problem of "sin" in the context of the Christian Church, as their counterparts in the West."[21]

We also discounted the possible "broadening-of-the-mind" effects[22] of international travel because so few of our participants had studied abroad[23]:

|  | No travel outside China | Less than 3 months | 3 months to one year | More than a year |
|---|---|---|---|---|
| Females | 93% (no.=67) | 6% (no.=4) | 0% (no.=0) | 1% (no.=1) |
| Males | 97% (no.=98) | 2% (no.=2) | 0% (no.=0) | 0% (no.=0) |

Research in the West offers abundant evidence that having a gay or lesbian relative or close friend is the most significant factor in a heterosexual's acceptance of sexual-minority persons.[24] Once again, this could not have been a major influence on our participants, as relatively few of them claimed knowingly to have a gay or lesbian acquaintance and even fewer claimed to have a close gay or lesbian friend or relative:

|  | No lesbian acquaintance | No gay acquaintance | No close lesbian friend or relative | No close gay friend or relative |
|---|---|---|---|---|
| Females | 83% (no.=68) | 89% (no.=73) | 96% (no.=77) | 95% (no.=78) |
| Males | 91% (no.=106) | 86% (no.=99) | 97% (no.=112) | 96% (no.=111) |

Li's research led to a similar conclusion: "Whether we admit it or not, homosexuality is a reality across the world, and the visibility of homosexuals reflects how accepting a society is toward them. But the Chinese Academy of Social Sciences (CASS) survey found that only 7.5 percent of the respondents admitted having known any homosexual."[25]

### SOCIAL JUSTICE ISSUE RESPONSES

The liberalness of our participants surprised us. While they gave us somewhat lower scores on the more personal issues—same-sex marriage, adoption, child custody in the event of divorce—than on the others, they were still considerably higher than results reported by other researchers in China. Specifically, we asked our participants whether they agreed that gay and lesbian individuals:

## 1. Should be allowed to marry their same-sex partners.

In our survey, 82% of our female and 70% of our male participants agreed.[26] We regard these numbers as highly significant because same-sex marriage has not been approved by the state and there is little prospect of it happening in the near future. As Li, a tireless advocate for same-sex marriage, has said: "Gay marriage is not something that our country can accept at this stage of its cultural development. History will change when it must. And perhaps I will only be able to be a bystander when the change comes, rather than a participant."[27] The results of a national phone survey in 2007 were discouraging: "On legislation for same-sex marriage, the CASS respondents seemed … conservative with 70 percent rejecting the idea."[28] She also reports on a second CASS online survey, which found that 60 percent of the Chinese respondents approved of same-sex marriage. She speculates that the difference in the results between the two surveys may be attributed to the fact that "a large percentage of Chinese 'netizens' are young, well-educated, and urban dwellers."[29] We see our research as corroborating her interpretation. A younger generation may be looking at same-sex marriage differently from its forebears.

## 2. Should be allowed to adopt children.

In one of his studies, Herek concluded that "overall, heterosexual women [in North America] were more supportive than men of … adoption rights for gay people."[30] In a 2005 study on medical students in Hong Kong, Hon et al. found that "less than half (46%) thought they (homosexual partners) should have equal rights in adopting children."[31] In another 2005 study, Cen Guozhen, a Shanghai Normal University professor of psychology, reported that "few (young) people agree with allowing homosexual couples to adopt children.[32]

Our results are markedly different. First, both our male and female participants strongly supported the right of sexual minority people to adopt children. Second, the parity between the positive responses of our female and male participants (F=70%; M=68%) was remarkable. Though these results are the lowest we recorded on our seven social-issue questions, they are higher than other available research results in China.

### 3. Should be eligible for child custody in event of divorce.

With China's divorce rate surging,[33] the issue of how to resolve child custody cases has become significant. Again, our participants strongly supported the right of gays and lesbians to apply for custody. Interestingly, this is the one category of social issues in which our male respondents scored higher (M=76%) than our female respondents (F=70%), though both scores are relatively high.

### 4. Should be free from discrimination in housing.

Our participants resoundingly rejected discrimination in housing (F=91%; M=88%).

### 5. Should be free from job discrimination because of their sexual orientation.

In one study, Herek concluded that, "Overall, heterosexual women were more supportive than men of employment protection ... and more willing to extend employment benefits to same-sex couples."[34] While China has no law protecting sexual minorities against job discrimination,[35] our female and male participants were overwhelmingly opposed to job discrimination and with near identical percentages (F=94%; M=91%).

These numbers are very close to those compiled by Li. Recalling a 2007 CASS telephone survey, she wrote that "with respect to equal employment rights for homosexuals, 91 percent of the respondents offered their support." She offered this explanation: "Although many Chinese people disapprove of homosexuality, they favor equal employment rights for homosexuals, because working is the basic means of a human being's survival, and our moral baseline entails the respect for another's right to work."[36]

### 6. Should be free from police harassment because of their sexual orientation.

As in many Western countries, the police in China play a forceful role in "the regulation of desire." Li sketches the situation that prevailed in China for many years. Despite the introduction of market reforms and China's shift to a "rule of law" in 1979, the Chinese police continued to apprehend, search, interrogate, and even detain people for engaging in consensual homosexual acts throughout the 1980s and 1990s. In the absence of any specific laws on homosexuality, persons apprehended for engaging in acts of same-sex love tended to be caught up in general policing campaigns to ensure "public security" and were generally charged with the more generic crime of hooliganism.[37] Interestingly, in a state where the heavy hand of the police is widely felt, our participants gave this position the highest approval rating of all seven issues (F=94%; M=94%).

**7. That same-sex persons from foreign countries should be allowed to immigrate to China to join gay and lesbian partners (provided the former meet all the other usual conditions for immigration).**

Our female (F=81%) and male (M=80%) participants strongly favoured the right of same-sex partners to be reunited in China.

The parity between the responses of our female and male participants across all of the issues is worth noting because they run counter to a "gender gap" that runs through most of this research in the West. On only two issues was there any noticeable difference: our female participants scored 6% less than their male counterparts on the question of child custody in the event of divorce and our females scored 12% higher than our males on the right of same-sex partners to marry.

Surprised by these findings, we looked for background factors that might suggest explanations. To do this, we stipulated that students would be defined as "liberal" if they answered affirmatively on at least five of our seven issues. The results of this exercise also surprised us:

|  | Females | Totals | Males | Totals |
|---|---|---|---|---|
| **7 out of 7 times** | 40% (no.=33) |  | 44% (no.=51) |  |
| **At least 6 out of 7 times** | 24% (no.=20) | 65% | 18% (no.=21) | 62% |
| **At least 5 out of 7 times** | 15% (no.=12) | 79% | 16% (no.=19) | 78% |

Almost 80% of all participants were found to have chosen the liberal options at least 5 times out of 7. Li has said that a CASS "survey found that Chinese society, on the whole, is tolerant."[38] Our results would lead us to believe that this young generation is very tolerant. For each issue, we developed a hypothesis which might explain the trends we were uncovering. We based our hypotheses on Western research and experience, as very little research of this kind had been undertaken in China.

**HYPOTHESIS 1. Those with more years in university are likely to be more "liberal" on social policy issues.**

Several studies support our belief that university experience broadens the mind. Kim et al., for example, concluded that "as the students gained more educational experiences, they tended to develop more liberal values leading to greater acceptance of homosexuality."[39] Lambert et al. asked, "Does education open students' minds and in doing so increase their acceptance of diversity in others?" and answered, "The results of this study suggest yes, at least in terms of attitudes towards gays and lesbians."[40] In a Canadian study, Schellenberg et al. confirmed that "attitudes toward homosexuals improved with time spent at college."[41] Our hypothesis was not completely confirmed in our study:

|  | Liberal | Not liberal |
|---|---|---|
| 1st year students | 75% (no.=88) | 25% (no.=29) |
| 2nd year students | 85% (no.=46) | 15% (no.=8) |
| 3 years or more students | 77% (no.=20) | 23% (no.=6) |

What is notable, however, is the high percentage (75%) of first-year students who fall into the "liberal" category. This rises to 85% for second-year students and falls back to 77% for third-year students.[42]

**HYPOTHESIS 2. Those who have one or more gay or lesbian acquaintances, close friends, or relatives are more liberal on policy issues than those who do not.**

Many researchers point to this factor as perhaps the most significant in producing a tolerant populace. Altemeyer "highlights the beneficial effects of knowingly knowing a homosexual."[43] Kardia concludes that "getting to know lesbians, gay men, and bisexual people was a primary mechanism through which students' attitudes changed."[44] And Herek and Glunt found that "interpersonal contact was a powerful predictor of attitudes toward gay men."[45] Very few of our participants claimed to know a gay or lesbian person, yet those who had neither a relative nor close friend were frequently as liberal as those who did.

|  | Liberal | Not liberal |
|---|---|---|
| Has a close friend/relative | 79% (no.=11) | 21% (no.=3) |
| Has neither a close friend/relative | 77% (no.=118) | 23% (no.=35) |

Our hypothesis was not confirmed.

**HYPOTHESIS 3. Female participants are more liberal on social policy issues than male participants.**

Western research has demonstrated overwhelmingly that in our culture females are more liberal than males. Altemeyer's clear statement can stand for a generation of researchers: "Females have always proved more tolerant than males toward homosexuals in my studies."[46] In a comparative study involving British and Chinese students, Higgins et al. reported that "although the British students held more permissive attitudes toward homosexuality than did their Chinese counterparts, it appeared that women seemed to be more accepting than men of homosexuality in both countries."[47] In our study, the percentage of females and males in the liberal category is virtually identical.[48]

|  | Liberal | Not liberal |
|---|---|---|
| Females | 79% (no.=65) | 21% (no.=17) |
| Males | 78% (no.=91) | 22% (no.=26) |

Our hypothesis was not supported.

**HYPOTHESIS 4. Those most liberal on social policy issues come from major cities (defined as 10 million or more) and, the corollary, those least liberal on policy issues come from smaller cities and towns.**

It is commonplace in North America to believe that those who live in rural areas are more homo-negative than those in urban areas. That is what Higgins and Sun believed they had confirmed in their research in China.[49] By contrast, we found that those who came from cities like Shanghai and Beijing were not as liberal as those from smaller cities and towns. In fact, when we moved from the top of our population list—"10 million or more"—to the bottom—"less than 5,000," we found the degree of liberalness rose:

|  | Liberal | Not liberal |
|---|---|---|
| 10 million or more | 70% (no.=37) | 30% (no.=16) |
| 10 million to 1 million | 81% (no.=25) | 19% (no.=6) |
| 1 million to 100,000 | 87% (no.=52) | 13% (no.=8) |
| 100,000 & 5,000 | 91% (no.=10) | 9% (no.=11) |
| Less than 5,000 | 88% (no.=22) | 12% (no.=3) |

Our hypothesis was not supported.

**HYPOTHESIS 5. Those in the humanities are more liberal on social policy issues than those in the pure and applied sciences.**

Kim et al.'s research led them to conclude that "students who studied education scored significantly higher than those students who studied business,"[50] and Schellenberg found that "compared to science and business students, students in the faculties of arts and social science had more positive attitudes toward gay men."[51] In our study, students in the humanities and the pure and applied sciences had identical scores for liberalness:

|  | Liberal | Not liberal |
| --- | --- | --- |
| Students in the humanities | 78% (no.=35) | 22% (no.=10) |
| Students in the pure and applied sciences | 78% (no.=69) | 22% (no.=20) |

Our hypothesis was not supported.

**HYPOTHESIS 6. The most liberal on social policy issues come from families whose parents have higher levels of education.[52]**

We placed a parent with some post-secondary education ("higher level of education") as an "A" and a parent whose education did not include any secondary education as a "B."

| | |
| --- | --- |
| Liberal participants whose fathers were "A's": | 74% (no.=52) |
| Liberal participants whose fathers were "B's": | 80% (no.=93) |
| Liberal participants whose mothers were "A's": | 77% (no.=41) |
| Liberal participants whose mothers were "B's": | 78% (no.=105) |

What we see is that the level of education had no bearing on whether their child was liberal on sexual orientation policy issues. Our hypothesis was not supported.

We then turned to assess our students' perceptions of sexual orientation prejudice on their campus, their willingness to intervene in the presence of negative comments, and factors that affected their perceptions and their actions. We began by asking how often they hear "fag talk" and where.

|  | Females | Males |
| --- | --- | --- |
| Frequently/Often | 18% (no.=14) | 14% (no.=19) |
| Sometimes | 38% (no.=31) | 30% (no.=35) |
| Rarely/Never | 44% (no.=36) | 55% (no.=63) |

While females and males reported just about the same level in the "Frequently" and "Often" categories, males responded more often than females in "Rarely" and "Never" categories. Overall, the incidence of "fag talk" is considerably lower than levels reported for North American universities and high schools.

Where did students hear most "fag talk"? Participants reported the highest frequency on university grounds and dormitories. Interestingly, little of it was heard around sports facilities.

|  | Classrooms | | University grounds | | Dorms | | Sports facilities | |
|---|---|---|---|---|---|---|---|---|
|  | F | M | F | M | F | M | F | M |
| **Frequently** | 0% | 2% | 2% | 5% | 2% | 11% | 0% | 3% |
| **Often** | 10% | 1% | 11% | 4% | 10% | 17% | 7% | 6% |
| **Sometimes** | 29% | 11% | 50% | 34% | 53% | 27% | 13% | 15% |
| **Rarely** | 42% | 42% | 34% | 37% | 29% | 26% | 36% | 41% |
| **Never** | 19% | 44% | 3% | 21% | 7% | 135 | 44% | 35% |

Did our participants regard the use of this language as offensive? If it could cause pain, there could be moral grounds for intervening.

|  | Not offensive | A little offensive | Quite offensive | Extremely offensive |
|---|---|---|---|---|
| **Females** | 1% (no.= 1) | 44% (no.= 36) | 22% (no.= 18) | 12% (no.= 10) |
| **Males** | 3% (no.= 4) | 33% (no.= 38) | 32% (no.= 40) | 7% (no.= 8) |

Only 5 of our 200 participants were prepared to claim that such slurs were "not offensive." When we combined "quite" and "extremely" categories, 34% of our females and 39% of our males agreed such language was offensive. One wonders what the numbers would be if our sample had been made up entirely of gays and lesbians.[53]

We asked our participants how often they thought anyone would intervene in the presence of "fag talk?"

| | |
|---|---|
| **Always** | 0% |
| **Most of the time** | 3% |
| **Some of the time** | 17% |
| **Rarely** | 39% |
| **Never** | 41% |

Clearly, general intervention rates are low: 80% of the time, intervention rarely or never occurs.

How often did our participants claim they intervened?

|  | Female | Male |
|---|---|---|
| **Always/Often** | 21% (n=12) | 9% (n=7) |
| **Rarely/Never** | 79% (n=46) | 91% (n=69) |

These numbers are no better than their estimation of intervention rates from the general populace whether on or off campus—this in spite of the fact that they understood that the language was offensive and likely to cause pain.

We wondered whether those in the humanities intervened more often than those in the pure and applied sciences. The differences were not appreciable:

|  | Humanities | Pure and applied sciences |
|---|---|---|
| **Frequently/Often** | 19% (n=6) | 12% (n=7) |
| **Rarely/Never** | 81% (n=26) | 89% (n=54) |

However, those who had a gay or lesbian friend or relative intervened four times more often than those who did not have such relationships. Conversely, those who had neither relationship seldom intervened:

|  | Has close friend/relative | Has neither |
|---|---|---|
| **Frequently/Often** | 30% (n=5) | 71% (n=12) |
| **Rarely/Never** | 8% (n=7) | 92% (n=92) |

If our participants intervened in a case of homophobic remarks, did they think they would receive support for intervening?

| *From their friends?* | Yes | No |
|---|---|---|
| **Females** | 68% (n=55) | 31% (n=25) |
| **Males** | 65% (n=71) | 36% (n=39) |

| *From classmates?* | Yes | No |
|---|---|---|
| **Females** | 68% (n=55) | 32% (n=26) |
| **Males** | 61% (n=67) | 39% (n=43) |

| From professors? | Yes | No |
|---|---|---|
| Females | 57% (n=45) | 41% (n=32) |
| Males | 46% (n=50) | 46% (n=50) |

| From family? | Yes | No |
|---|---|---|
| Females | 35% (n=27) | 60% (n=47) |
| Males | 41% (n=44) | 54% (n=58) |

| From onlookers? | Yes | No |
|---|---|---|
| Females | 21% (n=16) | 72% (n=54) |
| Males | 28% (n=31) | 65% (n=71) |

In large numbers, our students felt that they could turn to their friends and classmates for support, but, as one moves down the list, support from professors, family, and anonymous bystanders drops dramatically.

Was there any correlation between scores on our "liberal index" and rates of intervention? We found that 19 (14%) of "liberals" would intervene "always" or "most of the time," while 84 (62%) would "rarely" or "never" intervene. This is not particularly encouraging. On the other hand, when we looked at those who were not "liberal" in our sense, all claimed that they would rarely or never intervene. A high degree of liberalness would appear to be one positive variable.

Given these background conditions, we were interested to learn the reasons students would give for the actions they would or would not take if they heard words such as "fag," "faggot," "dyke," "homo," "queer," and/or "gay" directed at someone on campus.

In cases where they would intervene, the most common explanations given by both males and females were grounded in the language of ethics and human rights (principles of respect for persons, equality, freedom, and the dignity of all persons). For example, they wrote:

> People have no right to discriminate against gay and lesbian people due to their sexual orientation. Everyone should show respect for each other. Gay and lesbian people have a right to love and choose the one they love. We cannot treat them differently because of their sexual orientation. I wish that everyone would respect gay and lesbian people.

It's people's freedom to choose their sexual orientation. Even if we do not support gay and lesbian people, we cannot offend them. We do not have the right to insult or disturb their lives. Using words to insult gay and lesbian people infringes greatly on gay and lesbian people's rights. No matter what kind of sexual orientation they have, their rights should be protected. Everyone should show respect for each other. I did not realize this issue before, but now I am more attentive to it.

G&L behavior is a normal social phenomenon and it is nothing strange. I feel gay and lesbian people are as normal as heterosexual people. There are a lot of people who do not really know gay and lesbian people, but just follow others in insulting them. I feel they are ignorant, and they do not know what is right and what is wrong.

Long live understanding! Everyone has their freedom to choose their life styles, and gay and lesbian people do no harm to the stability of society. Oppression is not the only way to deal with this problem and it is definitely not the best way either.

G&L people are as equal as others. It is a basic norm to respect others.

Several simply took the position that being gay or lesbian was just normal:[54]

G&L people are normal. Maybe after several years, they will be accepted by others.

Some thought that being gay or lesbian was a matter of choice while others thought that it was biologically determined. Either way, they produced arguments to support tolerance:

Everyone has the right to choose their sexual orientation. We cannot insult others because of their different sexual orientation.

It is their freedom to choose their sexual orientation and it has nothing to do with others.

I definitely will intervene because G&L people are
born to be so and they have no choice and we should
not insult them.

Sexual orientation is determined by many factors
and we cannot insult G&L people because of something they cannot control.

Finally, many said they would intervene simply on grounds that
insulting people is rude:

I look down on those who insult others no matter who
they are insulting. It is definitely rude to humiliate others.

I feel it is really rude and boring to insult others and
I feel sorry for G&L students, so I will intervene.

We were just as interested to learn the reasons given by our participants for not intervening in the presence of homo-negative language.
Three positions were frequently repeated:

- It has nothing to do with me.
- Most times, students are just joking around.
- The terms are sometimes not insulting.

The first reflects a Kohlbergian level-one "moral argument": actions are
evaluated only by how they affect the speaker/agent. In the second, an
action is not reprehensible if it is not meant seriously (no matter what
hurt it might cause). The third is reminiscent of the defense many
teenagers offer in this country when they are challenged about their
use of "That's so gay." Several female participants argued that, if they
intervened, they would be taken to be lesbians themselves and this was
not a prospect they relished. Another group defended not intervening
because it would be ineffective and, what is more, it might disrupt social
harmony yet change nothing. In their own words:

Although I know it is wrong, I do not want to meddle
in it.

I do not think I have the right to intervene because it has nothing to do with me and it does not hurt my position.

The G&L issue is very sensitive. Although I have sympathy for them, if I intervene, people will think I am gay. What's more, intervening … will not provide G&L people with a better life. My intervention can change nothing.

If I intervene, others will think that I am gay as well, or others will think I have a mental problem.

Sometimes when we mention these words, it is just a joke and we do not truly mean it. It is not necessary to intervene when it is a joke.

First, insulting gay and lesbian students does not happen very often. We talk about this phenomenon in our dorms, and we do not talk about a specific person. It has nothing to do with whether or not it is insulting. Second, if I do see that someone is insulting gay and lesbian people, I will not intervene because it has nothing to do with me. I will feel sorry for gay and lesbian people, but I will not intervene.

We asked our participants whether they thought an "out" student felt *safe* on their campus. More than one-third of our males and a fifth of our females thought their campus was unsafe.

| | Extremely/quite safe: | Quite/Extremely unsafe |
|---|---|---|
| **Females** | 16% (no.=13) | Females 22% (no.=18) |
| **Males** | 14% (no.=16) | Males 35% (no.=41) |

When asked a more pointed question—Would an "out" student feel *welcome* on your campus?—the results were generally more negative:

| | Extremely/quite welcome | Quite/extremely unwelcome |
|---|---|---|
| **Females** | 0% (no.=0) | 41% (no.=32 |
| **Males** | 3% (no.=3) | 51% (no.=52) |

For both females and males, the welcoming numbers drop precipitously and the unwelcome numbers climb sharply from those recorded in answers to the previous question. The prospects of a positive experience for an out gay or lesbian student entering this university are bleak indeed.

Our participants caught the difference between their university being "safe" and it being "welcoming." For example, one of many students wrote in this vein:

> My university is very open. Everyone is treated equally, at least in public. Therefore, an openly gay or lesbian person will not be discriminated against, at least I don't think so. It is a safe place, but it is not very welcoming for G&L students.

Another echoed:

> No one will care about G&L people's privacy that much and it is safe for G&L students. But it is surely not a welcoming place.

By contrast, one student spoke eloquently and positively about his university:

> My university welcomes diversity. Different thoughts and values are respected and accepted here. In this kind of liberal atmosphere, students are open, tolerant, and understanding of all kinds of diversity ... G&L students can make friends and join campus activities just as others.

But many others presented a dark side of student opinion, referring to gays and lesbians as "abnormal," "weird," "different," "psychological deviants," and "disgusting."

One offered a general assessment of universities and aimed criticism at their own administration:

> Most people cannot accept G&L people, even in some so-called advanced universities. What's more, univer-

> sity administrators do not want to accept new ideas and
> they have more negative perspectives on G&L students.

One was even more pointed and personal in her criticism of what she perceived as a leadership vacuum in her university:

> Sigh! People at this university have been so cowardly.
> Even (the name of a senior administrator) is too timid
> to be open about his sexual orientation.

### CONCLUSION

In response to one question on our survey, one student wrote, "Chinese society is developing very fast and people's perspectives on G&L people are changing, too."

Changes in the past twenty years have been sweeping and the pace is accelerating. Some landmark indicators have been very public:

1997  Law reform decriminalized "homosexuality" by eliminating it from the "hooliganism" statutes.

2001  The Chinese Society of Psychiatry removed "homosexuality" from its Chinese Classification and Diagnostic Criteria of Mental Disorders manual.

2001  The first Gay and Lesbian Film Festival was staged in Beijing—although it was closed by the police after three days.

2003  Fudan University offered a course entitled "Homosexual Health Social Sciences" for medical students—the first of its kind.

2005  Fudan University offered an optional undergraduate course entitled "Introduction to Gay and Lesbian Studies"—a first for non-medical undergraduates.

2005  Hong Kong Judge Michael Hartmann ruled that laws against gay sex for men under 21 who engage in sodomy are unconstitutional; the government decided not to appeal the court ruling.

2006  Sun Yat-Sen University in Zhuhai officially approved the Happy Together club, an on-campus forum that organized lectures and movies on gay culture.

2009  The Beijing Queer Film Festival went off without a hitch (it had been closed by authorities in 2001 and 2005 and police harassment continues[55]).

2009  The Shanghai Gay Pride Festival was successfully launched.

Our research tells us that beneath these very visible events a seismic shift in public opinion is taking place—at least among a new generation of university students. Our most dramatic and surprising discovery was the very high percentage of students who took a liberal stance on sensitive public policy issues. We proposed a number of Western-derived hypotheses designed to offer possible explanations for our participants' liberal judgments and were amused when our hypotheses were confounded in all but one case. We were impressed by the number of students who relied on human rights principles to justify their positions.

We were disappointed, but not surprised, by low intervention rates in cases where students were confronted with anti-gay slurs, but we reminded ourselves of the very high priority Chinese people place on maintaining social harmony. To challenge someone is to disrupt social peace. Intervening is a very uncommon practice in Chinese society, so much so that one male student said, "I have never seen anyone intervene, so I won't intervene either." Finally, we wondered about a sentiment that many students shared with us: "University students are open and they respect G&L people. G&L people do not need to worry about being discriminated against." The next generation of research should consult directly with sexual minority students to see if they concur.

**NOTES**

1    "Homophobia" is a relatively new term in Chinese. It does not appear in the 1986 and 1999 editions of the *Concise English-Chinese Dictionary* (Toronto: Oxford University Press, 1986, 1999). For this reason, we have used "sexual orientation prejudice" in the title. See, for example, Yinhe Li recounting the view of one of her "informants" in "Regulating Male Same-sex Relationships in the People's Republic of China," *Sex and Sexuality in China*, ed. Elaine Jeffreys (London and New York: Routledge, 2006), 82–101 at 99: "While previously unaware of the existence of homophobia, (he) said that he now saw that it permeated all of the print and broadcast media.... (He) concluded, "I do not know how the English-language term 'homophobia' should be translated into Chinese. But it seems to me that China is 100 percent homophobic." A new term, "tong xing lian kong ju zheng," which

literally means "the symptoms of being afraid of gays," can now be found in the *Online Chinese-English Dictionary* at www.iciba.com (accessed August 27, 2011). In English, Gregory M. Herek recommends the use of "sexual prejudice" because it conveys no assumptions about the motivations underlying negative attitudes ("The Psychology of Sexual Prejudice," *Current Directions in Psychological Science* (American Psychological Society) 9, no. 1 (2000): 19). Similarly, Colleen R. Logan argues for "homo-prejudice" as an alternative to "homophobia" because "there is little, if any, evidence to support anti-homosexual characterizations as a phobia" ("Homophobia? No, Homoprejudice," *Journal of Homosexuality* 31, no. 3 (1996): 31).

2    Louis Crompton, "Imperial China 500BCE–1849," *Homosexuality and Civilization* (Cambridge: Cambridge University Press, 2003). See also Bret Hinch, "China," *Gay Histories and Culture: An Encyclopedia*, ed. George E. Haggerty (New York: Garland Publishing Inc., 2002), 184-88 and Fang-Fu Ruan, "China" in *Sociolegal Control of Homosexuality: A Multi-nation Comparison*, eds. Donald J. West and Richard Green (New York: Plenum Press, 1997), 57–66.

3    Though in "Ming Tales," Crompton (*Homosexuality and Civilization*) is "struck by the range of social classes involved: students and school inspectors, merchants, a porter, and a common soldier" (219).

4    Crompton, "Ming Tales," 217.

5    See Frank Dikotter, *Sex, Culture and Modernity in China: Medical Science and the Construction of Sexual Identities in the Early Republican Period* (London: Hurst and Company, 1995) and Erick Laurent, "Sexuality and Human Rights: An Asian Perspective," *Journal of Homosexuality* 48, no. 3/4 (2005): 163–225.

6    For a fascinating account of the transfer of Western thought about sexuality, see Howard Chiang, "Epistemic Modernity and the Emergence of Homosexuality in China," *Gender & History* 22, no. 3 (2010): 629–657. See also Jin Wu, "From '*Long Yang*' and '*Dui Shi*' to '*Tongzhi*': Homosexuality in China," *Journal of Gay & Lesbian Psychotherapy* 7, no. 1/2 (2003): 117-143.

7    We accept Chou Wah-shan's rejection of the term "homosexual" when characterizing same-sex eroticism in the pre-1911 era: "Chinese culture recognizes the differences between same-sex and opposite eroticism, but sex is not a ground on which to classify people. The traditional Chinese world did not dichotomize sexual desire into a gender binarism of same-sex desire and opposite-sex desire. In traditional China, same-sex desire activities are portrayed in predominantly social, rather than sexual terms...." "Homosexuality and the Cultural Process of *Tongzhi* in Chinese Societies," *Journal of Homosexuality* 40, no. 3/4 (2001): 27–46 at 29.

8    Hinch, "China," 187.

9    In *Sociolegal Control* (63), Ruan cites the *Criminal Law of the People's Republic of China*, Article 106 that read: "All hooliganism should be subjected to

arrest and sentence." The inclusion of homosexuality within the scope of article 106 was removed in 1997 about the time Ruan's article was published.

10    See Li, "Regulating Male Same-sex Relationships," 86: "The harsh treatment and excessive administration penalties that were meted out to homosexuals during the Cultural Revolution period was a product of the time. As is well known, this was a period in which the rule of law was non-existent and Chinese society was plunged into chaos. Although that era has past, just like the passing of a nightmare, it has nevertheless left a deep scar both in the minds of the people and on social consciousness in general. Certainly, the harsh treatment that was meted out to many homosexuals during this period has had a continued impact on their lives. Moreover, it promoted the existence of homophobia in Chinese society. This problem has yet to be resolved...." For an account of the extent to which all manifestations of love and sex were repressed during the Cultural Revolution, see Emily Honig, "Socialist Sex: The Cultural Revolution Revisited," *Modern China* 29, no. 2 (April, 2003): 143–75.

11    Yinhe Li, "Debate: Homosexuality," *China Daily*, July 25, 2011. http://usa. chinadaily.com.cn/opinion/2011-07/25/content_12973300.htm (accessed September 30, 2011).

12    The fact that 70% of respondents thought there was something wrong with being homosexual does not necessarily imply that sexual minorities would be discriminated against, but follow-up questions about family and social policy issues were warranted.

13    When asked for reasons why they thought an older generation held such negative views of sexual minorities, more than half our participants referred to "traditional culture," "traditional ethics," "Chinese ethics," "social ethics," or "conservative views." Other responses in descending order of frequency:
- has insufficient knowledge/understanding (20)
- believes that the behaviour of gays and lesbians is abnormal (16)
- finds gay and lesbian behaviour shameful/disgraceful/disgusting (12)
- holds majority-minority views (12)
- believes that gay and lesbian sexual orientation is against the law of nature (8)
- adheres to the adage that "sex without offspring is the greatest sin" (8)
- possesses a stereotype of heterosexual male-female roles (7)
- believes that there are serious health issues (6)

14    Dalin Liu, Man Lun Ng, Li Ping Zhou, and Erwin J. Haeberle, *Sexual Behaviour in Modern China—Report on the Nationwide Survey of 20,000 Men and Women* [English edition] (New York: Continuum, 1997), 191 and 192.

15    Y.T. Cui and L.F. Liang, "The Countermeasures and Multi-dimensionality Analyses of Mental Disorders among College Students in the Socialist Market Economy," *Proceedings of the Third Pan-Asia Pacific Conference on Mental Health* (Beijing: China Association for Mental Health, 2001), 26–40. Cited in L.T. Higgins and Chunhui Sun, "Gender, Social Background, and

Sexual Attitudes among Chinese Students," *Culture, Health, & Sexuality* 9, no. 1 (January, 2007): 31–42 at 34.

16   L.T. Higgins, M. Zheng, Y.L. Liu, and C. Sun, "Attitudes to Marriage and Sexual Behaviors: A Survey of Gender and Culture Differences in China and United Kingdom," *Sex Roles* 46, no. 3/4 (2002): 75–87 at 86. We interpret "should be allowed" to mean "should be legal."

17   East China's College Students Surveyed on Sex Views. We interpret "should be permitted openly" to mean "should be legal." http://english.people.com. cn/200201/18/eng20020118_88916.shtml (accessed July 3, 2012).

18   Reported by Vicky Xu in "Homosexuals better-accepted, but not for child-adoption rights," *Shanghai Daily News* (November 18, 2005). http:// english.eastday.com/eastday/englishedition/specials/node20815/userobject1ai1658123.html (accessed November 10, 2011).

19   Often Internet sites do not give many details about the sample size and categories of respondents. More importantly, none of the articles we uncovered reveal what standard of "more liberal" was used. http://www.chinadaily. com.cn/english/doc/2006-02/01/content_516625.htm (accessed October 19, 2011).

20   Bob Altemeyer, "Changes in Attitudes toward Homosexuals, *Journal of Homosexuality*" 42, no. 2 (2001): 63–75; Kam-lun Ellis Hon, Ting-fan Leung, Anthony Pak-yuen Yau, Sze-man Wu, Maxim Wan, Hoi-yee Chan, Wing-ki Yip, and Tai-fai Fok, "A Survey of Attitudes toward Homosexuality in Hong Kong Chinese Medical Students," *Teaching and Learning in Medicine* 7, no. 4 (2005), 344–48 at 346: "[Medical] students with a religion ... were more likely to be negative toward issues such as marital rights, child adoption"; Rhoda E. Howard-Hassmann, "The Gay Cousin: Learning to Accept Gay Rights," *Journal of Homosexuality* 42, no. 1 (2001): 127–47 at 145: "[Religious belief] made it difficult for many to accept gay marriage, and made it difficult for a few to show any tolerance whatsoever toward gay sexuality"; Mark E. Johnson, Christine Brems, and Pat Alford-Keating, "Personality Correlates of Homophobia," *Journal of Homosexuality* 34, no. 1 (1997): 57–69 at 57: "Religiosity was significantly correlated with more biased beliefs about the origins of homophobia, greater affective discomfort around gays, less endorsement of human rights for gays and lesbians, and greater homophobia"; Diana Kardia, "Student Attitudes toward Gay and Lesbian Issues: The Impact of College," *Diversity Digest* (Summer, 1998): "...this study found that fraternities and student religious groups are two peer environments that countered the more general trend on campus." http://www.diversityweb .org/Digest/Sm98/attitudes.html (accessed June 17, 2011).

21   Gary Sigley and Elaine Jefferys (1999), "Interview: On 'Sex' and 'Sexuality' in China: A Conversation with Pan Suiming," *Bulletin of Concerned Asian Scholars* 31, no. 1 (1999): 50–58 at 54.

22   See Martin Forsey, Susan Broomhall, and Jane Davis who challenge the value for students of international study abroad: "Broadening the Mind?:

Australian Student Reflections on the Experience of Overseas Study," *Journal of Studies in International Education* 16, no. 2 (2012): 128–30.

23   Just because so few of our participants had not traveled abroad does not mean that they were immune to influences from the West. New technologies have made it possible for Western media to penetrate the "Bamboo Curtain." When the Chinese government banned the distribution of the film *Brokeback Mountain*, so many pirated copies circulated that the acronym "BBM" quickly entered popular speech, as in "That is a BBM situation," or "She is a BBM ally." When our participants were asked to indicate the sources from which they gained the most information about gay and lesbian issues, films and the Internet received the highest ratings:

| FEMALES: | | MALES: | |
|---|---|---|---|
| Film | 94% (77) | Internet | 82% (96) |
| Internet | 72% (59) | Film | 80% (93) |
| Discussion with friends | 71% (58) | Discussion with friends | 68% (80) |
| Newspapers/magazines | 66% (54) | Newspapers/magazines | 64% (75) |
| Literature | 66% (54) | TV | 56% (65) |

24   See Bob Altemeyer, "Changes in Attitudes," 73: "…I would highlight the beneficial effects of knowingly knowing a homosexual"; Gordon Allport, *The Nature of Prejudice* (Garden City, NY: Doubleday, 1958); Gregory M. Herek and Eric K. Glunt, "Interpersonal Contact and Heterosexuals' Attitudes toward Gay Men: Results from a National Survey," *Journal of Sex Research* 30, no. 3 (1993): 239–244 at 242: "Interpersonal contact was the best predictor of attitudes toward gay men"; Gregory M. Herek and John P. Capitanio, " 'Some of my Best Friends': Intergroup Contact, Concealable Stigma, and Heterosexuals' Attitude toward Gay Men and Lesbians," *Personality & Social Psychology Bulletin* 22, no. 4 (1996): 412–24; Kardia, "Student Attitudes": "…getting to know lesbians, gay men, and bisexual people was a primary mechanism through which students' attitudes changed."

25   Li, "Debate: Homosexuality."

26   These numbers are somewhat higher than those recorded by Kam-lun Ellis Hon et al. in "A Survey of Attitudes toward Homosexuality" in which two-thirds of the study's Hong Kong medical students thought homosexuals should have equal marriage rights.

27   Li has proposed a *Chinese Same-Sex Marriage Bill* as an amendment to the marriage law at the Chinese People's Political Consultative Conference in 2003, 2005, 2006, and 2008 to legalize same-sex marriage. None has succeeded thus far, as she has been unable to find enough co-sponsors for the motion to be placed on the agenda. The attitude of the Chinese government towards homosexuality can be best summarized in the "three

no's" policy: "No approval; no disapproval; no promotion." Quoted from the Peking Duck blog by Richard Ammon, February 07, 2007 (http://blogs.mcclatchydc.com/china/2007/02/gay_marriage_in.html (accessed November 14, 2011). In 2012, she started yet another effort: http://www.gaystarnews.com/article/leading-chinese-scholar-seeking-support-gay-marriage-bill-again040312 (accessed July 4, 2012).

28  Li, "Debate: Homosexuality."

29  Li, "Debate: Homosexuality."

30  Gregory M. Herek, "Gender Gaps in Public Opinion about Lesbians and Gay Men," *Public Opinion Quarterly* 66, no. 1 (2002): 40–66 at 40.

31  Hon et al., "A Survey of Attitudes," 344.

32  Reported by Vicky Xu, *Shanghai Daily News* (November 18, 2005). Unfortunately, no figures were provided in the report to quantify what Cen meant by "few (young) people."

33  "China's Divorce Rate Continues to Climb," *The Independent*, June 17, 2010.

34  Herek, "Gender Gaps in Public Opinion," 40.

35  Ties Van de Werff, "The Struggle of the Tongzhi: Homosexuality in China and the Position of Chinese Comrades," *Urgency Required: Gay & Lesbian Rights are Human Rights*, eds. Ireen Dubel and Andre Hielkema (The Hague, Netherlands: Humanist Institute for Development Cooperation), 2009, 172–180 at 176.

36  In the same *China Daily* article ("Debate: Homosexuality"), Li fails to resolve some contradictory results in one of CASS's 2007 surveys. She wrote: "One question was: Should a known homosexual be allowed to take up a schoolteacher's job? The respondents who said 'no' slightly outnumbered those saying 'yes'.... When it came to 'whether parents should require a school to replace a teacher who is a homosexual,' more than half of the respondents stuck to their prejudice...." This does not sound like "equal employment rights for homosexuals" which 91% claimed to have supported, nor does it appear to be consistent with the 80% who agreed that "homosexuals were equal to heterosexuals." Equal but not equal.

37  Li, "Regulating Male Same-sex Relationships," 86.

38  Li, "Debate: Homosexuality."

39  Bryan S.K. Kim, Michael J. D'Andrea, K. Poonam, Kiaka J. Sahu, and A. Gaughen, "Multicultural Study of University Students' Knowledge of and Attitudes toward Homosexuality," *Journal of Humanistic Education and Development* 36, no. 3 (1998): 171–83 at 179.

40  Eric G. Lambert, Lois A. Ventura, Daniel E. Hall, and Terry Cluse-Tolar, "College Students' Views on Gay and Lesbian Issues: Does Education Make a Difference?" *Journal of Homosexuality* 50, no. 4 (2006): 1–30 at 24.

41  See E. Glenn Schellenberg, et al., "Attitudes toward Homosexuals," 139–152. See also Kardia in "Student Attitudes" who reports on a survey of 1000 first- and fourth-year students (1990–94) in which she found a liberal shift.

42 Because the sample of third-year students falls to 20, it may not be sufficiently large to be reliable.

43 Altemeyer, "Changing Attitudes," 73.

44 Kardia, "Student Attitudes."

45 Gregory M. Herek and Eric K. Glunt, "Interpersonal Contact and Hetero-sexuals' Attitudes," 242. See also Annie L. Cotton-Huston and Bradley M. Waite, "Anti-homosexual Attitudes in College Students: Predictors and Classroom Interventions," *Journal of Homosexuality* 38, no. 3 (2000): 117–33; Larry M. Lance, "The Effects of Interaction with Gay Persons on Attitudes toward Homosexuality," *Human Relations* 40, no. 6, 1987: 329–336; and Joel Wells and Mary L. Franken, "University Students' Knowledge about and Attitudes toward Homosexuality," *Journal of Humanistic Education and Development,* 26, no. 2 (1987): 81–95.

46 Altemeyer, "Changes in Attitudes," 66. See also Gregory M. Herek, "Heterosexuals' Attitudes toward Lesbians and Gay Men: Correlates and Gender Differences," *The Journal of Sex Research* 25, no. 4 (1988): 451–77; Gregory M. Herek and John P. Capitanio, "Sex Differences in How Heterosexuals Think about Lesbians and Gay Men: Evidence from Survey Context Effects," *The Journal of Sex Research* 36, no. 4 (1999): 348–60; Johnson et al. (1997), "Personality Correlates"; Vittorio Lingiardi, Simona Falanga, and Anthony R. D'Augelli, "The evaluation of homophobia in an Italian sample," *Archives of Sexual Behavior,* 34, no. 1 (Feb, 2005): 81–94; Trish Pratte, "A Comparative Study of Attitudes toward Homosexuality: 1986 and 1991," *Journal of Homosexuality* 26, no. 1 (1993): 77–83; and E. Glenn Schellenberg et al., "Attitudes toward Homosexuals."

47 L.T. Higgins, M. Zheng, Y.L. Liu, and C. Sun, "Attitudes to Marriage and Sexual Behaviors: A Survey of Gender and Culture Differences in China and United Kingdom," *Sex Roles* 46, no. 3/4 (2002): 75–87 at 86.

48 Hui Cao, Peng Wang, and Yuanyuan Gao have come to a similar conclusion: "...there was no significant difference found in the perceptions and attitudes about homosexuality between the female and male students" in "A Survey of Chinese University Students' Perceptions of and Attitudes towards Homosexuality," *Social Behavior and Personality: An International Journal* 38, no. 6 (July, 2010): 721–28 at 727. They point out that "this result diverges from that of Yan, Liu, and Yu (2002) who found that the attitudinal difference was significant between male and female university students," citing Yan, Y., J. Liu, and Y. Yu, "Knowledge and attitudes towards homosexuality in students of normal universities and colleges," *Health Education in China,* 18 (2002): 645–647.

49 Higgins and Sun, "Gender, Social Background, and Sexual Attitudes."

50 Bryan S.K. Kim et al., "Multicultural Study of University Students' Knowledge," 175–76.

51 E. Glenn Schellenberg et al., "Attitudes toward Homosexuals," 139. By contrast, in a study involving 500 students from three universities in China,

Cao et al. concluded that "generally speaking, the science students had much more knowledge about homosexuality and more tolerant attitudes than did liberal arts students" ("A Survey of Chinese University Students' Perceptions," 727).

52 We defined a "high level of education" as a father or mother having completed some post-secondary education and "little education" as having completed secondary school or less.

53 To our knowledge, this research—giving voice to gays and lesbians themselves—has never been systematically undertaken on campuses in China. This indictment includes our own research. The studies we found are all about asking "straights" what they think of "gays."

54 It is worth keeping in mind that the Chinese Psychiatric Association had removed "homosexuality" from its diagnostic manual of mental illnesses just five years before in April 2001. Interestingly, three of our participants turned the diagnostic manual on its head by suggesting the those prejudiced against gays and lesbians were the ones with mental illness issues: (1) "...people who insult gay and lesbian people are not psychologically healthy"; (2) "Those who insult gay and lesbian students have a personality problem"; and (3) "Those who insult gay and lesbian people are not psychologically healthy."

55 Though police harassment continues: http://shanghaiist.com/2011/06/22/beijing_queer_film_festival_2011.php (accessed July 4, 2012).

## "I Won't Discuss Who I'm Dating": Same-Sex Celebrity Gossip as Social Control

WES D. PEARCE

### POPULAR CULTURE AND GOSSIP

They're *all over* Hollywood! They all *know* each other!
They had this *pajama party*, and the police *raided* it![1]

David Ehrenstein recalls that this was how he learned that Rock Hudson was a *"ho-mo-sex-u-al"* and the news was breathlessly transmitted by his nine-year-old playmate Susan. She had learned about it from her parents who had read about if in *Confidential* and if that was the case then it must be so. Since the beginnings of celebrity gossip the public has been fascinated, titillated and scandalized to learn the intimate details surrounding the sexual escapades and practices of their favourite stars. Author and screenwriter James Ellroy suggests this interest stems from the size and scale of the Hollywood art form:

you're dealing with a bunch of characters whose gifts are erotically derived. They're 'larger than life' 'cause they're forty-foot faces up on the screen. Their lives are supposed to be our lives. And what's the most interesting thing about people? It's their sexuality.... I don't give a shit about anything pertaining to the movies, [...] All I want to know is who's a homosexual, who's a nymphomaniac, who's a lesbian, who has the biggest dick, and who is the woman who will fuck absolutely anybody—the driver, the car park, the boy who delivers the pizza. That's all!"[2]

Drawing upon scholarly writings, articles from popular magazines and gossip filled web-sites, this chapter argues that celebrity gossip, and more specifically same sex celebrity gossip, is not simply symptomatic of the golden ages of Hollywood and Broadway but is a complex cultural action made in response to conflicting middle class values, homophobia, a suspicion of acting and internalized homophobic insecurities. While the *National Enquirer's* annual "Who's Gay and Who's Not" edition might not provoke the outrage or sales that it once did, controversies such as Jody Foster's speech at the 2013 Golden Globe ceremony or Ramin Setoodeh 2010 article for *Newsweek* continue to demonstrate that even today, same sex celebrity gossip remains a powerful method of social control, containing and at times curbing the opportunities that gay and straight and queer actors, are able to pursue.

In his article on the culture of celebrity and Charles Lindbergh, Charles Ponce de Leon traces the development of "celebrity culture" back to the 1830s when "the penny press began publishing gossip and brief human-interest stories about various local and regional notables."[3] The demand was so great that by the 1850s the interview had become a regular feature of mass circulation journalism and in the 1880s and 1890s Joseph Pulitzer pioneered many of the innovations that have become mainstays of "celebrity journalism." Ponce de Leon argues that the tabloid journalism that emerged in the 1920s became a defining moment in the creation of American celebrity culture: "For many educated Americans, tabloid journalism was emblematic of a steep decline in public morals, the quintessential product of a society lacking dignity and good taste.... [B]y directing attention to the private lives of prominent individuals, tabloid journalism had shattered conventions that had enabled such figures to keep their private affairs out of public view."[4]

Tabloids operated with the assumption that their reading public had (or has) a right to know *"what was he really like?"* As such, tabloid journalists became "driven to get exclusives, they began to publish unauthorized material, including nasty exposés."[5] Further, Ponce de Leon argues that central to this journalistic approach (and to celebrity discourse past and present) is the underlying assumption in "American culture that wealth, power, and social prestige were morally corrosive."[6] The reception of tabloid journalism was constructed on Puritan/middle-class notions of containment, of ensuring that celebrity "not getting a swelled head."

While sociologist Jörg Bergmann argues that attempting "to fit the phenomenon of 'gossip' into a theoretical context of explanation" will inevitably be unsuccessful,[7] Ponce de Leon seems to suggest that the sole purpose of celebrity gossip is social control: ensuring that "the celebrity" conforms to "respectable, middle-class values" or, conversely, pays a price for this transgression. One of the results of this social policing, although certainly not an intentional one, was that sexuality became an area of discourse—or more specifically, deviant sexuality became a focus of tabloid journalism.

This celebrity-driven journalism evolved during the glory days of the great Hollywood studios. "From the very beginning, Louella Parsons dominated gossip about the movie industry. In 1925, she came to Hollywood where she enjoyed a virtual monopoly on celebrity news.... She had the power to make or break an actor by giving or withholding publicity."[8] Eventually, Parsons lost her "gossip monopoly" when "has-been, over the hill actress, Hedda Hopper, began writing her own version of Hollywood gossip, which millions of Americans read on a daily basis."[9] The two became bitter rivals, but both claimed to operate within a "strict system of ethics regarding what to print."[10] Correctly or not, Parsons always believed that she was the more ethical of the two: "I've kept secrets and watched others profit from my keeping them. I've covered up infidelities and scandals and seen them publicly proclaimed, frequently by the protagonist himself."[11]

The gossip stylings of Louella and Hedda eventually went out of vogue, *but not* America's appetite for celebrity gossip, and nothing better typified this new thirst for middle America's right to know than Robert Harrison's *Confidential Magazine*. In 1955, *Confidential Magazine*, sold over 5 million copies with lurid headlines such as "The Wife Clark Gable Forgot" (July 1955) and "Why Jo Di Maggio is striking out with Marilyn Monroe" (August 1953). In his biography of Harrison, Samuel Bernstein writes, "The shocking subject of homosexuality was a *Confidential* mainstay," noting that the publisher had "boundless enthusiasm for homosexual exposés."[12] Yet, perhaps ironically, Bernstein argues that Harrison "believed that he never wrote anything that could have really hurt anyone"[13] and, upon careful reading, many of the supposed "exposés" that targeted Tab Hunter and Liberace really do not say much at all.

Contemporary gossip about the deviant sexuality of certain celebrities can be titillating, scandalous, or outrageous, but it is almost always far more personal and vulgar than anything that *Confidential Magazine* or Louella Parsons could ever have imagined. Whether one believes Parson's ethical claim or Harrison's statement of innocence, both would be shocked by the state of contemporary celebrity journalism—a discourse in which the deviant or transgressive sexual practices of today's celebrities is seemingly always knowable and within easy reach.

## HOLLYWOOD, SEXUALITY AND MIDDLE AMERICA

The American film industry has, since its infancy, been focused on telling, retelling and selling the mythology and iconography of America; it is a mythology (and industry) that is hyper-masculine. Whether its stars are colonizing the frontier, celebrating the criminal underworld, retelling (or re-creating) war narratives or saving the world from aliens or super villains, Hollywood and, by extension, America has defined itself, and continues to define itself, upon a foundation of white masculine hetero-normativity.

In David Ehrenstein's *Open Secret: Gay Hollywood 1928–2000*, Mel Brooks is quoted, "Gays were always a fact in this industry—a rampant, wonderful, joyous fact,"[14] and yet Ehrenstein's book makes clear that this "joyous fact" has never been warmly received. In conversation with David Ehrenstein, pioneering queer activist Harry Hay remembers the days of Hollywood's Golden Age quite differently, recalling "there was never dialogue of any sort between Hollywood and the gay and lesbian movement. *Never....* the industry felt that families in, say, Iowa would not buy Hollywood movies if it were known in any way that *these* people were 'tainted'."[15]

The website GLBTQ argues that the banishment of William Haines (the first "out" Hollywood actor and a man who refused to "play by the studio rules"), the establishment of the Motion Pictures Producers and Distributors of America (1922), and the subsequent enactment of the Hays Production Code (1930) forced all actors of ambiguous sexuality into the closet.[16] Not surprisingly, in an industry where (at least publicly) an essential characteristic of film stars is heterosexuality, the treatment of deviant sexuality as something to be scorned, mocked and hidden away continued unabated. In *Liberace: An American Boy*, Darden Pyron argues that even in the 1950s and 1960s, "closeted" behaviour was a necessity:

> homosexual exposure equaled professional, economic ruin. It was what prompted the actor Anthony Perkins into "deep closet maneuvers to hide the fact of his boyfriends and male lovers" even abroad, where no one recognized the *Psycho* star. "You couldn't be too careful in those days," Perkins's manager, gay himself, agreed. "In those days," recalled another member of this demimonde, "if you had sex with a man, that put you in a category from which you could not deviate. You were a fruitcake, and destined to be that all your life"... George Cukor, one of Hollywood's most famous—and barely closeted—gay men, put it another way: "In those days you had to be very virile or they thought you were degenerate."[17]

For Hollywood stars, a sexual identity that deviates from the heteronormative has never been permitted. In the mid-1990s, Jill Abrams, "out" producer for CNN's *ShowBiz Today* argued, "If you're an actor it's very important that you appear to be heterosexual, because that's the majority of this country. That's where the dollars are coming from, and they need to believe in their fantasy world that they can have you. If they think you are totally unobtainable, it won't work."[18]

"Hollywood," as John Clum argues, "conveyed a paradoxical dual image ... the film studios wanted to be seen as the purveyors of middle class values.... But Hollywood was also famous as the center of conspicuous consumption, social mobility, and sexual profligacy."[19] If a star's scale tipped too much towards the unseemly, career disaster could follow. As Laurence Mark explains, the necessity to maintain the image of a star's heterosexuality, and by extension his masculinity, is because both are linked to the notion of studio profits and "relatablity"; relatability in the American heartland does not include male movie stars who "do" other male movie stars.[20]

This, one could argue, is the reason why so much time, money and energy was spent protecting to greater or lesser degrees the "reputations" of such stars as Tab Hunter, Sal Mineo, Charles Laughton, James Dean, Montgomery Clift, Kevin Spacey and perhaps most famously, Rock Hudson. It is, according to Bernstein (and others), widely accepted that in early 1955 Universal Studios made a desperate deal with Bob Harrison and *Confidential Magazine*; "kill any story about Rock Hudson's late night lavender life, and The Studio would offer up another star as a sacrificial lamb. That's supposed to be the skinny on how Rory Calhoun's mug shots made it to the cover of the May 1955 issue, complete with the macho star's arrest and prison record."[21] Ironically, *Confidential Magazine*'s exposé of Calhoun's criminal past, like the exposé of Robert Mitchum's 1948 arrest for smoking marijuana, only furthered his reputation as "a man's man" and helped further his career.

In the past two decades no one has spent more time fending off the persistent rumours of his sexuality and defending his heterosexuality than Tom Cruise. Cruise has launched and won several lawsuits over "libelous" claims that he has participated in sexual activities involving other men (which, one could argue, is quite different from claiming that Tom Cruise is gay). The most famous of these court cases was his $100 million suit against gay porn star Chad Slater (aka Kyle Bradford) and the celebrity magazine *Actustar*.[22] Shortly after the Bradford trial, Cruise filed another $100 million suit against *Bold* publisher Michael Davis who, at that time, claimed to have in his possession a tape of Cruise engaging in "sexual acts" with an unnamed man. Again, faced with a $100 million lawsuit, Mr. Davis quickly changed his story and said that "the videotape did not exist."[23]

Shortly after the Bradford suit was filed, Tom Cruise's lawyer Scott Fields wanted to ensure that the public understood that these actions were not motivated by homophobia but rather a concern for the truth and especially for the mental health of Cruise's progeny. Fields was quoted as saying that "[Tom] is a great respecter of homosexual rights, but he's not gay, and he's ready to prove this in court ... [he] is tired of it and it hurts his children. It's something that will be there forever. And damn it, he's going to stop it."[24] The gossip site *SweatPantsErection* has noted (with glee) that Tom Cruise and his numerous attempts to prove his heterosexuality in court echo the actions of another famous celebrity, reminding readers that Liberace also sued (and won) when "reports were made that he was gay."[25]

Hollywood, as far as the image presented to, and received by, "Middle America," is straight. The extent to which Cruise and others have gone to defend their heterosexual and masculine images reveals the importance and value that North American society places on hetero-normativity; more importantly, the actions of these stars indicate the value of hetero-normativity as a commodity. As Goldstein argues, "imagine if Russell Crowe cultivated a similar [hip straight guy] persona. Would he still be believable as the millennial version of a man's man? This is the heart of Cruise's suit: The implication that he is gay could destroy his credibility in action films."[26] More recently, *Newsweek* reporter Ramin Setoodeh wondered why, given that color blind casting is now widely accepted by American society, sexual orientation should limit a gay actor's choice of roles? As he answers himself, "[t]he fact is, an actor's background does affect how we see his or her performance— which is why the Denzels or the Tom Hanks-es of the world guard their privacy carefully."[27]

The at times outlandish responses to the gossip around same-sexuality constantly reinforces the notion that "passing" for straight and masculine (even for a heterosexual actor) is an important part of an actor's identity. Setoodeh hypothetically questions "if an actor of the stature of George Clooney came out of the closet tomorrow, would we still accept him as a heterosexual leading man? It's hard to say. Or maybe not. Doesn't it mean something that no openly gay actor like that exists?"[28] In other words, "how can any real man identify with a goddamn pansy?"[29]

The desire, or as Setoodeh would argue, the necessity, to be seen as "a man" or to "pass" as "a man" or as masculine, as opposed to "a fag," can put enormous pressures on an individual. This pressure does not simply prevent Hollywood stars from being totally engaged in their work as artists, but forces further compromises with their life. Yet, as has been argued, and continues to be evidenced in popular culture, as Rupert Everett recently made clear, remaining in the closet is an important part of maintaining a successful film career (a fact aided and perhaps made easier by the threat of same-sexuality gossip).[30] Hollywood maintains heterosexuality and hyper- masculinity in the same way that professional sports and country music reward such behaviour and punish transgressors.

## THEATRE, ACTORS AND SODOMY

Acting, unlike sports, or even country music, has historically been a site of hetero-normative and masculine resistance which further problematizes the sexual image of the actor. Dating back to (at least) the Elizabethan Age, acting has been a problematic site for the middle classes insofar as they have assumed that the theatre is full of sexual deviants, and yet this same public is extremely uneasy about the reality of sexual deviancy and theatre artists. In their book *Passing Performances,* Robert Schanke and Kim Marra draw attention to the popular notion that theatre, "has long borne the reputation of being a haven for homosexuality"; in reaching this conclusion they draw on Nicholas de Jongh's work which links this modern tension between "homosexuality and the theatre to the Puritans, who demonized ... the actor's body in public performance, linking it to prostitution and the worst of all cardinal sins, sodomy."[31]

As a by-product of this historic paradox, the function of gossip (especially when connected to notions of same sexuality) within the world of theatre operates differently than in the world of Hollywood. In 1953, while appearing in *A Day by the Sea,* the recently knighted Sir John Gielgud was arrested, convicted and fined ten pounds for "persistently importuning for immoral purposes." He had escaped immediate attention because he had, as was common practice, provided a false name to police at the time of his arrest. He was recognized during his court appearance and the incident soon became fodder for the London papers. Gielgud was, to say the least, humiliated by the publicity and extremely concerned about how this would affect the production. However, on the night the story broke, his first entrance was met with a standing ovation that stopped the show. As the show continued its run, he was often met with sustained applause both in the auditorium and by fans at the stage door.[32] The press continued to use Gielgud's arrest as evidence of the degenerates who work in theatre, thus allowing journalists to write vigorously and slanderously about the "homosexual menace." Gielgud's career continued, more or less unabated. He eventually won an Oscar, was named as a member of the British Academy of Film and Television Arts fellowship, appointed to the Order of Merit (by Queen Elizabeth II) and perhaps, more importantly, in 1994, he attended the ceremony when the West End's Globe Theatre was re-named the Gielgud Theatre.

The comparative ease (and this term is used with some reservation) with which Gielgud survived this incident can be partially explained by the nature and role of theatre gossip. If one of the major functions of Hollywood gossip is to maintain social control and thereby the illusion of heteronormative iconography with the threat of public "outing" and a ruined career as punishment for those who don't "play by the rules," the primary function of theatre gossip is to reinforce the validity of moral (and social) norms. By highlighting episodes like Gielgud's entrapment, theatre gossip reinforces the cultural ideology of who does theatre.

Because its role has typically been to confirm what a limited readership already knew, theatre gossip has never had the same allure as Hollywood gossip. The popular columns of Walter Winchell (such as "Your Broadway and Mine" that appeared in the *New York Graphic*) notwithstanding, theatre gossip has never had the power to destroy careers. In America, the power to make or break careers was controlled by the theatre critics of New York's daily papers and select national magazines such as *Time* and *New Republic*. These critiques, when they occurred, were not the somewhat veiled references to sexuality often used by Parsons or *Confidential Magazine*, but venomous, hysterical, articulated and homophobic attacks against all homosexual elements on Broadway. Not surprisingly, given the power of the word in theatre, the usual targets were playwrights. Such attacks could hardly be called "gossip," as they formed a well-orchestrated and relentless attack against gay playwrights such as William Inge, Tennessee Williams and Edward Albee (Inge suffered a breakdown after Robert Brustein's scathing article in *Harper's*). Yet for all the hatred written by these columnists, the content of their many articles remained strikingly similar: there are homosexuals in the theatre!

Recalling de Jongh's discussion, I would argue that theatre, much more than film or television, is transgressive insofar as it demands that the viewer gaze upon the performer's body. The performative body is live (therefore erotic) and "othered"; as such, it is a [potential] threat to the viewer. Alan Cumming argues, "You'll more readily try something completely bizarre on Broadway than you might in a movie. I mean, makeup galore and lipstick on my nipples—I do that on Broadway ... but would I do it on the screen?"[33]

Theatre is understood and critiqued as being more "authentic" and as such, considerably more dangerous. David Wayne asks, "Why does theatre attract more gay actors than the movies? I think it's due to the camera. Not that the camera doesn't lie—it does, often. But California people are more apt to place stereotypes in front of the camera. Theatre has more leeway, more faith in an actor's ability to make believe. Casting for the stage is nowhere as rigid and discriminatory."[34] Viewed as an authentic performative act, theatre is much more dangerous than film or television. Historically, critically and culturally, theatre has arguably been read as feminine.

## WHO DOES THEATRE?

There is a certain inherent "un-ease" among those who create theatre. The ideas perpetuated by celebrity (and even non-celebrity) same-sex gossip and middle America's misreading of "who does theatre" creates enormous pressures on queer and non-queer actors, which often leads to extremely negative and unhealthy attitudes. I would argue that the latent homophobia within professional theatre can be understood as a direct, if not necessarily conscious, response from heterosexual men who feel they have to prove that their masculinity is not in question. In other words, heterosexual men who work in theatre often feel the need to repeatedly demonstrate that they are straight, that they are not part of the "gay theatre mafia," and that they share no part of the cultural assumption that theatre is "gay." Heterosexual actors do this to avoid the sting of same-sex gossip.[35]

This behaviour can manifest itself in many ways. One of the most benign is referenced by Kaier Curtain who comments that he finds it interesting that "when plays with gay protagonists have been produced on Broadway, the program often made clear that the author was married and had fathered children."[36]

In *Place for Us,* D.A. Miller deconstructs the opening scene from *Gypsy*:

> More pertinent is the general law of the musical theatre that Jocko's particular irregularity merely makes exceptionally explicit. This law ordains that, though male and female alike may and indeed must appear on the musical stage, they are not equally welcome there: the female performer will always enjoy the advantage

of also being thought to *represent* this stage, as its sign, its celebrant, its essence, and its glory; while the male tends to be suffered on condition that, by the inferiority or subjection of his own talents, he assist the enhancement of hers.[37]

In Miller's essay, the stage/performing space is constructed as female and the passive (though resistant) ogling auditorium is further understood as male; by necessity such a construction involves complex issues of identity and transgression, including a musical-theatrical regime that feminizes access to the performing space; men who access the stage, be it as characters or actors, must necessarily remove and leave behind the masculine theatre while embracing (or at least accepting) the feminine stage.[38] Theatre, as Miller argues, is gendered. To a hetero-normative society, the lives of the stars of theatre and of Broadway musicals (as reinforced by celebrity gossip) are non-threatening because their work, located in gendered performance practices historically understood as feminine, are, unlike their counterparts in action movies, without power.

Of course, in order to function properly, gossip requires not just a teller but also a listener. The success by which same-sex gossip is used by the media to either punish or re-enforce actors is aimed at and supported by the audience of such gossip. The aspect of gossip, this notion of "social control," as Ponce de Leon argues in his article, can be equally effective in containing and controlling audiences. Movie gossip, especially deviant sexual gossip, is aimed at a particular audience which, not coincidentally, is the audience of the next block-buster playing at the movie-plex. It can be argued that the listeners, readers and viewers of Parsons and Hopper, *Confidential Magazine* and TMZ are (historically) one in the same. Further, this target audience and the gossip-mongers are products of a mass culture, one that is uneasy with notions of deviant transgression. Conversely, theatre audiences since the mid-twentieth century have been read as being more educated, more urbane and more literate. In short, more deviant than their movie-going counterparts, and therefore it is not surprising that theatre audiences and those who read theatre gossip are more likely than not to accept this deviant sexuality. In such a reading, both audience, performers (and to an extent the gossipers) celebrate, perhaps even flaunt, the known deviant sexuality of the theatre and of theatre artists.

As referenced earlier, in May 2010 *Newsweek's* cultural critic Ramin Setoodeh published a piece entitled "Straight Jacket"[39] in which he asked why can't gay men play straight? His argument took particular aim at *Glee's* Jonathon Groff and Sean Hayes' performance in *Promises, Promises* and seemed to many readers to be suspicious and deeply insulting. The article was met with much scorn, and the openly gay Setoodeh[40] was the subject of numerous critiques and scathing articles.[41] In subsequent interviews (and possibly only to save face) he claimed that he was trying to highlight the double standard that seems to exist in the entertainment industry: "known" heterosexual actors are lauded for playing gay (even if the portrayal is not that successful), but it is understood that "known" homosexual actors cannot be perceived as playing heterosexual characters.[42] In the ongoing media maelstrom that followed the article he, along with Dan Savage and Amanda Bearse, appeared on an episode of the Joy Behar Show in which Savage claimed that it was the perception of movie audiences that prevented gay actors from being accepted as straight romantic leads, not their ability to convincingly portray straight romantic leads. Savage claimed: "we've accepted that on Broadway for years, but still movie audiences won't."

At the beginning of the second decade of the twenty-first century, it is certainly reasonable to ask, "who cares about an actor's sexuality; aren't we beyond this?" Setoodeh writing of Sean Hayes' performance in *Promises, Promises* claims that all reviewers (save him) "ignored the real problem—the big pink elephant in the room" and continued,

> But frankly, it's weird seeing Hayes play straight. He comes off as wooden and insincere, as if he's trying to hide something, which of course he is. Even the play's most hilarious scene, when Chuck tries to pick up a drunk woman at a bar, devolves into unintentional camp. Is it funny because of all the '60s-era one-liners, or because the woman is so drunk (and clueless) that she agrees to go home with a guy we all know is gay?[43]

Having seen the production of *Promises, Promises* that Setoodeh is writing about, I would argue that Sean Hayes was more believable as Chuck

Baxter than Christine Chenoweth was as Fran Kubelik, and what Hayes proved was that he is one of the great physical comedians working today, with an endearing stage presence that is rare. And yet none of this is in Setoodeh's article. Instead, working his own form of homophobic same-sex celebrity gossip into the mainstream press, Setoodeh demonstrates that far too many people still care. Michael Musto cares, but for a completely different reason, writing of the elaborate games and coded language closeted stars still use when avoiding questions of their sexuality: " Whenever a subject tells me, 'I won't discuss who I'm dating' or 'I resent labels,' I generally know not so much that they're passionate about privacy but that they're gay, gay, gay."[44]

It seems, argues Ehrenstein, "For all that's happened to alter gay and lesbian life across America over the past two decades, same-sexuality is still regarded as an acceptable 'secret' in Hollywood. And it is *secrecy*, rather than 'privacy,' that is the issue."[45] Regardless of an actor's sexual orientation, it is almost impossible for a Hollywood actor to not (at some point in his career) become ensnared in the (sometimes) vile world of same-sex celebrity gossip.[46] This gossip contains and restricts, ensuring that social order is maintained regardless of the cost to the individual (or individuals) involved. Conversely, the relative safety that theatre and the Broadway musical provides can become problematic, maintaining a performative "gay ghetto," a ghetto that, like the glass closet of Hollywood, is maintained and supported by celebrity gossip.

**NOTES**

1    David Ehrenstein, *Open Secret: Gay Hollywood 1928–1998* (New York: Harper Collins, 2000), 2.

2    Cited in David Ehrenstein, *Open Secret: Gay Hollywood 1928–1998* (New York: Harper Collins, 2000), 19.

3    Charles Ponce de Leon, "The Man Nobody Knows: Charles A. Lindberg and the Culture of Celebrity," *Prospects* 21 (1996): 349.

4    Ibid., 357.

5    Ibid., 351.

6    Ibid., 357.

7    Jörg R. Bergmann, *Discreet Indiscretions: The Social Organization of Gossip* (New York: Aldine de Gruyter, 1993), 34.

8    Jack Levin & Arnold Arluke, *Gossip: The Inside Scoop* (New York: Plenum Press, 1987), 64.

9    Ibid., 65.

10    Ibid., 66.

11    Louella O. Parsons, *Tell It to Louella* (New York: Putnam, 1961), 316.

12    Samuel Bernstein, *Mr. Confidential: The Man, His Magazine & The Movieland Massacre That Changed Hollywood Forever* (New York: Walford Press: 2006), 2.

13    Ibid., 148.

14    David Ehrenstein, *Open Secret: Gay Hollywood 1928–2000* (New York: Harper Collins, 2000), 302.

15    Ibid., 46.

16    GLBTQ: *An Encyclopedia of Gay, Lesbian, Bisexual, Transgender, & Queer Culture* (http://www.glbtq.com/arts/film_actors_gay.html ([retrieved March 10, 2010]).

17    Darden Asbury Pyron, *Liberace: An American Boy* (Chicago: University of Chicago Press, 2000), 228.

18    Ehrenstein, *Open Secret*, 243.

19    John Clum, *Something for the Boys: Musical Theatre and Gay Culture* (New York: St. Martin's Press, 1999), 68.

20    Ehrenstein, *Open* Secret, 172.

21    Bernstein, *Mr. Confidential*, 118.

22    www.Buzzle.com        (http://www.buzzle.com/editorials/1-21-34073.asp [retrieved March 13, 2010]).

23    www.SweatPantsErection.com (http://www.sweatpantserection.com/tom-cruise-gay.html [retrieved March 13, 2010].

24    www.Dealmemo.com "Tom Cruise Courts Another Victory" (http://www.dealmemo.com/Legal/Tom_Cruise_Courts_Another_Victory.htm [retrieved March 15, 2010]).

25    www.SweatPantsErection.com (http://www.sweatpantserection.com/tom-cruise-gay.html retrieved March 13, 2010]).

26    Richard Goldstein, "Cruise Control: Why Is It Libelous to Call an Action Actor Gay?," *The Village Voice* May 8, 2001 (http://www.villagevoice.com/2001-05-08/news/cruise-control).

27    Ramin Setoodeh, "Straight Jacket: Heterosexual Actors Play Gay All the Time. Why Doesn't It Ever Work in Reverse?" *Newsweek Web Exclusive* (April 26, 2010) (http://www.newsweek.com/id/236999).

28    Ibid.

29    Goldstein, " Cruise Control."

30    Carole Cadwalladr, "I Wouldn't Advise Any Actor Thinking of His Career To Come Out," *The Observer* (November 29, 2009). In this article Rupert states: "The fact is that you could not be, and still cannot be, a 25-year-old homosexual trying to make it in the British film business or the American film business or even the Italian film business. It just doesn't work and you're going to hit a brick wall at some point. You're going to manage to make it roll for a certain amount of time, but at the first sign of failure

they'll cut you right off" (http://www.guardian.co.uk/film/2009/nov/29/rupert-everett-madonna-carole-cadwalladr).

31   Robert A Schanke and Kim Marra, *Passing Performances: Queer Reading of Leading Players in American Theatre History* (Ann Arbor: The University of Michigan Press, 1998), 9.

32   Alan Sinfield, *Out on Stage: Lesbian and Gay Theatre in the Twentieth Century* (New Haven: Yale University Press, 1999), 165.

33   Boze Hadleigh, *Broadway Babylon: Glamour, Glitz and Gossip on the Great White Way* (New York: Back Stage Books, 2007), 18.

34   Ibid., 315.

35   Pearce, "Performing and Culture," 255–71.

36   Kaier Curtin, *We Can Always Call Them Bulgarians: the Emergence of Lesbians and Gay Men on the American Stage* (Boston: Alyson Publishers, 1988), 327.

37   D. A. Miller, *Place for Us: Essay on the Broadway Musical* (Cambridge: Harvard University Press, 1998), 71.

38   Ibid., 81.

39   The piece first appeared online on the *Newsweek* website (http://www.newsweek.com/2010/04/30/straight-jacket.html) on April 26, 2010 and was subsequently published in the May 10, 2010, print copy of the same magazine.

40   Setoodeh makes no secret of his sexual orientation and in the ensuing maelstrom, this became central to both the criticisms of the article and his own defense of the article:

> Immediately, a number of gay blogs picked up my essay and ran excerpts from it out of context, under the headline that I was antigay. It went viral. Chenoweth wrote a letter to NEWSWEEK calling the article "horrendously homophobic," even though she went on to acknowledge that I am openly gay. It went even more viral. In the meantime, commenters [sic] on the Internet piled on the attacks. Many of them said they hadn't even read the original article (some of them did) but they all seemed to agree on the same point: that I was an idiot.
>
> Over the weekend, I became the subject of a lot of vicious attacks. I received e-mails that said I will be fired, anonymous phone calls on my cell phone and a creepy letter at my home. Several blogs posted my picture, along with a link to my Twitter feed. People commented about my haircut, and that was only the beginning. I was compared to Ann Coulter and called an Uncle Tom. Someone described me as a "self-hating Arab" that should be writing about terrorism (I'm an American, born in Texas, of Iranian descent) http://www.newsweek.com/2010/05/10/out-of-focus.html (retrieved November 25, 2010).

41    Kristin Chenoweth immediately came to the defense of her co-star with an opinion piece that was sent to (and published by) *Newsweek* and quickly re- published (and cited) by a variety of on-line and print sources; "Kristin Chenoweth: *Newsweek*'s Sean Hayes Piece 'Horrendously Homophobic' (http://www.huffingtonpost.com/2010/05/10/kristin-chenoweth-defends_n_570537.html [retrieved November 23, 2010]), "Kristin Chenoweth 'Offended' by Ramin Setoodeh's Homophobic Article in *Newsweek*" (http://www.afterelton.com/people/2010/05/kristin-chenoweth-offended-newsweek [retrieved November 23, 2010]), "Kristin Chenoweth: *Newsweek* Article was 'Horrendously Homophobic' (http://broadwayworld.com/article/Kristin_Chenoweth_Newsweek_Article_Was_Horrendously_Homophobic_20100507 [retrieved November 23, 2010]). Further, there was a strong and vocal number of critical responses by a number of cultural commentators and actors, see for example: "Cheyenne Jackson and Michael Urie Rip "Newsweek's Ramin Setoodeh For 'Gays Can't Play Straight' Article" (http://www.afterelton.com/blog/waymanwong/cheyenne-jackson-michael-urie-rip-ramin-setoodeh [retrieved November 23, 2010]), "Ramin Setoodeh Tries to Defend his Newsweek Article" (http://perezhilton.com/2010-05-11-ramin-setoodeh-tries-to-defend-his-newsweek-article [retrieved November 23, 2010]) and "*Newsweek's* Ramin Setoodeh Can't Stand Sissies" (http://www.vanityfair.com/online/daily/2010/05/newsweeks-ramin-setoodeh-cant-stand-sissies.html [retrieved November 25, 2010]).

42    http://www.newsweek.com/2010/05/10/out-of-focus.html (retrieved November 23, 2010).

43    Setoodeh, "Straight Jacket."

44    Michael Musto, "The Glass Closet," *Out Magazine* (May 2007) (http://out.com/detail.asp?id=22392).

45    Ehrenstein, *Open Secret*, 126.

46    Nancy Collins, "Sex and the Single Star: John Travolta," *Rolling Stone Magazine* 402 (August 18, 1983). In this article Travolta, seemingly aware that one of the consequences of being young and attractive will be same-sexuality gossip and speculation, states: "That's a notorious rumor... They say that about me, Marlon Brando, every male star, especially the first year you become a star. It wears off after a while, but I've heard it said of just about everybody."

# PART II

# NEGOTIATING
# **SELF (SELVES)**

"It is not easy to find happiness in ourselves,
and it is not possible to find it elsewhere."
— AGNES REPPLIER

## Small Boy DREAMS (an excerpt)

KELLY HANDEREK

This play was the result of a six-month sabbatical. During that time, for three to four hours each morning I placed my thoughts, struggle, identity, childhood, quest for purpose and reflective questioning down in words to shape and sort the queer existence of my young life. Childhood friends, sexual partners, family, teachers, accidents, lovers, career and theatre formed the situational narrative of this journey, which charts a path that ends with the death of my mother.

The interior web is more important than the outer narrative. This web reaches to touch the flexible relationships that move in and out of life as success and loss, powerless and powerful to shape and mold us without the knowledge that we are being thrown around on the wheel of life and fashioned into a world that can accept and still mostly chooses not to understand that we are, as gay men, wired differently. Or are we? The most profound feeling of aloneness and loneliness hung around me when I wrote this and for some years now I've not been able to return to the work because the shadow of loss seemed inescapable. I was without resilience or the lift of life. Only within the last few months have I begun to feel the courage to shape, cut, return to and synthesize the pattern so as to place this work in a more fluid form. So, today I am feeling purpose as you read this and hope that each young man in a small world will know that the future can be good.

My thanks to Susan Ferley, artistic director of the Grand Theatre, London, Ontario, and David Oyie, past artistic director of Buddies in Bad Times. Both artists have supported this work with a Toronto workshop of this play at Buddies in Bad Times with the amazing actor/ artist Ronnie Burkett as the sole voice. All the artists concerned gave thoughtful response to this work and have assisted in realizing the play that is still emerging today. Bless you. Jayden Pfeifer read the script in its early stages and his voice was a good jumping-off point to the first early drafts. My characters are the fragments of past friends—some gloriously here on this planet and some long-departed. All of them form the fabric of a life and each are as dear to me as family. Today I give my thanks to the University of Regina Queer Initiative and the Speakers Series that allowed excerpts of this play to be spoken within my university context and provided an open space and platform for any to hear what might be of interest, within the world that is open and out to us.

KELLY.  Well ... Stop.
        Please don't
        The Knife ... Please ...
        Put it down

                                    DANNY.  But I'm not sure if I
                                            Can live like this.


KELLY.  Many do ... Away from here ...
        You just need to go away
        from here. To get away.

        Away is good ...
        It's larger, more people.
        Like you, like me.

When I found him that evening in the kitchen with the knife in his hands
he would have taken his life.

        I was thirteen.            He was fifteen.

His eyes were red and the decision was clear. His face was a tangle of self-
loathing and disgust for the pleasure we had enjoyed.

We were at his Grandma P's—housesitting. Asleep on the screened
porch with many lilac trees separating us from a quiet street in Medicine
Hat that only cats would walk down after 10:00 p.m.

        It was summer.            It was dry.

Slow breath, and heavy eyes welcomed the late afternoon heat that
drifted into evening and made my young mind wander away from piano
lessons or chores around the house that kept this thirteen-year-old in the
good graces of a weekly allowance ...

        Yes ... wander away from family concerns

                And wander into my body, my sexual discovery, my need ...

But the picture of my blonde blue-eyed best of best childhood friend with the bone-handled bread knife out of its special drawer and the steel blade moving toward his pale wrist.

> **KELLY.** STOP
> You don't ever need to do this
> You are too talented
> Too Beautiful
> Too Good
>
> Why?

> > **DANNY.** It's a world that doesn't
> > want us.
> > Our kind—My family
> > won't get it.
> > And you—You seem
> > so confident…
> > self-assured.

> **KELLY.** Some days.

> > **DANNY.** And I've done this to you.
> > I've made you…

> **KELLY.** No you didn't.
> Don't be silly—do you
> think I was…. Oh….
> get real.

I've wanted to be with you ever since we first met. Be with you in every way. The look of your smile and your wrinkly face, the gentle voice, your big laugh and your grace. There is something with your body—the way it/ you move… long strides as you walk. You connect to this world. I see how you are with friends, family and others. They love you. You are a happiness in the day.

You are a happiness in my day.
(*tear up*).

A happiness, a brother, a guy who I feel close to—so very close. I want to always be near you and in you.

> **DANNY.**  I love it when you're
> inside me.
> Oh...

We spoke these words above the edge of a whisper so the still breeze would not scream our secret to this little world though it seemed the wise would already know.

> **DANNY.**  You mean you are...
> And me having sex with
> you for the first time didn't
> turn you...

**KELLY.**  (*smile*) No.

My fantasy world has felt you in the centre of it since we first met. When we look at each other eye to eye in a group of people or when alone—you seem to say—don't worry, we will be together. And we are. And since we have... you... it... has given me happiness. A freeing... a something so new. To feel in body, touch, mind. So new a feeling in my body of what it is to touch and be touched—the staying power of care. A lasting gift

Special

The touch of a hand

Lips
And body

The warmth of a feeling (smile) is you.

As the knife went away, those honest words sprung from the moment of truth. Yes, I meant every word. No holds barred. And yes, I spoke so deep and complete my childhood truth that he put away the knife, forever, and he reached for my hand and we stumbled off to sleep.

Good Nite.

We would never discuss that time again—and he continues well to this very day—my childhood happiness (*blow a kiss*). Thanks!

(*space*)

Mysterious, dark voiced, handsome good looks, he seemed a rich prince from a different place and time.

We competed together in the festival—Speech Arts-section—and although he was like me, adopted, he was more of a lover than me. His chocolate-brown eyes were deep pools active with restless thoughts, soulful journeys
     —where—?
          oh where are you dreaming?

A low truth was the central core of his voice—it seemed to catch the ear of the world. At sixteen he was considered a man in every way— the shock of a black/blue hair seemed to crown his bright brow and fur everywhere.

**KELLY**. Wow.

                              **DEAN**.    What?

**KELLY**. You've got really hairy arms.

                              **DEAN**.    Yeah.

**KELLY**. Neat.

DEAN. (*grimace*) You think
it's neat?

KELLY. Well sure… it's you!

DEAN. You're good at that dramatic
stuff—at festival.

KELLY. Oh?

DEAN. Yeah.

KELLY. When you speak—sounds like you
wrote the stuff—and so vivid.
Your Dad's my doctor isn't he,
Dr. Rahaaman?

DEAN. (*pause*)… yes.

KELLY. He's wonderful. So great.
I always feel good when I
leave his office—he's so
caring and…

DEAN. I know, he's that kind of
person always. I hope to
be like him when I grow up.

KELLY. Yeah… a doctor?

DEAN. We'll see.

KELLY. You're so much like him.
You both have a gentle
good way about you.

DEAN. I'm adopted.

**KELLY**.  Me too.

**DEAN**.  (*Taken aback*)
Really? Strange.

**KELLY**.  Don't you hate it:
when everybody asks—"
"what's it like to be adopted"
—As if we know.

**DEAN**.  Plus, it's just me—no
brothers, no sisters.

**KELLY**.  Yeah. Me too.

**KELLY**.  Don't you hate it: when everybody
Says "what's it like to be the only
child—no sisters, no brothers—just you."

**DEAN**.  Yeah.

**KELLY**.  I tell them more gifts at birthdays
and Christmas.

**DEAN**.  True. Only we don't
celebrate Christmas,
we're Jewish.

**KELLY**.  I work for Mr. Levinson who
runs the music store. (Well, he
and his wife Bea.) They're Jewish,
do you know them?

**DEAN**.  (*grimace/smile*) A—sure.

**KELLY**.  He's a great boss. Tells
wicked jokes and always asks
questions.

DEAN.     What do you mean?

KELLY.  You know. "How are you?"
Then waits and listens or
"How was school today?"

He cares… He listens.

We could listen to records,
Come over… sometime.
What kind of music do you like?…
I just got "Born to be Wild"—
Steppenwolf and Bette Midler's
"The Divine Miss M."

DEAN.     (*wait*) Never heard
of them…
(*half smile*)
But sure… sure

(*space*)

I wonder why? (*Slow release of breath*)

You see he found out his father had terminal cancer and had only, at best, a year to live. I understand that he never got on with his mom. Why? I don't know, they seemed to clash. So one weekend when his mom and dad were away, he shot himself. In this room. I didn't know they had guns or that he knew how to hunt. Five months later Dr. Rahaaman died and one year later his mom hanged herself in the garage. The whole family gone. Dean—gone. We never had a chance to listen to music or get to know each other. Dean—gone. Why? I still miss him—His gentle strength and truth—His honest style of self.

Our world is less without Dean, Dr. Rahaaman and his Mom.

(*space*)

♪ The show is about to begin
The show is about to begin

Please stand to sing "O Canada"
Please stand to sing "God Save the Queen"

Children's Theatre

Decked out in one of the four ill fitting court jesters costumes
complete with turned-up pointed toes—with bells.

Oh yes, Bells—everywhere
Wrist bells, elbow bells
Hat bells, knee bells

The idiot's stick with bells

♪ The show is about to begin.                O… so true.

Two shows daily
For THREE consecutive Saturdays
ADMISSION twenty-five cents

Opened your eyes to a one-hour version of Cinderella, The Pied Piper of
Hamelin, Christmas Carol, The Wizard of Oz and Davie Star. Performed at
the Public Library Auditorium. With painted flats—all cobbled together
from previous plays, rich jewel-colored costuming—mis-matched from
various periods in history but each looking fairytale in style. Sound
effects, lighting and wild make-up, all performed by children.

Yes, my first stage role—"The Mayor of Munchkin City"

This was the play version of Oz (no music) or as the advertisement read

"The Story as it was meant"

All of us misfits gathered together. Children telling stories to younger
children. We were the odds and sods of the city who felt more at home

on stage, in the yearly musicals, festivals or singing at church halls than we did watching Lanny McDonald play with tigers.

On two-show days… we were allowed out of costume for lunch to go the three blocks to either Woolworth's or Kresge's. My parents allotted me enough money to join the cast and purchase a grilled cheese sandwich, with fries, a salty pickle and a real chocolate shake.

So there we were: The Witch, the Green-Faced Guard, Dorothy, Tin Man, Lion and the Mayor of Munchkin City chowing down to grub in street clothes and full make-up. Giving the Saturday shoppers gossip and amusement as they poked around for bargains.

Oz was such a hit that Cinderella would follow it.

Advanced ticket sales were brisk.

Cinderella—the magic tale of transformation, good fortune, rags to riches, happily ever after and a handsome prince.

Well—it was lean pickings to find a "handsome" prince so the director asked if I would tackle the challenge.

My, my, what folly.

I would be a jolly prince
A pudgy prince,
A guy who got way too close to palace pastries and should knock off the gooey cheese at lunch let alone the chocolate shake.

However

Why not?

Black leotards, black ballet shoes, and a black tunic—so far so good. Until the stage director says to the costume wrangler—"He doesn't look 'royal' enough."

Voila—gold metallic fabric now adorns my tunic and all is well with the Kingdom.

Off goes the prince of pudge to capture Cinderella.

We coast through two weeks without caustic comment or any munchkins muttering about the girth of the Prince—so—I'm all in tack.

> However, it was the afternoon show—our closing performance and sitting two rows from the front on the aisle I spy a disgruntled customer.
>
> And as I come down the aisle searching for Cinderella, my instructions were: come quickly into the theatre calling for Cinderella, run down the aisle carefully balancing the glass slipper on the velvet blue pillow—with gold trim—to match my tunic.
>
> Run to extreme house left, return to centre and then run extreme house right (*do this*)
> Exclaiming:
>
> > (while in conversation)
> > "I am Prince Charming and I am looking for my Princess who left behind
> > Her glass slipper at the Ball—
> > Where oh where could she be?"

Or something to that effect

My direction from Palmer Huckle:
"Speak loudly and clearly using your upstage hand cupped as a megaphone as if calling across the land."

> "I am Prince Charming… BIG
> (*the actor repeats both the moves and the text*)

A flickering flame of discontent in row two is scowling at me—

Oh dear the pudgy prince will be punctured and persecuted.

(*Repeat*) "I am Prince...."

(*with actions*)

And as I am crossing to extreme house right I place the pillow and slipper centre stage on the edge and continue my search, but I sense all is not well in make-believe land—I lose my eye line on the little grumbletonian and as I am about to call out at full throttle again for my lost princess...

I hear a knock... knock-knock centre stage

as I look to see what has tickled the children and adults alike. My friend from row two, obviously a budding thespian, if not a critic, stands at the edge of the stage—glass slipper firmly in hand.

(*actor uses knuckle to create a pattern of the action*)

"Plastic—I thought so," he exclaims with the concrete smile of a scientist.

(*small space*)

This little children's theatre gathered so many exotic people around its every production. Some became fast friends, others close chums, but none more interesting than dear Lilah Head. Den mother. Retired ballerina and now full-time actress and Avon representative.

At a stately home on Riverside overlooking a brambled overgrown garden sloping down to the South Saskatchewan River, we gathered each Sunday afternoon for games and laughs.

Lilah appeared, greeted us at the door, sixty-plus years, full pink tutu, and crinoline. The track played a rather dog-eared version of Swan Lake, the parlour was cleared of the antiques and off she went—a small show of dexterity—a potted performance of memories of youth culminating in four pirouettes and the big fanfare—the full splits.

Applause.

Then a swift game of mahjong and a supper of stuffed marrow.

I think I thought I fell through a looking glass—but seldom wanted to return.

She occupied the house with her husband John—a gentle scholar now substitute teacher turned-out with thin grey tie, oxford button-down shirt and a lambswool green Bayfield pullover spotted with leftovers of yesterdays meals. Joining the two humans in the six-room house were four birds, three dogs and twenty-some cats. Yes, all indoor cats.

Yes, most of them lived in one room.

You see, dear Lilah was a collector of creatures—whether lost or alone she wanted to offer refuge to those who had lost their way.

Much like all of us—

Our group was comprised of all the kids from the theatre company who did or did not get cast in the upcoming play or musical. We met each Sunday around 2:30 p.m. and became a human menagerie of friends and family to each other.

Within a few years, we began to be known, among ourselves, as The Gang.

Myself—the youngest. And during weeknights when homework was quickly concluded, off we would go in Rhonda Hermon's large Parisienne to the A & W, then cruised the town before heading home.

Away from our parental tormentors, we talked about people we liked and disliked at school, developed special languages—code—known only to The Gang, drove through the cemetery to try to scare each other, and enjoyed the odd world of outcasts in our small town.

The dominant force of The Gang was Rhonda—she had the car and the most formidable personality. Debbie was the worrier and usually played the Mom roles in the plays although she thought she should play the ingénue. Gerry was a sound or backstage guy—he had no interest in any formal education, but taught himself to play by ear and in his basement getaway we always listened to the Planets at full blast. M.J. (Mary Jane) was short, sweet and forever optimistic—I knew her from church so she was always my "get out of the house free" card with my parents.

**MOTHER**. Will Mary Jane be there?

**KELLY**. Yes—Mother.

**MOTHER**. Well, she's a lovely person. You can go.

And there was Danny.

He was the prize of the group—everyone wanted to be around him.

Tall, blonde, lanky, with a huge smile. His family, brothers and sisters all were blest with a winning grin. Father and Uncle—it would make politicians jealous how a simple smile made people melt.

Have you noticed that a blonde can get away with such bad behaviour/ say the most outrageous thing and like Jupiter it slides off as a gossamer-soft arrow—without an intended target.

As The Gang grew up together, we would grow apart—then close—then apart again. Who was traveling away to school—to university—and who would forever stay home—locked in the comfort of Medicine Hat and its simple ways. That beautiful, warm community that is still nestled in a land that time forgot with folks who wanted a gentler path—they are in a word—content and connected to each other in caring ways.

For the girls the dream was who was hoping to marry and to whom.

For the boys—what was to be the work—and where.

When girls and boys drift into men and women, they see in front of them a possible journey that bends as dreams fly away and reality creates a path that calls each to a different destiny.

Wherever the girls and boys of youth may be.

Rock on—

Ride Hard and Dream Deep.

(*space*)

Dishwasher, music store clerk, clothing salesman, speech arts teacher, waiter—these were the part time jobs of my teenaged life.

Each new season, the boxes of styles would reveal: daring colours, jaunty jackets, fresh looks that would draw the "trendsetters" of Medicine Hat to look great for that special hit.

The owner/manager suggested I tackle the small display windows to spice it up. Yes! I brought every idea of autumn I could find to layer, droop and festoon the window with—"I am autumn—Dammit!"

The poor clothes didn't have a chance:

New clothes: 5　　　　Autumn theme: 19

My creation was met with raised eyebrows from the Boss but a doctor's compliment saved the effort and I was offered the large in store window and finally the front showcase—I had arrived.

**GEORGE**. May I look at some socks?

**KELLY**. Yes…
　　　Sir… over here.

I didn't know if I should call him sir.

> GEORGE. Thanks.
> You can go on with what
> you were doing. I'll just look
> around for a Mo. (*space*)

And then he giggled.

(*small space*)

Humm.....

Odd, then as I watched him looking over the socks, touching them, considering both colour and lengths, I was strongly aware he was looking at me.

Did I do something wrong? Confused and interested—I got on with the daily tasks.

> BOSS. They're beautiful—aren't they?

> GEORGE. (*high laugh*) You scared the
> Devil out of me (*laugh*)
> Where did *you* come from?

> BOSS. Sorry, didn't mean to startle.
> Those socks are… art.
> However , I've just opened the
> new argyle collection, 'Heaven'—
> let me get you a pair.

And with that his quiet soft Bally butter leather shoes carried him to the back office as quiet as a ghost and he returned quickly with three pair of socks draped over his arm—as if showing a diamond necklace.

> GEORGE. Oh my (*high laugh*)
> They are…yes. Those.
> BOSS. Kelly, ring these
> up will you?

> KELLY. Sure.

Boss glided back into his office, proud of his ornate haberdasher flair and simple sale.

            **GEORGE**. Your name is Kelly?

**KELLY**. "Kelly". Yes. It was my
mother's maiden name—
so now I'm stuck with it.

            **GEORGE**. Try George. (*smile*)
Georgie Porgy. (*laugh*)

He had one of those most distinctive laughs (LAUGH) a stand out in a crowd laugh (LAUGH) a look-at-me, look-at-me trill (LAUGH) followed each time by an incredulous smile as if to say—Why are you looking at me?

            **GEORGE**. (*Whisper/confidential*)
Does the Guy always
parade the socks like
they are limp ballerinas…
such a dandy!

**KELLY**. Yeah. Both Jay and his
wife must have learned this
—somewhere.

            **GEORGE**. Wife? *He* has a wife?

**KELLY**. And three kids. (*wait*)
(*frown/confusion*)

            **GEORGE**. …too bad. Kelly, do you
have a wife?

**KELLY**. No, I'm in high school.

            **GEORGE**. Me too. You want to meet
for coffee—Saturday?

KELLY. I work. Here.

GEORGE. Movie? Saturday Night?

KELLY. My parents are away at a
wedding so they've asked
me to stay home and take
care of the dog.

GEORGE. Great. Can I come
over (*laugh*) to visit?

(*wait/frown/confusion*) (*small smile*)

KELLY. Well, sure.

GEORGE. Good. See you at 7:00.

And out the door he went. Socks in bag. Hey—he doesn't even know
where I live.

[*DOORBELL DOORBELL DOORBELL X 6. FAST AND DEMANDING.*]

KELLY. Okay. Okay.

GEORGE. I'm here (*laugh*).

KELLY. Yeah. So I hear. Come in.

GEORGE. Nice place.

KELLY. So, I show him around. The
cheap tour and as he looks
around the room quickly he
returns to me. My eyes. I
feel uncertain yet
interested.

GEORGE. I've brought some chips.
Pop—stuff.

KELLY. Thanks. We can stay here
or go downstairs to the
rumpus room.

The rumpus room was all one big room. A well-stocked bar at one end and comfortable couches, chairs and television at the other with space in the middle to dance. Large neighbourhood celebrations, at New Years, Anniversaries. Plus it hosted my piano, which seldom enjoyed the touch of my fingers. A paneled wall of pictures showed off Family, my father's World War II regiment and his success as a piper.

GEORGE. Hey your Father wears a
dress. (*laugh*) I've always
liked pipebands and the
idea of men playing and
marching in tune, kilts
flying, knees exposed to
the sun.

Oh, my God—Look at that
bar. Now that's a stocked
bar. Let's have a drink.

KELLY. No.

GEORGE. Something clear so we can
add water/top it up and no
one will know—(*laugh*)

KELLY. Well…

Hours passed. Music played. Lights dimmed. Cards came out. A friendly game of "strip poker." My heart started pounding with excitement and uncertainty. Fear and fantasy. The mind raced—what would happen? Would I be able to stay soft and be contained or would my hard-on belie my interest or was I interested? Ah, the flights of fantasy of a teenage boy.

Off to the races. I had never played this game before and within a few hands only my babe blue Y fronts were standing at attention—telling my truth. Another loss. Another laugh and off they came.

Hello.

We pushed away the cards. Started to touch each other. Me in the buff. George with his pants on. Shoulders, arms, bones, and boners awkward and wonderful. I traced his bones on his back and ran my fingers over the ridges of his backbone up to his bristly, bushy head of hair. His skin was cool to touch and then my arms wrapped around him and my hands landed in the flesh of his back. A shock of embarrassment, a defect in his body. Acne. He froze and looked concerned.

> **KELLY**. Don't we all have things about
> our body we wish were different?
> … it's a map of who we are.

With those words he stood up, offered me his belt buckle to undo. As if to say you may have lost at cards but you've won. My fingers stumbled, and I felt incompetent at this gentle offer—then I recovered and slowly began to enjoy un-buckling, un-buttoning and un-dressing our naked youth.

Our love-making—deep in feeling, laughter, tender holding. These holdings were like Angels wrapping assurance around each other—this comfort and courage swept away adolescent worries like:

> "What are you going to do when you grow up?"…
> "Do you have a girlfriend?"…

The nightly whispers across the kitchen table of Mother and Father airing worries of making ends meet that seemed to haunt my dreams and their daily worlds. My dad's idea of money was—don't spend, do without, and try to save. My mother's idea was—we deserve nice things/beautiful spaces/buy the best, it will last and endure—why else would we work so tirelessly hard? Mother won the fiscal plan, she made more money. Dad lived with worry, the bills and the tensions.

However, my youth with George and Danny, friends and play pals, allowed me to escape the home fires and fall into the sleepovers of young love. Floating sexual times in each other's basements, bedrooms, midnights on a golf course. These were the young summers of adolescent love that drifted through the high school years making learning, parents and life so much happier.

(*space*)

George has gone from our world and planet. Swept away by the plague which steals the brothers, sons, husbands, daughters, wives and friends that define our lives. Bless Them All.

I miss George so deeply. His honest quick words unblocked by social masks, his soaring laugh.

(*small space*)

His warm touch—his spirit

*[something wrapped in tissue paper comes out of a plain box]*

I have this to celebrate his life *[the package is not revealed]*.

It was 1989. I was working in Ontario, he tracked me down and asked what was my favourite colour.

KELLY. What?

GEORGE. Favourite colour! What's your favourite colour. Tell me then I'll tell all about what's happening.

**KELLY**. Red.

> **GEORGE**. I wish to leave each of my
> friends something to keep
> them… to keep them
> warm. You see. It got me.
> Some days I didn't play by
> the rules and… I'm dying.

**KELLY**.  Oh. George.

A short time later this came in the mail from Vancouver. With a note—(expose a scarf of one foot in length/handmade/Red)—"It's all I can manage."

Yes… it's all I can manage. Some days I feel that—is exactly where I am.

> Where are the angels to solve this?
> Why are so many friends lost to it?
> When shall it become an entry in history?

> So…

George… Stephen… Dale… (*invite the audience with a breath to say a name*) and all the people who have become names whose lives are dancing in your minds now. Those beautiful people…

> Shall we say their names quietly now—
> On the breath of our lips
> Like a gentle kiss to be close to them
> And honour them with a cold tear

To say that they are with us now. In echoes of sounds, words, memories, pictures, feelings we give them our love.

And listen for them … (*do this*)?
To speak our name … (*do this*)?
Or laugh

Yes, George … laugh.

My friend told me that she was off to Toronto to visit a dear one who was ill …

Upon her return her spirits were vexed as the visit was glorious— laughter, tears, memories and long lingering smiles, but underpinning her happiness was the knowledge this would be the last visit. They kissed goodbye.

The day she heard of Richard's passing she chose not to go to work, stayed home, played all the music they enjoyed throughout their friendship, watched two of their favourite movies and slept heavy with the joy and sadness of a lived life.

(*telephone rings*)

**MARIANNE.** He came to me in my dreams. He was dancing … it was raining but not on him. He stood in the sunshine and light. Welcomed each handshake. I was at a distance and could see him from behind. When I went to him to say hello, he turned and where the marks were on his face there was a moon/stars and sun. Flickering with colour, energy. He smiled and said:

let's dance!

# Eros and the Erotic in the Construction of Queer Teacher Identity[1]

JAMES MCNINCH

This chapter situates itself in cross-disciplinary work that combines action research into my own teaching practice, and my own conflicted but privileged identity as a gay man (my "queer locatedness" as André Grace [2000] calls it), with more traditional elements of media studies and critical pedagogy. The circle around this reflection is defined by ruminations on the subject of the relationship between eros and the erotic, media representations of teachers, and morality and mortality in identity and pedagogy.

For rhetorical purposes Aristotle configured intense pleasure into two peaks: sexual intercourse and thinking. Alan Bloom (1987) commented that the human soul is a kind of parabola spread between these two peaks, displaying "tropical variety and ambiguity" (137). This classic split between mind and body permeates the popular imagination and media representations of teacher identity, but does little to define the spiritual and physical connection ("the body electric" as Whitman called it) between the erotic (sexuality) and eros (passionate desire). Since Socrates and Plato, the homoerotic element of the teaching relationship has animated discussions of how the quest for wisdom and goodness comes from passionate desire. Bloom's own conflicted and closeted homosexuality both explains and undermines his strident attachment to a romantic conservative canon and Platonic duality.

My own "coming out" in 1992, Frank Oz's film *In & Out* (1997) and several other cinematic images of teachers—and the death of my father in 1999—form the catalytic triangulation for this discussion of queer teacher masculinity. I offer several tentative conclusions: the role of a queer teacher is more conflicted and problematic than that of a heterosexual; good teaching, defined as that which positively influences learning, is not possible unless there is an element in it of seduction. However, in understanding eros, it is important to see that it is teachers who are seduced by their students, not the other way around as Hollywood would have us believe. Good teaching—defined as ethical teaching—celebrates differences by exploring them. An exploration of eros and the (homo) erotic in teaching leads to a new appreciation of the sweetness of morality and the stench of mortality along the parabola connecting the body and the mind, and of the construction of a queer teaching identity. This discussion may contribute to our understanding of the tensions inherent in being a queer in the classroom and "que(e) rying and queering" the classroom, as S. Anthony Thompson (2004), following Sears (1992), so aptly calls it (273).

## CONSTRUCTING THE CULTURAL CONTEXT

As an openly gay, well-educated, middle-aged Canadian Caucasian male, I find it seductive to think that a sense of my own masculinity has been accepted in Canada, not just under the law, but in the profession of teaching and by society at large in the everyday.

> *During mid-term break in February, I am sitting in one of the infamous "blue chairs" on the gay beach at Puerto Vallarta Mexico surrounded by other white Canadian and American "fags" who congregate in this "gay mecca." I have escaped Canadian winter to indulge in the middle-class luxury of fruity alcoholic beverages brought to me through deep sand by young Mexican men earning a tough living. My peers from around North America parade on the beach in bathing trunks designed to show off their "baskets." Obese men who stroll look as if they*

*are naked because their guts hide their groins and swal-
low the string of their bikinis. Behind sunglasses my peers
"cruise the 'talent'" and gossip about which guys are hot
and who's not and who's a bottom and who's a top. Then
the topic drifts to where we will eat tonight and who is
going to Anthropology, the gay strip bar, where buff short
young hairless Mexican men strip on top of the bar and
then lap dance for pesos to be stuffed into their g-strings by
the customers from Timmons and Gatineau and Regina.*
— FROM THE AUTHOR'S DIARY

This chapter reflects a privileged queer "lifestyle." Conceived first as a seminar on cinematic images of teachers, it is more an "ethnography of one," as Ursula Kelly (1997) in *Schooling Desire* (25) calls it.

bell hooks (1994) has noted that "professors rarely speak of the place of eros or the erotic in our classrooms" (191). On the premise of meta-physical dualism, we teach to the mind and ignore the body.[2] Yet such politically divergent critics as hooks herself, who speaks of "students desperately yearning to be touched by knowledge" (199), and Alan Bloom (1987), who longed for the days when students were "physically and spiritually virginal … [whose] lust was mixed into everything they thought and did" (135), understand that "acts of learning and teaching are acts of desire and passion," as Barreca and Morse (1997) so aptly put it: "The personal history that both student and teacher bring to the place of instruction informs the tenor of the relationship" (viii).

How much more problematic then is the connection between the mind and the body for gay and lesbian educators who are "othered" and defined by their difference? Our sexuality pulls us into the limelight of the body politic. We are understood by our sexual difference because, as Elliott (1996) says, our public identity is "predicated upon [our still] private taboo sexual practices" (704). Any call to restore passion to the classroom is a greater challenge to those whose sexual identity is prob-lematic, i.e., the queer in the academy.[3]

Almost a quarter century ago Robert Wexelblatt (1991) understood the implications of the metaphor of teacher as lover endemic in our understanding of academic manliness. "Let us be clear from the start: the whole issue of meaningful emotional attachments and/or sexual relations is tangential to the question of the structural eroticism of professing" (10). If we profess, we are owning up to something, like guilt or innocence, say, or a longing for both eros and the erotic, or perhaps something more pedagogically comprehensible—quite simply a desire for passion in the teaching/learning milieu.

Many, including Wexelblatt, have understood teaching metaphorically as a form of courtship:

> The professor is polite, for his or her intentions are "honorable." The professor attempts to win the students' affections by means of gifts (a paper extension or interesting anecdotes, say). ... The courtship may well take more directly pedagogical shapes: a complaisant manner in the classroom, the use of first names, showing excessive regard for jejune interpretations..., a subtle running-down of competitors, other disciplines, other professors. (13)

The metaphor strengthens because of the secrecy and furtiveness of encounters in academia. Teaching, usually behind closed doors, is like a conspiracy, a dirty little secret. It moves to greater intimacy:

> group-bound secrecy is fostered in "our class" which meets as if for a tryst. The relationship between professor and students is exclusive, enlivened by private references and in-jokes; it has its own history... . This is close to professing as seduction, a more general strategy of erotic manipulation. (14)

The trope of cavalier courtliness, with its allusions to chivalric codes of honour, dignifies such manipulation by masking it in an aura of romantic enchantment. This feminizes pedagogical seduction by harkening to a patriarchal view of the process: the imposition of knowledge is, we are assured, to be alluring and safe and gentle.[4]

At the extreme end of this continuum of such ravishment is the violence of rape. The image of poor Leda taking on perhaps, as Yeats put it, "His power with His knowledge" is a more apt metaphor for the asymmetrical power relationships which have defined student-teacher relationships. As a university student in the 1960s, I recall the rhetoric:

"they [the old, the establishment, monopoly capitalism] are fucking us, man," mowing us down like some grim reaper. Resisting the rape, the more political of us idealized liberation in the form of Ché Guevera; the more literary of us held on to Holden Caulfield, a *Catcher in the Rye*, a saviour of our naiveté; for the most romantic of us there was Blake, who would sing us songs of innocence.

Bredbeck (1995) cites Jane Gallop's discussion of the "student body." Subject to the empty vessel syndrome, in traditional pedagogy, "a greater man penetrates a lesser man with his knowledge. The student is empty, a receptacle for the phallus; the teacher is the phallic fullness of knowledge" (169). From here it is a short step to having "been had"; the expert, the guru, speaks, the disciple listens and they become one: a particularly insidious form of academic nepotism regardless of age or sexual orientation.

John Glavin (1997) rails against the role of seducer imposed by the ideal of the good, i.e., the responsible and controlling teacher, and the good, i.e., passive but demanding student, who clamours: "Take me.... Charm my resistance. Captivate my indifference. Please me, entertain me, divert me, fascinate me, thrill me—seduce!" (12). Teachers with the ability to manipulate rapport into learning in this construct are reduced to used car salesmen or drug pushers, ready to make the sale and close the deal—an entrepreneurial image of successful masculinity. For Glavin (1997), all successful teaching, either "abusive or seductive," is inevitably corrupting. Drawing on Walter S. J. Ong, who called abusive teaching "agonistic" (bullying and cajoling students into learning with threats, punishment and competition), Glavin reminds us that this hyper-masculine model is reflected in "a Latin etymology at least," of "testing and testament," from testis, testicles (14) which the OED confirms originated possibly from "evidence of maleness."

So how do queer teachers wade their way through such heterosexual mire? The queer literary canon has always been witness to the older man as the initiator, someone who teaches and who, at the same time, longs for the beauty and innocence of youth, like Aschenbach's love for Tadzio in Thomas Mann's *Death in Venice* (1911). Closeted, many queer teachers have felt forced to merely mirror repressive norms, ironically and tragically becoming paragons of agonistic teaching, in which self-inflicted sado-masochistic homophobia becomes an excuse for teaching that resembles the theatre of cruelty in its brow-beating and belittling of those who don't conform or rise to expectations of conformity, if not brilliance. The teacher as tormentor, in whom the goal of passionate desire is twisted by repressed eroticism, has a long and ignoble past. Alberto Manguel's *History of Reading* (1998) is full of stern and brutal men and women throughout the ages who with pleasure would spare no rod in the name of teaching and learning.

Glavin (1997) himself prefers "romantic" teaching because it implies passion and revelation, "the crucial capacity to feel and to communicate enjoyment of the self" (16) ... and that enjoyment guarantees in turn the student's enchantment" (17). The lack of a defined power relationship in this statement is, in itself, seductive to those who might wish to structure the teaching and learning paradigm along more egalitarian lines. Gay and lesbian educators have been drawn to this kind of romantic definition because it implies inclusivity. There's a promise of hugs and the warm fuzzies of diversity education that suggest that none need be excluded; indeed we might even dare to celebrate our differences together. Are sexual difference and orientation any more difficult in the classroom than other fundamental differences such as class, ethnicity, religion, race or gender?

Joseph Litvak (1995) reminds us that the classic masculine/feminine split in the role of teacher and student is particularly problematic for the gay and lesbian teacher, whether or not they are out. "Maybe [we] have to accept the fact that [we] can't simultaneously *épater les bourgeois* and charm their pants off," but the antithetical positioning between "teaching as opposition and teaching as seduction is no less deconstructable than any other" (29). From a feminist perspective, the old metaphors of seduction, romantic or otherwise, don't work, even in a heterosexual paradigm. From a queer perspective they are even more problematic.

First as a high school and then a college and now a university teacher and administrator, I have come to understand over the past thirty years that it is students, at all levels, who exert real power along the teaching/learning continuum. Students grant us permission to teach; without that permission, that is, the offering of their readiness and receptivity, the act of teaching is reduced to a solo act. It is like trying to play catch with a two-year-old: lop-sided, unfair, and mutually frustrating and unfulfilling. Or to use a queerly unsettling metaphor, given this context: without student consent and participation, agonistic teaching is like an act of masturbation: pleasurable perhaps, but alarming, undignified, and inappropriate if done in a public place. That is why so much bad teaching *is* embarrassing. It *should* be done behind closed doors. It is awkward in its portentousness and garish in its presumptuousness—much like the sweaty fumbling and lurching late at night in the back of a '62 Galaxy to which I inflicted high-school girls in the name of "going steady" to prove I was straight. As a teacher-educator, I have seen individuals making their often painful transitions from student to student-teacher to teacher, adopting often very inappropriate stances that presume to know what masculinity and femininity are all about as they try on roles of authority figures in the classroom.

Similarly, in my role as an instructional developer aiming to improve the quality of instruction in the university, I have seen professors struggle with the assumptions about and nature of their highly gendered roles. My aim was to help them make the unconscious more conscious, the self-conscious more conscientious, and the private more public and thus more accountable. When you focus less on performativity, that is, the "acts" of teaching, and more on the learner and learning outcomes, good teaching becomes ethical behaviour, with social and political implications, not just personal ones. I understand teaching occurring on the line where the public and the private intersect; indeed, making public of the private, making the personal universal, making of the unique a universal sign or symbol, is a common reading of all creative ventures, which I also see teaching to be and what animates my teaching, despite what the media has determined a teacher to be.

But as a homosexual, making the personal public has had, I suggest, greater implications than for a heterosexual. Teaching, unlike many other aspects of academia, is an "up front and in your face" activity. We expose ourselves, not physically, but emotionally and intellectually, and then don masks and roles and costumes in order to teach, constantly checking that our flies aren't down and our slips aren't showing. Yet, ironically, the metaphor that comes to me in making sense of my teaching experience is a traditional masculine metaphor grounded in war and struggle: Success in the pedagogical arena is hard fought, often the odds are stacked against you, ground is gained slowly at a great cost; there are battles, the wounded and maimed, heroes and survivors, and sometimes the sweet smell of victory.

So even my tropic constructions are conflicted: the personal in becoming public becomes a metaphor that is both sexist and heterosexist. I am the general leading the students into some war zone. In rejecting what I would like to assume is an imposed way of thinking, I began to look for other metaphors for teaching that were closer to my own sense of (perhaps an ideal) self. In sharing this search with colleagues I hear many metaphors for teacher: builder, gardener, caretaker, doorman, window-cleaner, match-maker, dinner-party host, jazzman, stage manager, ship captain, stand-up comic, and snake-oil salesman, to name just a few. Wendy Steiner (1995) concludes, "Muzzled, hobbled, [professors] trim the wick of their passion to make the flame of learning glow. It is little wonder, then, that most non-academics look upon professors as figures of fun, contempt, or disgust" (165). The martyr is one image that teachers often identify with.

It is a powerful and appealing—if self-indulgent—image for anyone who historically has had to endure (often closeted and self-abusive) personal and systemic discrimination and victimization. Yet the martyrdom of the priest taking vows of chastity remains for most an impossibly idealized virtue.[5]

### REIFIED CINEMATIC IMAGES OF TEACHER

Erotic irony is the subject of the 1997 film *In and Out*, which galvanized for me a sharper understanding of the relationship between queer teacher role and identity within the parameters of eros and the erotic. Frank Oz's movie casts Kevin Kline as Howard, a teacher of English in a bourgeois high school in a small town in contemporary Middle America.

I revisited this media artefact in light of my emerging queer sensibility and my new position as an older man who is no longer a student of teachers but a teacher of students. The cultural repertoire remains the same but the point-of-view is different and my sense of my own manhood has profoundly changed. Positionality and context determines how we read media texts but also how media texts, in turn, read us. Di Piero (2003) points out that masculinity is by definition conflicted and over-determined by the discrepancy between hegemonic ideals of manhood and identity as it is lived on the social plane by real human beings (3). Because whatever is meant by "queer" is by definition not part of hegemonic patriarchy, and indeed challenges "fatherly knowledge" (Hoagland, in Libretti, 2004: 170), this reading of popular culture addresses the tension between the personal and the public, the social cauldron in which we perform identity.

Outed by a former student-turned-actor during the broadcast of the Academy Awards, Howard is forced to deal with students, colleagues, his parents, his fiancée, and ultimately his own admission that yes, he is gay. Complete with a typically unrealistic Hollywood ending where the entire school celebrates his new identity, *In and Out* is a lovely romantic comedy, a true "fairy" tale. Howard's transformation from geeky English teacher, replete with bow tie and bicycle clip, to a happy, openly gay man begins with a kiss from Prince Charming (a television news personality played by Tom Selleck). The kiss allows Howard to experience an epiphany, a sense of wholeness, presumably for the first time, between eros and the erotic and between body, mind, and spirit. Gadamer would call this "the revelation of the possibility of the embodiment of the ideal in the real by transforming the scattered, fragmentary nature of the everyday world into a moment of harmony, lucidity, and ... presence" (Alexander 1997: 332-333).[6] Sexual orientation makes little difference to this longing and applies to all involved in the teaching-learning paradigm.

Myths and fantasies about what teachers are like and what society might wish they were form part of the cultural milieu of our educational context. *In & Out*, with its strident acceptance of an English teacher's gay identity, ends on an upbeat note. Presumably, however, Howard will have to follow his new lover to the big city. Despite the popularity of queer characters in television programs such as *Glee*, *Modern Family*, and *Will and Grace*, living happily ever after as an openly gay teacher in Middle America is not yet the stuff of comedic media representations of queers who teach. The positive spin on gay teacher identity in *In & Out* is still outnumbered by more typically negative caricatures of teachers, regardless of their sexual orientation. In coming-of-age movies, adolescent audiences take satisfaction and find revenge in portraits of teachers as idiots, boors, and malevolent beings—vampires, aliens, or simply exhausted nerdly shells, like "anyone, anyone"—the brilliantly parodied answer-seeking history teacher in *Ferris Bueller's Day Off* (1986).

Each generation draws on a filmic or televised view of teaching that can be variously sentimental, idealistic, romanticized, and even funny. Eve Arden, playing Connie the English teacher in *Our Miss Brooks* in the 1950s, first on radio and then on TV, captured the wise-cracking tough cookie with the heart of gold and became an icon of popular but implicit lesbianism, if only because her attempts to win the attention of the male biology teacher fail miserably. The message, reinforced by the principal (played by Gale Gordon), is that in being sharp and funny and intelligent, she is not attractive to men. In the 1960s I remember watching a cute and imperturbably sincere Tony Franciosa play *Mr. Novak* and wishing my own high school English teachers might be like him. For others, *Welcome Back, Kotter*; *To Sir, with Love*; *Blackboard Jungle*; *Goodbye, Mr. Chips*; *The Prime of Miss Jean Brodie*; *Mr. Holland's Opus*; *Stand and Deliver*; *Dead Poets Society*; or *Mona Lisa Smile* will resonate. Each one of these movies can be critiqued for the inaccurate, heterosexual and often heterosexist view they give of teaching and education.[7] The recently released comedy *Bad Teacher* (2011), starring "teacher" Cameron Diaz as a hard-drinking, pot-smoking, manipulative and sexually aggressive heterosexual looking for a rich man to hook up with, is perhaps the most depressing depiction of teacher in the past thirty years, and stands at the very least as an indictment of the sorry state of the status of teachers in schools in America today. The movie ends with this foul-mouthed reprobate being promoted to the role of guidance counsellor because of her supposed understanding of the social and sexual problems of kids in schools today. This intuitive ability is demonstrated when she takes off her bra and gives it to a 12-year-old boy who can thus prove to his buddies that he got to first base with some girl. Yikes.

Such reified images of teacher exist and define our context. In the public imagination, good teachers are born, not made. Through the authority of our personalities (whether as nice guy or clown or rebel or absent-minded professor, to name only a few) we are supposed to be successful at teaching. In popular culture, success as a teacher is highly constructed as a gendered and sexual identity. Eros and the erotic are present on the screen but only heterosexually. Examples of such successful teaching is constructed without preparation, planning, reflection, action or scholarly research, but simply as a gift of faith, inspiration and dedication, and dependent on one's performance as "straight" man or woman.

A decade and a half ago Barbra Streisand produced, directed, and starred in *The Mirror Has Two Faces* (1996), an indicative study of this kind of teaching. Despite the artifice of the ugly duckling's inevitable transformation to beautiful swan (a Barbra motif that defines her as quintessential, like Cher, to gay iconography), Streisand's character,

Rose Morgan, a university English professor, is proposed pedagogically as an example of good teaching. In lectures she has hundreds of students eating out of her hand because she is funny, self-deprecating, apparently honest, relevant, and direct, and she can, as if by magic, call on any one of the hundreds of beaming students by first name whenever she wants. It is not mere chance that the subjects of the only lecture we see her give are romantic love and sex. Receptive because of the topics, students (and we the audience) become consumers of a theatrical performance—inspirational at best, but pedagogically unsound and blatantly untrue. Despite her supposed intellectual prowess, she confides to students that in the end romance is superior to sex because "it comes down to fucking feeling good" (a deliberately ambiguous phrase). Her success in convincing her audience of this truth proves she can walk that tightrope between eros and the erotic. The vulgarity of the apparently personal appeal, acting, acting out, and publicly embracing heterosexuality is to be considered highly appropriate and an example of good pedagogy. Imagine a queer teacher doing that, in either the media or in reality.

Pity the poor math professor, fall guy Greg Larkin, played by Jeff Bridges, who on a ruse seeks Barbra's advice on teaching ("make it something kids can relate to," she says). Mumbling to himself at the blackboard, Bridges doesn't hear female students lamenting his lack of interest in their flirting. One concludes disparagingly, "He must be gay". But the other quickly retorts, "Oh no. He's too boring to be gay."

Indulging in such stereotypes, pedagogical success by Hollywood's standard is achieved through the power and cult of personality. Teachers portrayed like this make claims to authoritarian constructs and the American dream of success through willpower, ambition, and using their powers of seduction. Bauer (1998) calls such intuitive teaching "the erotic manipulation of desire." We see this vividly in the 1995 film *Dangerous Minds*, which is loosely based on the memoirs of inner-city high school teacher LouAnne Johnson. The heterosexual female teacher, played by Michelle Pfeiffer, is the potential victim to be seduced by or succumb to the torrid predatory sexuality of the class leader, Emilio, the Hispanic James Dean character. Instead (and isn't it lucky she has some training as a Marine), teacher seduces students with her mental stamina and physical strength. She wins them over by teaching them martial arts. She adopts an agonistic stance that plays on a model of machismo with a highly honed erotic edge. In other words, she beats Emilio at his own game to assume the leadership position of power in the classroom. Once she gains the trust and respect of the class she is able to soften to a more nurturing and vulnerable persona and the movie spins into a muddle of sentiment and sentimentality, authentic if only because there is as much frustration and failure as there is success in this particular view of pedagogy. Lipstick lesbian or dominatrix, the teacher cannot be seen to "win" in such an environment.

In comparison to the heterosexual sex and pedagogy promoted in these films, *In and Out* seems so "heart-warming" because a gay man is able to be a respected teacher of English and drama and a basketball coach and come to acknowledge his homosexuality first privately and then publicly. Eros and the erotic have merged in an idealistic if unrealistic way. But this is a new way of gendering pedagogy, even if it is mere fantasy. As a media text of popular culture it designs to educate—literally to lead us—didactically to understand that the explicit naming of sexual or erotic orientation need not compromise the eros of passionate teaching. Indeed, as an out gay male, Howard's new self should, in a hermeneutic sense, allow him to strive more freely for beauty and truth by coming to better understand the "other," his students who are the subject and object of passionate teaching.

### TEACHING ASEXUALLY IN THIS CULTURE

By default, then, teachers are part of a mythological media construct that defines us. The identity of teachers is even more conflicted than this cursory glance at the more obvious elements of popular culture's view of teachers might superficially suggest. In teacher education and in instructional development I had, for all sorts of reasons, chosen to make my sexuality a non-issue. Part of me said it shouldn't matter, that my sexuality is a private issue and no one else's business. Pragmatically, such a stance is easier than having to deal with students' fears or ignorance or faculties' misconceptions or good intentions. Pinar (2001) suggests that such closeted denial subverts curriculum as "currere," meaning to challenge and interrogate the status quo, in a form of "social psychoanalysis" (2). At the same time I eschewed the authority of the power figure, despite (or rather because of) my years and experience.

Yet new faculty and pre-service teachers alike still crave that "gift": to understand how the practice of narcissism can be transformed into the art of seduction so that they might "control," or at least successfully manage, the teaching/learning environment. Understandably, the preoccupation with control—of themselves, of the content, of the students—is a hallmark of novices finding their way, but it is also embedded in our understanding of hetero-masculinity. In the past I would have deliberately chosen to be neither an openly gay nor an authoritative teacher, even though I am both, because of the focus those perceived roles bring to the cult of personality. My construction and performance of straight high school teacher in the 1980s looked like this: big Bee Gees hair, tight flat-front pants, pink cotton button-down shirts and baby blue ties. This norm was not mere fashion; it presented a particular "cool" sexuality (in contrast to two of my English teacher colleagues, Mr. McPherson, who was never without his shabby, patched-at-the-elbows Harris Tweed, and Sister Jasmine, always in some variation of black wool). Like current student-teachers, I assumed my appearance paramount to meaning and intent. When I returned to the high school classroom to do action research, I was reminded that adolescents are quick to "judge a book by its cover."

What I would hope pre-service teachers would learn from me is that they can be successful by being more interested in the success of their students than in their constructed identity. So again, I am locked in a contradiction: I do have the authority of my experience and I am a gay man. Why did I deny this and what degree of "choice" or agency was involved in such a decision? Part of an answer may be because the sub-text of eroticism, involving seduction and power in the teacher/student relationship, leads to the narcissism of the "act" of teaching. Educators are vulnerable public figures, needing approval, prepared for derision, conflicted by the authority imposed by our roles, and fearful that we will or have become in the public domain something separate, and thus somehow invalid or inauthentic or distanced, from the personal self. Female pre-service teachers and new female university faculty members, for example, worry about becoming something they are not—"the hard-nosed bitch"—in order to lay claim to the authority of their role as teacher. But the same concern is echoed often by their male counterparts, particularly those who do not come easily to an aggressive or extroverted manner of the manly expert, charmer, or controller.

Novices understandably yearn to become the kind of dynamic figures that Hollywood plays back to us: vivid personalities for whom teaching is a "natural" act of passion where traditional constructions of gendered masculinity and femininity control the paradigm. In this context, and learning to project an identity, pre-service teachers may well believe they have more to learn from teachers portrayed in such films as *The Mirror Has Two Faces* and *Dangerous Minds* than they do from teacher education programs, or specifically from me—someone who has un-closeted his sexuality and refused to take on the role of authoritarian.

Kelly (1997) attributes the dearth of literature addressing eros and teaching to the general resistance by educators to any acknowledgement of desire in teaching. "As teaching subjects, teachers have been positioned within the same discourses of desexualization" (124). This has abetted those of us who for whatever reason chose to be closeted or circumspect about our sexual orientation and has bolstered the heterosexist norms that permeate the classroom. But what does this kind of symbolic castration or mutilation mean for our pedagogy? How can we speak from the heart or the gut if we are disembodied? As Joseph Litvak points out, "every classroom is an eroticized space: eroticized in different ways and with different effects, depending on the sex and gender of the students [and teacher]" (19).

From a homoerotic perspective, what do we make of the Greek concept of *agape,* that is, ultimately, "we become what we love"? Education is a form of *agape*: our destiny is in our desires, yet what we seek to possess soon comes to possess us in thought, feeling and action. The Greeks understood this in the raising of children and thus made the education of eros, passionate desire, the supreme aim of education—the desire for and to do "good." The result of such an education is supposed to be practical wisdom: the ability to distinguish between what we immediately desire and what proves truly desirable after reflection, that is, what is for the common good: values, laws, principles, and ethics. Schools and universities have prided themselves on bearing the burden of such ethical, discriminating responsibility. It was not merely a question of teaching the young delayed or sublimated gratification. It was a noble charge that lent integrity and thus dignity to the academy as an extension of many phallic or patriarchal narratives in our culture. For many this is, in itself, a romantic and seductive idea.

The ancient Greeks had an expression that captures the spirit and also some of the erotic charge of philosophical reflection: "You must come naked to wrestle." In what ways, as teachers, inviting our students to "wrestle with ideas," as we say, must we also come, metaphorically, naked to teach? Surely this requires a kind of preparation and a receptivity to the moment that implies vulnerability, regardless of gender constructs or sexual orientation. To be authentic we must dispense with masks and suits of armour. Isn't my sexual orientation part of this nakedness? Moreover, in what way, then, does the homoerotic animate the eros of the teaching of a gay man such as myself? How do I go about learning and explaining that to myself and to my students? Surely I am charged ethically to do so. I now understand that we diminish our potential for passionate desire (eros) if we dismiss our sexuality (the erotic), as I used to do, as nobody else's business, or just a matter of biology or politics, or (worse), as some conservative colleagues do, diminish or misrepresent it even further by presuming it to be an unfortunate "preference" or "lifestyle." The business of teaching is in metaphor, in making comparisons and contrasts, in learning to discriminate distinctions between one thing and another. If part of me as a man is defined as "nobody's business," what implications are there for my pedagogy when eros is the force that prompts the pursuit of wholeness?

Anti-oppressive educators such as Kumashiro (2000) and Tuitt (2003) have been inspired by bell hooks' (1994) adage that "education is the practice of freedom" (207). They encourage us to focus less on teaching for and about differences and concentrate more on teaching about oppression and privilege. The former continues to stigmatize and victimize "others" for their place and space in society; the latter encourages us to seek justice. Using curriculum as a series of windows and mirrors (Styles, 1996; McNinch, 2004) implies that we should look critically and appreciatively at ourselves as well as the many perspectives on the complicated lives of others. We need to help each other look in the mirror and to see out the windows to the world beyond.

When there is duplicity and deception on the erotic side of Aristotle's parabola, there can be grave moral implications for eros. Think of the lurid and salacious stories the media loves to tell: elementary and middle-years female school teachers taking children as their lovers and having children by them. Think, in turn, of junior high school administrators who have been charged across the country with collecting and disseminating child pornography through the Internet. Think, too, of the culpability of victim and perpetrator in sexual harassment cases that continue to emerge at universities between students and professors.[8] This "evidence," while it might be dismissed as marginal and exceptional, helps us to understand through the sensationalism of the media that eros is complicated not just by erotics but by asymmetrical power relationships. Fear and denial of all sexuality, not just homosexuality, continues to define the educational environment (McNinch, 2004).

A former university student of mine, a Métis man in his early thirties and an award-winning high school teacher and basketball and football coach working with inner-city Aboriginal youth for the past decade, was charged several years ago with a number of sexual offences involving teenage males. The teacher pleaded not guilty to all charges and, as of this writing, all charges but one have been stayed. In roles of teacher and coach, men in particular find themselves vulnerable and in potentially tragic positions. Some research shows that men are increasingly reluctant to enter the teaching profession for fear that, while they are doing their job, allegations of sexual impropriety may brand them forever as "perverts" (Harris, 2009). Such allegations stem from deeply conflicted and contradictory impulses and motives related to the construction of masculinity by both teacher and student (McNinch, 2011).

As my partner Michael has reminded me, as a closeted young teenager in small-town Saskatchewan in the 1970s, he would have been only too willing to jump into David Hasselhoff's *Knight Rider* smart car or jump up behind Erik Estrada on his motorcycle in *CHiPs* and leave his closeted and suicidal life behind. Assuming a simplistic binary of adult perpetrator and youthful victim serves to confirm and maintain the status quo relating to definitions of heterosexual masculinity. Congruency, rather than contradictions, between one's inner (erotic) and outer (eros) life might reduce the seriousness and implications of such allegations and entanglements.

Addressing issues of masculinity and schooling, Martino (2003, 2001) demonstrates how fear and denial of sexuality serve to undermine the success of boys in education. Queer educators might come to understand this through their own imbalanced position vis-à-vis the power relationships in schools and universities. Queer educators' own lack of voice, lack of power, and potential for victimization, link us, through struggle and eros, to all minority groups who have fought against prejudice and oppression: "We are in excellent historical company" (Elliott, 1996: 703).[9] Such a queer gaze is directed by insult and contempt and of "suffering the experience of a subordinate positionality," as Pierre Bourdieu calls it (in Eribon, 2004: 38).

Seduction becomes molestation because of the inequality between student and teacher. From Plato and Socrates to Shaw's *Pygmalion* (1916), or Morag Gunn and Brook Skelton in Margaret Laurence's *The Diviners* (1974), there has always been the potential for the erotic in teacher/student roles. The role of the governess, the live-in teacher, in Brontë's *Jane Eyre* (1847) and Henry James' *Turn of the Screw* (1898) shows the heightened, often hysterical, tension between eros and the erotic because of the ambiguous power relationships between master, servant and child. Who is seducing whom is the precise question that Brontë and James would wish us to ask. Think, too, of the title character in Flaubert's *Madame Bovary* (1857), the young virginal wife seduced into uxorial duties by a man who could be her father. Gay literature has always been witness to the older man who initiates the younger man in the vagaries of lust and love, like George, the British professor in Christopher Isherwood's 1964 novel, *A Single Man*. Plato, in the *Dialogues*, warns young men to take care not to confuse tenderness with romance; older men seek their own pleasure at the expense of the young.

There has always been the potential for the merely erotic in teacher/student relations because of the promise of both dependence and liberation. The old are mortal; the young are beautiful simply because they are not old. Think of the machinations of professor Humbert in Nabokov's *Lolita* (1958), or the pathetic longing of Aschenbach in Thomas Mann's *Death in Venice* (1912). Erotically, it is the Lolitas and Tadzios who have something to teach the sexually repressed bourgeoisie. But in the classroom, students the same age as Lolita and Tadzio have tyrannized many teachers in another way; that is, they have refused to be pedagogically seduced by them and often driven them from the profession. In my era, it was anglophone teachers of junior high French who seemed to suffer the worst fate: We "went through" five of them in one year, Grade 8, and took perverse pleasure in wasting these vulnerable "weaklings."

## PROVISIONAL CONCLUSIONS

How do we begin to put these pieces together? What is the relationship between eros and erotics and how does this play itself out for the straight and the queer teacher? Why does teaching continue to be about the art of seduction, particularly in media representations of pedagogy? Vygotsky (1986) spoke about "luring students into learning." Why, even in his alliterative metaphor, is a tool of eroticism the tool that will lead us to eros—the pursuit of the passionately desirable: truth, justice, and beauty?

I am struck by the image of the *berdache* in Aboriginal cultures: an individual who might be (in our terms) a homosexual or cross-dresser or transsexual or hermaphrodite and be accepted at face value by the community as a manifestation of the natural and spirit worlds and celebrated as a gift and a power and not shunned as a deviant or a pervert.[10] Through my teaching of First Nations and Métis literature I have learned that the erotic has no negative connotations; the wisdom of the shamans and the Elders fuses the corporeal and the ethereal. The ideal teacher in Native legends as well as contemporary fiction is no trickster, no Wesakeyjak, or shape-shifter, though the best teachers and storytellers will use such characters to their advantage. In the same way they will draw on sexuality as a wonderful endowment of richness, humour, and humanity, a gift where there are no "dirty" words to describe the body or denigrate sexuality.[11]

What a contrast that is to the image of the colonizing teacher, in literature and in history, not just as the seducer but as the abuser of cultural identity and individual children. Brian Moore's 1985 novel, *Black Robe*, vividly demonstrates the contradictions of guilt and sin imposed through the notion of the duality of mind and body. Spying on *"les sauvages ... like dogs coupling"* (54), Jesuit Father Laforgue is sexually aroused and ejaculates, and then flagellates himself with willows to punish himself for these sins and, symbolically, for all the sins of sexual molestation and physical abuse by clerics in residential schools in the nineteenth and twentieth centuries.

Despite rich beginnings for eros and the erotic in both Aboriginal and Greek cultures, we continue to regard pedagogy not as an embodied and intuitive search for wholeness but rather as a rational and technical pursuit of skills and competence that becomes normative through standardized testing of both students and teachers.[12] What kind of burden of responsibility for authenticity and identity do such assumptions impose on educators, particularly queer ones? Authenticity is judged by the power of applause or approval and students' rating of our performance. We need this approval or, like the actor on the stage, we fail. Thus teacher-educators encourage student-teachers to entice pupils with a "set," grab attention and learn to work the crowd with their bodies and their eyes, to play up to their charges, cajoling them to "work with me on this," "play ball" and hopefully gain trust for the engagement and seduction into teaching and learning.

Student-teachers who fail to establish their presence in the classroom (lacking "with-it-ness," their supervisors whisper) have failed to seduce their students with the power of their personalities. We see, too, academics floundering in their role as teachers, blinking blindly through the glare of the data projectors, caught like deer in headlights, clinging to the authority of their own texts, insisting on the primacy of ideas, refusing to believe that the dancer is the dance. Queer educators may appreciate what Jean-Claude Couture (1997) meant when he said, "Experience is a structure built by the text(s) of our stances taken in the world." But what if these stances, including our gender performativity, are in themselves inauthentic, or closeted, or unacknowledged? In failing to acknowledge, much less celebrate, the tension and synergy between eros and erotics, do we, particularly if we are gay or lesbian, encourage in ourselves and our students a false consciousness of what pedagogy is? How do we, with intentionality, reach for what Peter Grimmet (1997), in critiquing the mere busy-ness of schools, calls the "focally real"? Revisiting Freud, Britzman (2000) cites structural, pedagogical and psychical forms of resistance to Eros and asks, "Can sexuality ... be educated? And can education be sexed?" (34–35). Pinar (2001) suggests, and agrees with Britzman, that to effect change we should be creating anxious knowledge about such things as manhood and masculinity, concepts of identity that we know are inherently in flux, inherently unstable (11–13).

Aristotle's parabola of pleasure is not between sex and thought; such dualism may seem arcane and trite in our "holistic" age. The parabola exists because of our humanity: the tension plays itself out on a continuum between the young and the old, between immortality and mortality, between a lack of awareness and a growing consciousness, between the finite and the infinite, between the student and the teacher. When my alcoholic father hid the secret of his cancers for more than two years from us adult children, having insisted my mother take vows of complicit silence to this dirty little secret, he fulfilled his sex's and his generation's adherence to the Hemingway code of taciturn circumspection. ("Good living, like good writing, is like an iceberg—only ten percent is above the surface.") Today we might charge him with a profound fear of intimacy, only emotional—by turns gleeful or raging—when drunk. Now as a middle-aged orphan, I know I cannot ascribe to this model in my life, any more than I can accept Platonic duality in my teaching.

Teaching then, as the art of seduction, moves from receiver to sender, object to subject, from other to self. Teaching is seductive and alluring, not to the student but to the teacher. It is attractive to educators because it sets us clearly on the tightrope stretching between eros and the erotic and between innocence and wisdom, between the young and the old. In the students who greet us each September, forever the same age and saccharine as an ABBA song, and forever reminding us that we are no longer young, we see poignantly the struggles ahead of them with this business of living, of having and making a life.

It is we teachers, not our students, who are aware of our "mere" mortality. The reason secondary and post-secondary literary anthologies are full of poems about death and poems espousing the *carpe diem* sentiments of the Cavalier poets—and indeed why I am drawn to teach them—is because these are the issues with which we teachers are concerned. It is not our students who need to be encouraged to "gather ye rosebuds while ye may" or "seize the pleasures of the day" or "Come live with me, and be my love/And we will some new pleasures prove," or "tear our pleasures with rough strife," or to say "Death be not proud, though some have called thee/mighty and dreadful" and "Do not go gentle into that good night/... . Rage, rage against the dying of the light."

Queer Edmonton playwright Brad Fraser (1999) often speaks of and is drawn to the seductive powers of youth—their energy, their confusion, their passion, admitting he prefers to hang out with adolescents rather than with his peers. Partly embarrassed by and partly envious of the exhibitionism of Brad Fraser, I find him, with T.S. Elliot's Prufrock, as well as myself, "At times, indeed, almost ridiculous—/Almost at times, the Fool[s]. I grow old ... I grow old.../I shall wear the bottoms of my trousers rolled" (118–21).

For teachers, ageing teachers, and certainly queer teachers, the distance from brave tightrope walker to clown is but a foolish fall. This rumination on eros and the erotic in teaching as the art of seduction has revealed inchoate aspects of my identity as a gay man and my identity as a gay teacher, and has led me to interrogate eros and the erotic through an exploration of the media and mortality. Despite huge gains over the past decades, the role of the queer teacher has been and is still highly conflicted, in the past by the burden of the closet and Socratic dualism, and now by the burden of responsibility for modelling health and openness beyond stereotypes promulgated in popular culture with its obsession, like gay culture itself, with youth. I hope it is clear why youth is so seductive to the teacher. I have learned that those of us who have been knocked around by love and death, and shame and guilt and grief, usually conclude that we should be more tentative in our forays into the realm of "truth"—which teaching, in attempting to cultivate passionate desire for what "right" and "just and good," is all about.

Kelly (1997) suggests that in reclaiming eros we exercise caution:

> Such caution demands, minimally, that we ask con-
> tinuously of ourselves and our pedagogies what the
> sources of our passions and desires are, what effects
> our passions and desires have on others, and in what
> way our passions and desires might interface with
> desiring others in productive and non-productive
> ways. I suggest it is our responses to these questions
> wherein lies the specificity of an erotic character of
> our pedagogies. For this reason alone, it is important
> to analyze responses to cultural texts of teaching as
> a means of locating a reflexive sense of personal eros
> and teaching. (130)

But it is more than a matter of being useful to others and it is more than eros being the displacement of the erotic. Quoting Felman and Lacan, Kelly sees transference from teacher to student as "an emotional erotic experience" (133). What is often missed in such a discussion is the reciprocity of the process of identification and transference. bell hooks (1994) and others talk about this eroticism in the building of community and transformative visions. This visionary community-building is what queers have been doing stridently and courageously for at least the past three decades. We make sense together; in a pedagogical construct we also need to make sense to others if we, as queer educators, are to be included in the larger community of meaning-makers. Engaged in daily work, we embody a form of advocacy research for ourselves and all our students and struggle to queer and que(e)ry the curriculum (Pinar, 2001; Clarke, 1999; Sears, 1992). We must become ourselves, first for ourselves and then for all teachers, and most importantly for all our students, despite the ambiguity and ambivalence of the discourse in this still largely unmapped territory of eros and the erotic in the queer land of homosexuality.

Bauer (1998) concludes

> Much of the best of our intellectual work comes from the deepest commitments to our own sexual and political styles, charged as they inevitably are with desires for connection, intimacy, love. If this is an indecent proposal about our pedagogy, it is better made public than repressed. (316)

Parker Palmer in *The Courage to Teach* (1998) speaks of the need for the inner and outer lives of teachers to be congruent in order for us to maintain our integrity. This wholeness will show students how to define themselves "authentically and spontaneously in relation to the world," as Thomas Merton describes it (cited in hooks, 199). Roger Simon talks of the "pedagogy of the possible." As a political act, teaching must rest on "a fascination with the dignity of those whom we teach" (cited in Kelly, 6). For me this wholeness is in continuing to be charmed, intrigued, captivated, enchanted, in short, seduced by youth in all their brave, frustrating, naive, sweet ignorance. Regardless of our or their sexual orientation, students will not grant to us the permission to teach if we do not accord to them, and celebrate with them, the majesty they desire. This is the passionate desire of both eros and the erotic that we must cultivate: the desire to learn and to love; our mortality insists on it. Pedagogy is an act of privilege; gay and lesbian teachers must create their own pedagogical models and images and forget Hollywood. It has taken me thirty years to realize that teaching is an affair not just of the mind, but of the gut and the heart.

**NOTES**

1    An earlier version of this paper was published as "Queering Seduction: Eros and the Erotic in the Construction of Gay Teacher Identity," in *The Journal of Men's Studies*, Vol. 15(2), (Spring 2007), pp. 197–215. Reprinted by permission. Men's Studies Press, LLC. Copyright 2013.

2    "One of the radical transitions in Western philosophy which seems to have gone unnoticed, is how the modern era, from Descartes on, *"unsexed the mind*, that is, removed the relationship of understanding and meaning to Eros." See Thomas Alexander, "Eros and Understanding," (Chicago: Open Court, 1997), 339.

3    I use "gay and lesbian" and "queer" roughly as homonyms, although "queer" implies a stronger sense of critical consciousness and a much larger construct than the binary of gay vs. straight.

4    The debate a decade ago between "ludic" feminism [from *ludos*—play/pleasure] and "red" feminism is informative here. Teresa Ebert (1996) articulates well the classic Marxist view that speaks to the struggle for consciousness that oppressed minorities have experienced, as opposed to the "libidinal pedagogy" of the privileged. For Ebert "the pedagogies of pleasure" are a middle-class indulgence. Red pedagogy is "transformative and part of the praxis of class struggle" (816). See Teresa Ebert, "For a Red Pedagogy: Feminism, Desire, and Need," *College English* 58, no. 7 (1996): 795–819.

5    Cf. the 1996 Canadian film *Lilies*, in which Saint Sebastian figures prominently in an exploration of young homosexual love and betrayal. Alexander (1997) quotes Gadamer's focus on Plato's understanding of Beauty in the Symposium—a perfect instance of self-representation, whose "radiance" constitutes its "very being" (332). Beauty is one manifestation, then, of the "aesthetic lure in our quest for the experience of meaning. Through this we are tempted to the other…" (330). Radical theologians, such as Lutherans Concerned, who wish sanctity for gays and lesbians within the Church, connect the pain of homosexuality to the suffering of Christ to envision a "Gay Christ."

6    Alexander (1997) makes useful distinctions between Platonic Eros ("the drive for the ideal") and Freudian Eros ("sublimated sexuality") and what he sees in Dewey and Gadamer's work as a form of "Human Eros," that is, "this basic drive for experiencing meaning and value" (324).

7    See John Glavin (1997) for an incisive deconstruction of the role of the teacher as manipulator and seductive mentor in *Stand and Deliver* and *Dead Poets Society* (14–26), and Dale Bauer (1998) for a critique of culturally sanctioned sexuality in pedagogy in *The Mirror Has Two Faces*. Ursula Kelly (1997) does a good job of explaining identification and transference in *To Sir, with Love*. See also Claudia Mitchell and Sandra Weber (1999) for a discussion in chapter 5 of popular culture and teacher identity.

8    According to a survey in *Campus Canada*, 38% of male and 63% of female undergraduates still fantasize about having sex with a professor. See Intini (2000): 12–14.

9    Elliott (1996) sees the connections between the "corrosive character and … helplessness of women's shame," the "double-consciousness" articulated by W.E.B. DuBois as "the internalization of white racism in black consciousness," and internalized homophobia. Elliott reminds gay and lesbian educators that "many of us cannot avoid seeing ourselves as we have been taught to imagine that others see us [as somehow damaged goods]" (696).

10    For Norval Morrisseau, the Ojibwa artist, "a homosexual is one of the most gifted persons there is. I think all shamans are homosexual, or, anyway bisexual (in Martin, 1999: 42). See also for example, *Keeper 'n Me* (1994) by Richard Wagamese and the poetry of Louise Halfe (1996, 1998) for a sense of the rich strength of the elders.

11    I am indebted to colleagues Jo-Ann Episkenew and Heather Hodgson for helping me clarify this. See also Martin Cannon's seminal article, "The Regulation of First Nations Sexuality" (2004). Cf. Drew Hayden Taylor (ed.), *Me Sexy: An Exploration of Native Sex and Sexuality* (Vancouver: Douglas & McIntyre, 2008).

12    In Greek mythology Eros was the first god, born of chaos, the force behind creation. In other versions Eros is the son of Aphrodite, goddess of beauty and love, who becomes Cupid and marries Psyche (the soul) and has a daughter (Pleasure). The connection between Aboriginal and Ancient Greek mythology is illuminating. Eros in the Aristophanes myth of three-sexed humanity is male, female, and androgynous but then is split by the gods who feel threatened by them and thus leave the parts longing for the whole. Eros in this scenario is the force that prompts the pursuit of wholeness, a wholeness implicitly understood in traditional Aboriginal understandings of sexual identities.

## REFERENCES

### A. TEXTS

Alexander, T.M. 1997. "Eros and Understanding: Gadamer's Aesthetic Ontology of the Community." Pp. 322–45 in L. Hahn (ed.), *The Philosophy of Hans-Georg Gadamer*. Chicago: Open Court.

Bauer, Dale M. 1998. "Indecent Proposals: Teachers in the Movies." *College English* 60, no. 3: 301–17.

Barreca, Regina, and Deborah D. Morse (eds.). 1997. *The Erotics of Instruction*. Hanover: UP of New England.

Baxter, Magolda M. 1992. *Knowing and Reasoning in College*. San Francisco: Jossey-Bass.

Bell, Sophie. 1998. "Dangerous Morals: Hollywood Puts a Happy Face on Urban Education." *Radical Teacher* 54: 23–27.

Bloom, Allan. 1987. *The Closing of the American Mind* (Foreword by Saul Bellow). New York: Simon & Schuster.

Bredbeck, G.W. 1995. "Anal/yzing the Classroom: On the Impossibility of a Queer Pedagogy." Pp. 169-82 in George Haggerty and Bonnie Zimmerman (eds.), *Professions of Desire*. New York: MLA.

Britzman, Deborah. 2000. "Precocious Education." Pp. 33–59 in S. Talburt and S. Steinberg (eds.), *Thinking Queer: Sexuality, Culture, and Education*. New York: Peter Lang.

Cannon, Martin. 2004. "The Regulation of First Nations Sexuality." Pp. 95–108 in James McNinch and Mary Cronin (eds.), *I Could Not Speak My Heart: Education and Social Justice for Gay and Lesbian Youth*. Regina: Canadian Plains Research Center.

Chickering, A.W., and L. Reisser. 1993. *Education and Identity,* 2nd ed. San Francisco: Jossey-Bass.

Clarke, Paul. 1999. "Toward an Inclusive Community: Protecting the Human and Constitutional Rights of Homosexual Educators in Public Schools." *Journal Of Educational Administration & Foundations* 14, no. 1: 58–100.

Couture, Jean-Claude. 1997. "Impaired Driving." Pp. 109–20 in T. Carson and D. Sumara (eds.), *Action Research as a Living Practice*. New York: Peter Lang.

DiPiero, Thomas. 2002. *White Men Aren't*. Durham NC: Duke University Press.

Ebert, T.L. 1996. "For a Red Pedagogy: Feminism, Desire, and Need." *College English* 58, no. 7: 795–819.

Elliott, M. 1996. "Coming Out in the Classroom: A Return to the Hard Place." *College English* 58, no. 6: 693–708.

Eribon, Didier. 2004. *Insult and the Making of the Gay Self* (M. Lucey, Trans.). London: Duke University Press.

Fraser, Brad. 1999. Address and Readings. Faculty of Fine Arts Speakers Series. Riddell Theatre, University of Regina, February 4 and 6.

Garrison, James. 1997. *Dewey and Eros: Wisdom and Desire in the Art of Teaching*. New York: Teachers College Press.

Glavin, John. 1997. "The Intimacies of Instruction." Pp. 12–27 in R. Barrecca and D. Morse (eds.), *The Erotics of Instruction*. Hanover: UP of New England.

Gorney, Cynthia. 1999. "Teaching Johnny the Appropriate Way to Flirt." *New York Times Magazine* (June 13): 43–47.

Green, Jesse. 1999. "Gays and Monsters." *New York Times Magazine* (June 13): 13–14.

Grace, A. 2000. "Using Autobiographical Queer Life Narrative Research to Shape a Pedagogy of Space & Place." Session VI: Pedagogy. Canadian Lesbian and Gay Society of Academics. University of Alberta, Edmonton, May 26.

Grimmett, Peter. 1997. "Breaking the Mold: Transforming a Didactic Professor into a Learner-Focused Teacher Educator." Pp. 121–36 in T. Carson and D. Sumara (eds.), *Action Research as a Living Practice*. New York: Peter Lang.

Haggerty, G.E., and B. Zimmerman (eds.). 1995. *Professions of Desire: Lesbian and Gay studies in Literature*. New York: MLAA.

Halfe, Bernice. 1996. *Bear Bones & Feathers*. Regina: Coteau Books.

———. 1998. *Blue Marrow*. Regina: Coteau Books.

Hayden-Taylor, Drew (ed.). 2008. *Me Sexy: An Exploration of Native Sex and Sexuality*. Vancouver: Douglas & McIntyre.

Hill, Robert J. 1996. "Learning to Transgress: A Socio-historical Conspectus on the American Gay Lifeworld as a Site of Struggle and Resistance." *Studies in the Education of Adults* 28, no. 2: 253–79.

hooks, bell. 1994. *Teaching to Transgress: Education as the Practice of Freedom*. New York: Routledge.

Intini, John. 2000. "Sex on Campus." *Campus Canada* 16, no. 4 (Spring): 12–14.

Isherwood, Christopher. 1964. *A Single Man.* New York: Noonday Press.

Kincaid, James R. 1997. "Eroticism Is a Two-Way Street, and I'm Working Both Sides." Pp. 81–93 in R. Barreca and D. Morse (eds.), *The Erotics of Instruction.* Hanover: UP of New England.

Kelly, Ursula A. 1997. *Schooling Desire: Literacy, Cultural Politics, and Pedagogy.* New York: Routledge.

Kumashiro, K. 2000. "Toward a Theory of Anti-Oppressive Education." *Review of Educational Research* 70, no. 1: 25–53.

Laurence. Charles. 2000. "Bellow, Book, Cradle." *National Post* (January 22): B1+.

Libretti, Tim. 2004. "Sexual Outlaws and Class Struggle: Rethinking History and Class Consciousness from a Queer Perspective." *College English* 67, no. 2: 154–71.

Litvak, Joseph. 1995. "Pedagogy and Sexuality." Pp. 19–30 in G. Haggarty and B. Zimmerman (eds.), *Professions of Desire.* New York: MLA.

Manguel, Alberto. 1998. *A History of Reading.* Toronto: Random House.

Martin, Lee-Ann. 1999. *Exposed: Aesthetics of Aboriginal Erotic Art.* Regina, SK: MacKenzie Art Gallery.

Martino, Wayne, and Maria Pallotta-Chiarolli (eds.). 2003. *So What's a Boy? Addressing Issues of Masculinity and Schooling.* Maidenhead UK: Open University Press.

Martino, W., and B. Meyenn (eds.). 2001. *What about the Boys: Issues of Masculinity in Schools.* Buckingham UK: Open University Press.

McCourt, Frank. 1999. "Back to School, 1958." *New York Times Magazine* (September 12): 54–61+.

McNinch, James. 2012. "Que(e)rying Canadian Manhood: Gay Masculinity in the Twenty-First Century." Pp. 269–291 in Jason Laker (ed.), *Canadian Perspectives on Men and Masculinity: An Interdisciplinary Reader.* Toronto: Oxford University Press.

McNinch, James, and Mary Cronin (eds.). 2004. *I Could Not Speak My Heart: Education and Social Justice for Gay and Lesbian Youth.* Regina: Canadian Plains Research Center.

Mitchell, Claudia, and Sandra Weber. 1999. *Reinventing Ourselves as Teachers: Beyond Nostalgia.* London: Falmer Press.

Orwin, C. 2000. "Bringing Bloom's Laughter Back to Life." *National Post* (May 6): 7.

"Out of Control." 1998. *People Weekly* (March 30): 44–49.

Palmer, Parker. 1998. *The Courage to Teach: Exploring the Inner Landscape of a Teacher's Life.* San Francisco: Jossey-Bass.

Perry, William G. 1970. *Forms of Intellectual and Ethical Development in the College Years: A Scheme.* New York: Holt, Rinehart & Winston.

Pinar, W.F. 2001. *The Gender of Racial Politics and Violence in America: Lynching, Prison Rape, & the Crisis of Masculinity.* New York: Peter Lang.

Robertson, Douglas L. 1999. "Unconscious Displacements in College Teacher and Student Relationships: Conceptualizing, Identifying, and Managing Transference." *Innovative Higher Education* 23, no. 3: 151–69.

Steiner, Wendy. 1995. *The Scandal of Pleasure: Art in an Age of Fundamentalism*. Chicago: Chicago University Press.

Style, E. 1996. "Curriculum as Window & Mirror. The Wellesley Centers for Women SEED Project on Inclusive Curriculum." Retrieved April 20, 2003 from <www.wcwonline.org/seed/curriculum.html>

Thompson, S. Anthony. (2004). "Operation 'Special': Interrogating the Queer Production of Everyday Myths in Special Education." Pp. 273–88 in James McNinch and Mary Cronin (eds.), *I Could Not Speak My Heart: Education and Social Justice for Gay and Lesbian Youth*. Regina: Canadian Plains Research Center.

Tuitt, F. 2003. "Afterword: Realizing a More Inclusive Pedagogy." Pp. 243–68 in A. Howell and F. Tuitt (eds.), *Race and Higher Education: Rethinking Pedagogy in Diverse College Classrooms*. Cambridge: Harvard Educational Review.

Vygotsky, Lev. 1986. *Thought and Language* (Alex Kozulin, Trans.). Cambridge, MA: MIT Press.

Wagamese, R. 1994. *Keeper 'n Me*. Toronto: Random House.

Wexelblatt, Robert. 1991. *Professors at Play*. New Brunswick, NJ: Rutgers.

## B. FILMS

*Bad Teacher*. Dir. Jake Caston. Columbia Pictures, 2011.

*The Blackboard Jungle*. Dir. Richard Brooks. MGM, 1955.

*Dangerous Minds*. Dir. John Smith. Hollywood Pictures, 1995.

*Dead Poets Society*. Dir. Peter Weir. Touchstone, 1989.

*The Emperor's Club*. Dir. Michael Hoffman. Universal Pictures, 2002.

*Good-Bye, Mr. Chips*. Dir. Sam Wood. Denham Films, 1939.

*In & Out*. Dir. Frank Oz. Paramount, 1997.

*The Mirror Has Two Faces*. Dir. Barbra Streisand. Tristar, 1996.

*Mona Lisa's Smile*. Dir. Mike Newell. Sony Pictures, 2003.

*Mr. Holland's Opus*. Dir. Stephen Herek. Hollywood Pictures, 1995.

*Oleanna*. Dir. David Mamet. Goldwyn Co & Ch. 4 Film, 1995.

*Our Miss Brooks* (TV Series). Desilu Productions, 1952–57.

*The Prime of Miss Jean Brodie*. Dir. Ronald Neame. 20th Century Fox, 1969.

*A Single Man*. Dir. Tom Ford. Weinstein Company, 2008.

*To Sir, With Love*. Dir. James Clavell. Columbia Pictures, 1967.

*Stand and Deliver*. Dir. Roman Menendez. Warner Brothers, 1988.

*Waterland*. Dir. Steven Gyllenhaal. New Line Home Video, 1992.

# Camp fYrefly:
## Linking Research to Advocacy in Community Work with Sexual and Gender Minority Youth

ANDRÉ P. GRACE

n Canada, I live with a paradox. Since July 20, 2005, when the *Civil Marriage Act* (Bill C-38) extending the definition of marriage to include same-sex couples became law, I can get married. However, I still cannot walk down Whyte Avenue in the heart of my home city of Edmonton without the threat of a homophobe shouting the defamatory epithet "faggot" at me as he drives by in his truck. While such hate incidents still make me uncomfortable, I no longer find them unnerving. What is unnerving for me is the seemingly endless run of hate incidents and hate crimes that sexual and gender minority (SGM) youth and, in particular, gay male youth, experience everyday in the classrooms, gyms, and corridors of our nation's schools and in the malls, parks, and other common spaces where youth congregate.

SGM youth include lesbians, gay males, bisexuals, intersexuals, Two-Spirit Indigenous persons, and trans-identified persons who have minority status due to differences in sexual orientation and/or variations in gender identity and expression that fall outside hetero-normative categorizations of sex, sexuality, and gender as well as outside the normative and dichotomous categorizations created by the male/female and heterosexual/homosexual binaries (Grace, 2005a, 2008a,

2009). Almost everywhere they go, SGM youth can be denounced, demeaned, defiled, and left devastated. These youth are targets of cultural ignorance and fear that often culminate in self-directed, peer-instigated, and other forms of violence.

The current spate of gay-male youth suicides in Canada and the United States, which is a consequence of the cultural havoc that heterosexist/sexist systems and homo/bi/transphobic bullies wreak on these vulnerable youth, indicates emphatically that life can become too unbearable for some SGM youth trying to mediate the rather shaky construction that is our hetero-normative social democracy. What we are presently witnessing is an epidemic of SGM youth, predominantly gay-male youth, seeking a final solution to the woes of living in a world where symbolic violence (like name-calling and anti-queer graffiti) and physical violence (like gay bashing and assault and battery) constitute seemingly ceaseless daily outbursts from belligerent homo/bi/transphobic perpetrators, many of whom are also youth (Grace, 2007, 2009; Grace and Wells, 2005, 2009).

At the Institute for Sexual Minority Studies and Services, Faculty of Education, University of Alberta, both my research and intervention and outreach work with SGM youth unequivocally indicate that these youth remain a vulnerable and much-maligned population that is perennially targeted by exclusionary systems and heartless bullies (Grace, 2009; Grace and Wells, 2011). In this contribution to the URQI Speakers Series anthology, I discuss this reality as I speak to the ongoing need for Camp fYrefly, a summer leadership retreat that Dr. Kristopher Wells and I co-founded in Edmonton in 2004 as a university-community educational outreach project that focuses on meeting the needs of SGM youth (Grace and Wells, 2007a).

The camp is growing. In 2009 the first Camp fYrefly Saskatchewan was held in Saskatoon, with the second held in Regina as alternating host city in 2010. To date, there have been eleven camps held in the two provinces. Camp fYrefly emphasizes helping youth to grow into resilience with foci on individual development, socialization, learning leadership skills, and being safe and healthy. Camp fYrefly exists to provide a proactive response to the generally unhappy, unhealthy, and unsafe predicament of SGM youth.

As I discuss this dire social problem, I consider the recent suicide of Jamie Hubley, a 15-year-old gay youth from Kanata, a suburb of Ottawa,

Ontario. Jamie's untimely death provides another stark reminder that it is not getting better for many SGM youth in our schools. Indeed, schools can be hell on earth for these youth, and principals, teachers, and guidance counselors can fan the flames of this exclusionary hell. This is especially likely when these "caring professionals" feel that holding personal conservative moral values gives them permission to disengage from public ethical practices in schools. In the face of this danger, SGM youth like Jamie have long needed alternative spaces where the emphasis of involvement and social learning can be on thriving instead of just surviving.

Camp fYrefly provides such a counter-space to nurture SGM youth. It is a safe learning space where these youth can become happier and healthier as they accept themselves, embrace others as they build queer community, and engage in a queer public counter-pedagogy that helps them build assets, their "resilience toolbox," so they can mediate and even contest hetero/sexualizing school and community cultures that make them sick by stifling their healthy individual development and socialization. SGM youth who attend Camp fYrefly come to know this counter-space as an affirming ecology where they can find the recognition, acceptance, respect, affirmation, and accommodation that often eludes them in schools and communities.

### THE ONGOING NEED FOR CAMP FYREFLY

Despite the historical pigeonholing of sexual and gender minorities and our differences in culture and society, there has been a trend in Canada—especially noticeable since the 1998 Supreme Court decision in *Vriend v. Alberta* that granted equality rights to lesbian and gay Canadians—to make changes in law, legislation, and educational, health, and other institutional policies that respect and accommodate SGM individuals in various institutional and other life contexts (Grace, 2005b, 2007; Grace and Wells, 2011). This trend notwithstanding, heterosexism, sexism, and homo/bi/transphobia persist to inhibit the safety and security of SGM individuals, placing their health and well-being at risk. SGM youth are particularly vulnerable, especially those under the age of majority in our nation's schools, the healthcare system, community settings, and other sociocultural spaces where they are subjected to bullying, marginalization, and exclusion that entrench mistrust, alienation, nihilism (feelings of helplessness and hopelessness), and susceptibility to suicide ideation and attempts or completions as cultural markers of their disenfranchisement (Grace, 2005a, 2008b; Grace and Wells, 2005, 2009, 2011; Taylor and Peter with McMinn, Schachter, Beldom, Ferry, Gross and Paquin, 2011). These youth often experience physical, mental, and emotional health problems as they cope with stressors and risks that lead to dysfunction in their everyday lives (CPHO, 2011). Consequently, many SGM youth are unhappy and unhealthy in their lives, where such negative outcomes as cutting, eating disorders, drug and alcohol abuse, and suicide ideation, attempts, and completions comprise deleterious ways of coping (Grace and Wells, 2011).

*The Growing Suicide Epidemic: It Doesn't Seem to Get Better*
Suicide ideation, attempts, and completions are entrenched in the dark side of queer culture as ways to succumb to stressors as a matter of degree. Many SGM persons have waltzed with the suicide process or have been impacted by the suicide completion of a queer family member, relative, or friend. The fallout is immense, as my poem indicates:

**NO SOLUTION**

You lied to yourself
And you lied to the world
Then you sought the ether with a single bullet
Freaking because you could no longer dream here
It was no solution
You left behind your cosmetic brave face
To be imitated by those who loved but never knew you
You left your sadness in their eyes
To accompany their counterfeit smiles
And while those smiles were less perfect copies of the master's
They belied the same emptiness
You were Judas to yourself
Exacting your own death as the price of self-betrayal
A shotgun was your Judas tree
You left your hurt behind
To be carried by those you left between earth and fire
A hollow man
A man dead too soon
Only incites anger

The last words you scrawled were no testament
They were lost words
Lying words
A testimony to your hopelessness
Each syllable was meant to scourge those you blamed
As though the price you decided to pay would not be enough
No one made you gay
You were born that special way
You killed yourself
But you only wounded those you targeted
They were already living gay and their wounds gradually healed
And although there were scars
They carried on having survived your struggle
Their trauma subsided over time
And for them thriving became its phoenix

I wrote an earlier version of this poem, one with a less hopeful ending, a long time ago after a friend completed suicide. I was so incredibly angry. Perhaps I am still angry. Years later another man, a person whom I had dated, also decided to take this way out. Internalized homophobia can terrorize its victims to death. Societal homophobia can send them into the darkness and toward the devolution that leads to suicide ideation, attempts, or the finality of suicide completion. Somewhere in between these suicide completions, I had my own waltz with the suicide process, and I spent time in hospital under suicide watch. I could no longer deal with the horror of the barrage of systems and bullies that wanted to snuff out gay to relieve what I now recognize as their anti-queer fears and anxieties.

As I lay in my hospital bed, I remember being checked intermittently by healthcare workers who would shine a flashlight through a small window in the locked metal door to my room. They would point the piercing light in my face until I moved. It took a long time, but I found my way back. Nonetheless, suicide bewilders me to this day. I know some SGM persons can reach a point where they complete suicide because they can no longer bear to be battered by heterosexism, sexism, and homo/bi/transphobia. Irrevocably broken by systems and bullies, they see no other way to get away, permanently. Still it is paradoxical that this permanent solution, the expression of an overwhelming desire for peace, is achieved through suicide completion as the ultimate nihilistic expression of self-directed violence.

When SGM persons are young and vulnerable, homo/bi/transphobic bullying, which is a composite of the symbolic and physical violence that heterosexism and sexism induce, can exacerbate thoughts of suicide, leaving miserable youth to ideate about, attempt, or complete the process. What appears to be a current epidemic of gay-male youth suicides in Canada and the United States is providing blitzing reminders of this abject reality. Since being and acting gay in the world represent everything heterosexism and sexism seek to wipe out, gay-male youth are moving targets for homophobic bullying in their schools and communities, which they know as dangerous social and cultural spaces. Genderfucking and desiring or expressing love for another male are absolute no-nos for these youth. These constrictions intensify and specify challenges to the growth and development of this adolescent population who are naturally experiencing changes in so many ways. When the collective hell of heterosexism, sexism, and homo/bi/transphobia becomes too much, completing suicide can be the definitive end to the stories of the brutalization of gay-male youth. Indeed, suicide completion is the ultimate damage that heterosexist/sexist systems and homo/bi/transphobic bullies do to vulnerable gay-male youth.

On October 14, 2011, these systems and bullies claimed another victim when teenager Jamie Hubley became another queer angel. Here is an excerpt from the note he blogged to *catchmeblondy.tumblr.com* before his suicide completion. His words are as he wrote them. I refuse to sanitize them because that would be silencing Jamie in death, which would be one more assault on his queer integrity:

> I'm a casualty of love. Well, I'm tired of life really. It's so hard. I'm sorry. I can't take it anymore. ... Being sad is sad. I've been like this for way too long. I can't stand school. I can't stand earth. I can't stand society. I can't stand the scars on my arms. I can't fucking stand any fucking thing. ... I don't want my parents to think this is their fault either. ... I love my mom and dad. It's just too hard. I don't want to wait 3 more years. This hurts too much. How do you even know it will get better? It's

not. ... I hit rock-fucking bottom, fell through a crack,
[and] now I'm stuck. ... Remember me as a Unicorn.
... I'll fly away, mysterious, enigmatic, energetic, pure,
and graceful.

Once again I am so angry, and my anger is valid. I am angry that
another gay boy, one who already possessed many marvelous traits of
the mythical Unicorn, completed suicide. I am angry that, sometimes,
loving parents, as wonderful as they are, are not enough. I am angry
with the bullies. And I am angry with the adults, schools, and communities that gave these uncaring youth license to incapacitate and destroy
Jamie. Their indifference and inaction in addressing the homophobia
that Jamie experienced made his life a living hell. Yes, my anger is valid.

Jamie had loving, caring parents whom he loved. He said so. What
does it tell us about how bad school and his world were that their love
and support were not enough? On October 18, 2011, in the aftermath of
his son's death, Jamie's devastated and grieving father, Kanata South
city councilor Allan Hubley, released a statement, which was posted on
*thestar.com* website. This excerpt serves as a profound reminder of the
need to address homo/bi/transphobic bullying and the mental health
problems that many SGM youth experience as a consequence of the
trauma they undergo:

> This past Friday, our family suffered one of the worst
> experiences that can happen to a family when we lost
> our boy—Jamie. To make this even more difficult, his
> death was a result of suicide. ... Jamie was for most
> of his life a very happy and confident child. He was a
> compassionate person always looking to help others
> and [he] didn't have a mean bone in his body. Jamie
> often worked with me on community events and our
> many efforts to help others were made more effective
> with his ideas. From a very young age he wanted to
> make a better community and a better world. ... James
> had been suffering with depression and was receiving
> care from doctors at CHEO [Children's Hospital of
> Eastern Ontario] and counsellors. These professionals,
> along with James's family and friends, were trying to

help him learn to cope with his depression and other
issues, one of which was his struggles with his sexuality. He struggled with the idea that people can judge
you harshly even when you are trying to help others.
Jamie asked a question no child should have to ask—
why do people say mean things to me? ... Although
James had a great many people who loved and supported him, something in his mind kept taking him to
a dark place where he could not see the positive side of
life, which led him to this drastic and tragic decision
on Friday. Jamie is free of his pain now, and there is a
new angel, but we have paid too high a price. ... There
are some reports in the media and on social media
that James was bullied. This is true. We were aware of
several occasions when he felt he was being bullied. In
Grade 7 he was treated very cruelly simply because he
liked figure skating over hockey. ... Recently, when
Jamie tried to start a Rainbow Club at his high school
to promote acceptance of others, the posters were torn
down and he was called vicious names in the hallways
and online. We had meetings with officials at the
school and were working with them to bring an end to
it, but Jamie felt it would never stop. ... We will not say
that the bullying was the only reason for James's decision to take his own life, but it was definitely a factor.
... Bullying doesn't always take the form of physical
violence. Especially today with cyber bullying on the
Internet, children often feel there is no safe place to go;
even when they are at home they can still be victims.
... To this end, after my family and I have had some
time to come to terms with the loss of our beautiful
son James, I will be working hard to use my energy and
public position to help bring awareness and resources
to those groups working to stop the bullying and find
a treatment for depression.

The goals that Jamie's dad has—to prevent bullying and to help
SGM youth have access to mental healthcare—should be the goals of

every caring parent/caregiver and every caring professional working in educational, health, and other social institutions (Grace and Wells, 2011). Working to achieve these goals provides a constructive way to vent valid anger in the interest of making life better *now* for SGM youth. We have to be practical and productive today so all SGM youth will have a tomorrow and the possibility of being happy and healthy in the future.

*Camp fYrefly: A Social-Learning Counter-Space*
*Where SGM Youth Can Thrive*
Thriving is the desired phoenix that leaves the trauma that SGM youth experience in its ashes. Camp fYrefly has evolved into a four-day volunteer-based, residential-style summer leadership retreat where SGM youth can thrive (Grace and Wells, 2007a). SGM youth came up with the camp's name, with the acronym *fYrefly* standing for fostering, Youth, resiliency, energy, fun, leadership, yeah! In researching fireflies, youth learned that these insects can be found everywhere on earth except Antarctica. To develop, fireflies undergo metamorphosis and they produce their own light energy. Building on this metaphor, Camp fYrefly is a counter-space where SGM youth can learn about coming out, coming to terms, and growing into resilience in the face of the traumas they experience as consequences of heterosexism, sexism, and homo/bi/transphobia (Grace and Wells, 2007b).

Camp fYrefly focuses on building and nurturing SGM youth's leadership potential and personal resilience in order to help them become agents for positive social change in their schools, families, and communities. To our knowledge, Camp fYrefly is the largest youth leadership camp of its kind in Canada. It is affiliated with a major research university, which ensures research-informed programming, sound pedagogical principles, and strong fiscal management. Five themes comprise the framework that guides the development and delivery of the Camp fYrefly program:

1.  *Creating a socially just and inclusive community:* As citizens, we all have a social responsibility to foster a sense of community spirit and to take care of one another. Creating a community that is inclusive, welcoming, and harmonious is crucial to ensure that everyone is connected, included, and accorded respect and dignity regardless of their differences. At Camp fYrefly, we build a community that

demonstrates acceptance, accommodation, inclusivity, and respect through engagement with individuals from different ethnocultural backgrounds, faiths, beliefs, abilities, ages, socioeconomic backgrounds, sexualities, and genders. Presentations and workshops developed around this theme function to help SGM youth to build awareness and understanding of democratic and inclusive citizenship in innovative ways that address barriers to full participation in our society.

2. *Building resiliency and youth leadership capacity:* Engaging SGM youth in learning how to make significant contributions to their own lives and to their schools, families, and communities helps to build a strong, ethical, and just community for tomorrow. By helping them to develop a resilient mindset, SGM youth can make informed and healthy decisions about the issues and challenges that impact their lives and social interactions. Topics and workshops developed around this theme focus on social and cultural learning about human and civil rights, advocacy, media awareness, public speaking, peer-to-peer mentoring, sex and gender stereotyping, healthy living, protective factors, harm reduction, and leadership skill development.

3. *Helping youth to know their rights in order to empower them to address bullying, harassment, and hate incidents/crimes:* Knowing one's rights as persons and citizens comes with concomitant responsibility to advocate for others to advance a socially just society. Helping SGM youth to feel supported and empowered to address discrimination, bullying, harassment, sexual harassment, and hate incidents/hate crimes is key to change processes focused on nurturing the self as well as assisting schools, families, and communities. Presentations and workshops developed around this theme focus on personal well-being, social activism, anti-oppression, inclusive cultural work, healthy decision-making, safety, and coalition building.

4. *Learning through art, music, writing, performing arts, and games:* The arts have the power to open up both the heart and mind. At camp, SGM youth learn about themselves and others through creative exploration and expression. This helps them to develop new forms

of communication, understanding, and community building. Presentations and workshops developed around these themes often use arts-informed pedagogy whereby youth engage in song-writing, improvisation, dance, personal journaling, movement, poetry, photography, and learning leadership skills through games.

5. *Self and social development:* In a complex and rapidly changing world, SGM youth often struggle to find support, purpose, and a sense of space and place. Finding access to non-judgmental information about the issues that impact their lives is critical to self and social development. Presentations developed around this theme focus on personal development, personal wellness, self- and social-esteem, healthy minds and healthy bodies, spirituality, family (as they construct it), and overcoming internalized homophobia and transphobia.

All Camp fYrefly programming is guided by input from youth and facilitated by trained educators and youth workers in collaboration with a team of artists, dramatists, and community and youth leaders. The camp, guided by an arts-based educational philosophy, is jam-packed with dance, drama, music, writing, visual arts, empowerment and reflection exercises, anti-oppression work, personal growth opportunities, healthy socialization, and in-depth learning activities about specific youth topics and social issues. In sum, Camp fYrefly's arts-informed pedagogy focuses on four key areas: leadership, individual development, socialization, and health and safety linked to growing into resilience.

Camp fYrefly exists because caring adults believe that all youth are entitled to a world that embraces diversity instead of fearing it. For four days each year, we create that world, a world that lives out the fYrefly acronym. Camp fYrefly's philosophy and programming emphasize a by-youth-for-youth approach where adult facilitators mentor older youth to engage and support younger youth. In the spirit of advancing youth leadership, youth contribute to the development and delivery of the camp's wide-ranging leadership program in two important ways:

1. Youth attending Camp fYrefly are invited to provide feedback through camp evaluations and wrap-up meetings. Their feedback

helps organizers improve camp programming and services for the future.

2.  Youth, once they reach the age of majority (aged 18), can apply to become youth leaders who work with pods of 6 to 8 campers to mentor and support them in their individual development and socialization as SGM individuals. Youth leaders work to build trust and rapport among pod members so they feel safe and have a sense of belonging.

Camp organizers work extensively with SGM and allied youth and have substantial first-hand experience in recognizing how challenging adolescence can be for all youth, especially those who are coming out and coming to terms with their own sexual orientation and gender identities and differences. We hope to be able to help empower camp participants to envision a healthy and happy future that is free from fear, abuse, and discrimination. By developing a resilience toolbox that includes a network of friends and trusted adults, community resources, and strategies for thriving, we believe that SGM youth will be able to flourish and become leaders who advocate for social justice and inclusion in their schools, families, and communities. At camp, as these reflections provided by Camp fYrefly participants indicate, SGM youth begin to build a sense of self and the self-confidence and self-esteem that energize such thriving:

> I came and no one judged me or made opinions about me without getting to know me.
> I didn't have to be afraid. [As a lesbian] I could say 'my girlfriend' and nobody blinked an eye.
> All the Camp exercises helped me realize things about myself. It helped me put my inner demons to rest.
> People, new people treated me as a human being. I could have cried! No insults, no sneers, no conflict, just simple acceptance. It's the most amazing thing to know that total strangers can love you.

In a reflection written on the camp's graffiti wall, another Camp fYrefly participant considered how he is a multiple subject, linking this to his humanity:

> I am several minorities: Gay. Franco-Albertan. Québécois. Roman Catholic. Piccoloist.
>
> I am several majorities: White/Caucasian. Canadian. Albertan.
>
> My majority/minority status changes depending on where I am.
>
> But does it really all matter?
>
> At camp, I feel emancipated—free from labels, categories, closed boxes.
>
> I can be who I am—everything and nothing—without fear. No second-guessing.
>
> I AM HUMAN.

These heartfelt reflections of Camp fYrefly youth move me. They are my fuel. I hope that Camp fYrefly will continue to be a fun-filled, affirming, and accommodating social space where every camper can learn and grow into a stronger, healthier, happier, knowing, and more resilient person who is able to survive and even thrive when family, school, faith group, or community are unsafe life spaces. I believe that by supporting SGM youth, we are making the best possible investment in their futures and in the future of communities across Canada.

**CONCLUDING PERSPECTIVE: WHAT SGM YOUTH WANT**

In some ways SGM youth are like other youth, and in some ways they are unique. Like other youth, SGM youth are growing and developing. They are dealing with peer pressure and the intricacies of fitting into social and cultural spaces where possibilities for connection, collaboration, and building relationships and community may exist. However, SGM youth also have to deal with the systemically induced burdens that heteronormativity places on their sexual and gender differences. Youth with heterosexual privilege do not endure these burdens. After all, heterosexuality is a hegemonic construct deemed moral and socially desirable.

During adolescence when any difference can be problematic, sexual and gender differences, which go to the heart of being a living and functioning SGM person, pose extra difficulties and dangers for SGM youth. This is why gay schoolteacher Andrew Gadsby calls on us to confront the pink elephant in the classroom. As he reflected on the suicide completion of Jamie Hubley in an October 26, 2011 article posted on *the globeandmail.com* website, he provided this sorry assessment of what life in schools continues to be like for SGM students and teachers:

> Certain things I know about myself. For example, my name is Andrew and I'm 24. I'm a high-school teacher, I love hockey and I'm gay. I also know that when I read the story of Jamie Hubley or young victims like him, I could no longer remain silent. Bullying in schools isn't new. But, tragically, gay bullying often comes to the forefront only when it's too late to save another young man or woman from taking their life to escape daily torment. If gay is still taboo for some, gay bullying is the pink elephant in the [class]room. … As a teacher, I have seen vitriolic hate hurled at students, and heard the word "fag" spread around with utter disregard for its hurtfulness. That word can mean so many things: stupid, worthless, dumb, gay. Anyone hit with it knows its sting—how it can make them feel less than everybody else. … So what was so wrong with Jamie—why was he so tormented by his classmates that he thought taking his own life was the only way out? Because the 15-year-old "natural-born" performer preferred figure skating to hockey. That's it. It makes absolutely no sense. Yet sadly it does, at least if you spend any time in today's schools. Too often, homophobia is swept under the rug; sometimes it's even tacitly accepted. In my experience as a student, "gay" was a topic met with reproach, reservation or downright dirty looks. And now, as a teacher, it's hardly better. Early in my teaching career, I recall confiding to an associate that I was gay; she implored me to keep it quiet, as students might not react well. If an adult can be held hostage

to the bigotries of 14-year-olds, what hope is there of creating any sort of safe space for LGBT teens? Who, if not everyone, will protect our struggling youth?

Keeping quiet about sexual and gender differences is often the directive in families, schools, and communities as life spaces that have traditionally maintained the heteronormative status quo. The hegemony of heteronormativity as *de rigueur* in these social spaces often positions SGM youth as fear-filled outcasts in the very spaces that should nurture them. All these youth want is to be nurtured for the persons they are, which means they want to be respected and accommodated as they learn to be, become, and belong as SGM individuals in the world and in the institutions that make up the world. Like all youth, SGM youth want to be happy, healthy, creative, energized, accomplished, and free to be themselves. To help them grow and develop so they can reach their potential, Camp fYrefly provides this kind of nurturing. And while schools and other social institutions fail to respect and accommodate SGM youth, Camp fYrefly will continue to exist as a place for them, their place, a safe and happy place.

## REFERENCES

Chief Public Health Officer (CPHO). 2011. *The Chief Public Health Officer's Report on the State of Public Health in Canada 2011: Youth and Young Adults—Life in Transition.* Ottawa: Office of the CPHO. (Also available at http://publichealth. gc.ca/CPHOreport).

Grace, André P. 2005a. "Reparative Therapies: A Contemporary Clear and Present Danger across Minority Sex, Sexual and Gender Differences." *Canadian Woman Studies* 24, nos. 2, 3: 145–51.

——. 2005b. "LGBT Issues in Canada." Pp. 122–26 in James T. Sears (ed.), *Youth, Education, and Sexualities: An International Encyclopedia.* Westport, CT: Greenwood Publishing.

——. 2007. "In Your Care: School Administrators and Their Ethical and Professional Responsibility Toward Students Across Sexual-Minority Differences." Pp. 16–40 in William Smale and Kelly Young (eds.), *Approaches to Educational Leadership and Practice.* Calgary, AB: Detselig Enterprises/Temeron Books.

——. 2008a. "The Charisma and Deception of Reparative Therapies: When Medical Science Beds Religion." *Journal of Homosexuality* 55, no. 4: 545–80.

——. 2008b. "Psychotherapy." Pp. 212–15 in James T. Sears (ed.), *The Greenwood Encyclopedia of Love, Courtship, and Sexuality through History: The Modern World,* vol. 6. Westport, CT: Greenwood Publishing Group.

——. 2009. "Resilient Sexual-Minority Youth as Fugitive Lifelong Learners: Engaging in a Strategic, Asset-Creating, Community-Based Learning Process to Counter Exclusion and Trauma in Formal Schooling." In John Field (ed.), *Proceedings of the Lifelong Learning Revisited: What Next? Conference of the Scottish Centre for Research in Lifelong Learning, University of Stirling, Stirling, UK* (CD format, 4,041 words).

Grace, André P., and Kristopher Wells. 2005. "The Marc Hall Prom Predicament: Queer Individual Rights v. Institutional Church Rights in Canadian Education." *Canadian Journal of Education* 28, no. 3: 237–70.

——. 2007a. "Everyone Performs, Everyone Has a Place: Camp fYrefly and Arts-Informed, Community-Based Education, Cultural Work and Inquiry." Pp. 61–82 in Darlene Clover and Joyce Stalker (eds.), *The Art of Social Justice: Re-Crafting Activist Adult Education and Community Leadership*. Leicester, UK: NIACE.

——. 2007b. "Victims No More: Trends Enabling Resilience in Sexual-Minority Students." Pp. 79–88 in *Proceedings of the Education for Social Justice: From the Margin to the Mainstream—A Canadian Teachers' Federation Conference, Ottawa Marriott Hotel, Ottawa, ON.*

——. 2009. "Gay and Bisexual Male Youth as Educator Activists and Cultural Workers: The Queer Critical Praxis of Three Canadian High-School Students." *International Journal of Inclusive Education* 13, no. 1: 23–44.

——. 2011. *Sexual Minority and Gender Variant Youth and Linkages between their Mental Health and Sexual Health*. Prepared for the Public Health Agency of Canada, Ottawa, ON.

Taylor, Catherine, and Tracey Peter, with T. L. McMinn, Kevin Schachter, Stacey Beldom, Allison Ferry, Zoe Gross and Sarah Paquin. 2011. *Every Class in Every School: The First National Climate Survey on Homophobia, Biphobia, and Transphobia in Canadian Schools. Final Report*. Toronto, ON: Egale Canada Human Rights Trust.

# PART III

## NEGOTIATING
# PUBLIC SPHERE(S)

Do not follow where the path may lead.
Go, instead, where there is no path and leave a trail.
—RALPH WALDO EMERSON

## Repressed Identities: A Traveling Exploration of Sexuality, Gender and Place

CAITLYN JEAN MCMILLAN

I began my summer of 2010, prepared to embark on a study in "Representation, Embodiment and the City" with Marie Lovrod in a two-part travelling program with approximately ten other students. Introduced to Doreen Massey's theories of how "gendering of space and place both reflects and has effects back on the ways in which gender is constructed and understood within the societies that we live in,"[1] I wondered how each city forms an identity by the experiences it provides.

Spending a total of ten weeks in Saskatoon (Saskatchewan), New York (New York), Thunder Bay (Ontario) and Banff (Alberta), I attempted to observe how each public space was constructed to control and restrict public movement and expression through media, commercialization, architecture and urban landscaping. My experiences of gender and sexuality in each city resulted in the exhibition *Urban Liminal* with Niknaz Tavakolian's videos questioning age, nationality and gender, curated by Tabitha Minns at the Banff Centre.

My presentation, given for URQI's Speakers Series, consisted of my exploration and analysis of these four popular North American centres and the resulting work in *Urban Liminal*. Each of the cities has an identity of its own that affects how people live within the space. Landscape, architecture, population, location and weather all change how people move and live, influencing very different ways of socialization. Focussing on easily accessible public spaces, I began to understand the major differences in each city, while attempting to recognize the resulting change of behaviour. I set out to explore how these differences directly result in varied gendered and sexual expressions in those spaces. These influences create a unique social structure of gender and sexuality that is much more complex than I present here; however, there were some obvious trends of behaviour that I use to illustrate how gender and sexuality are influenced by the spaces they inhabit.

As we enter, as a public, into the spaces that haven't been constructed—specifically, nature spaces—our presence introduces our own ideas of gender and sexuality. This insertion of our own culture changes the space, whether temporarily or permanently. Within the urban spaces, however, I doubt our behaviour directly affects the spaces we inhabit. Occupation of space occurs in an attempt for social change, but we cannot physically change the public spaces around us. The major architecture and landscaping decisions are determined by those with more status, and these rarely match the needs of the entire community. Formed through time, by city planners, landscapers and architects, construction advances slowly, and rarely as a result of the direct actions of those who use the space. An understanding of the spaces that exist, however, may lead to an alteration of future construction.

My perception of each space is affected by my perspective, as an able-bodied, white, middle class, educated, queer female, further informed by the time frame when I occupied the city and what experiences I had while I was there. My conclusions are no more than personal speculation, based upon my experiences in each space. Yet each tells a story about social occupation of these urban spaces and how each city was formed by different location, population, and city planning, causing differences in behaviour. My intention is to read the gender and sexuality of these spaces, to allow understanding of the patriarchal dominance and heteronormative tendencies that exist.

## URBAN SASKATCHEWAN

At the time I was in Saskatoon, "Divas" was the only gay bar in the city. Tucked in the back alley of 3rd Avenue South, it was essentially hidden from public view. The entrance was without a window, lined by the neighbourhood's dumpsters. Perhaps this placement can be seen as holding a queer historical quality, with a safe and secure entrance away from the public eye; however, currently, it seems seedy and unsafe, putting queers at greater risk by placing them in a small, deserted, dark alley.

Inside, the demographic at the bar further emphasized the outdated entrance; seemingly heterosexual patrons were everywhere, co-mingling with the queer crowd. Many urbanites now consider the gay bar a fantastically non-judgmental dance bar, whose entry deserves more than a back alley.

A lot of Saskatoon's architecture and planning is steeped in the similarly patriarchal, heteronormative dominance of traditional city planning. Though Saskatchewan's urban spaces are fairly new, their continuing construction mimics the car culture model that seems to be problematic in many other North American cities. The pedestrian areas of Saskatoon are limited to the waterfront parks and surrounding areas, while car traffic is catered to in the rest of the city. At one position in the north core of Saskatoon, I found myself surrounded on all sides by large plain cement foundations that stretched approximately four feet above my head. The buildings' windows were enticing me to see inside, yet they were placed in a position that refuted my presence. Located far from the residential areas, and exposed to Saskatchewan's harsh cold winters, this architecture and positioning encourages car use for those who can afford it. These buildings, and the newer shopping centers that are being built, promote an indoor, car culture that, in turn, influences further construction of public spaces.

The pedestrian areas that do exist boast an impressive (foreign) green space, and are constructed to maintain and direct movement along the water. Known as the "City of Bridges," Saskatoon is distinguished from other prairie cities by its urban waterways, with its architecture built up for "accessibility" and culture; yet, the water is not accessible at all. Without being able to access the water as outlets for the summer heat, pedestrians wore bathing suits for display rather than function, and more often near roads than by waterways. This lack of accessibility, from the built-up architecture and natural landscape, influenced a very public display of sexuality.

Despite an open sense of sexuality, Saskatoon is constructed with a strong rural influence, and a strong sense of constructed gender and sexual expression. This enforces heteronormativity in a city that has enough queer population to now sustain two queer-friendly bars. The strong traditional gender expectations placed my identity as submissive, unimportant, and secondary to those with more money and privilege than I possessed. The spaces neither emphasized nor denigrated queer identities, but neither was there a place for queer pedestrians to congregate nor was there room for public expression of their identity. Their presence was invisible; they were unable to openly express their sexualities within the public spaces. I am sure queer people frequent the main urban areas of Saskatoon, but their presence was unsupported in comparison to the integration in New York.

## NEW YORK CITY

New York is similarly constructed in both city and nature to Saskatoon, except it is bigger, older and much more complicated. The massive city is far from being influenced by a rural way of thinking. Located on an international trade route, the city has become one of the largest and most desired locations in North America. Built and developed through time, New York City includes a variety of overlapping communities that offer many opportunities to experience gender in a different way from the expected norm. The condensed urban space allows for exposure to a lot of "other" identities, emphasized by the massive presence of pedestrians that mobilized each area. I experienced the availability of queer culture in particular as a culture shock, coming from the Prairies. The subway system in New York allowed fluidity between areas, making the city a truly pedestrian city, despite the built-up architecture. New York's public transit system has made commuting as a pedestrian very efficient. Pedestrian freedom pervades New York, resulting in a variety of expressions within one place. This has caused the binary of public and private to become much more flexible than the cold Canadian climate allows, emphasized by the open movement of people through consumerist and community spaces.

The accessibility of essentially every location in the city through the subway system enables a different kind of interactivity. Shops spill out onto the streets, in large contrast to the inaccessible concrete walls found in Saskatoon. The clubs are still located in back alleys like "Divas," but are placed there for exclusivity and availability, for any demographic, rather than restricted to the queer community. This blending of public and private, along with the sheer numbers that populate the city, has resulted in a strong, visible queer community. Social support for the queer community is as open and accessible as it is for many other social groups in New York. While I was there, I experienced a lot of gender-oriented events that were held in popular public spaces rather than hidden away. A drag show in the elegant foyer of the Brooklyn City Hall, an LGBT "Don't Ask Don't Tell" benefit concert in Central Park, and the visible movement of LGBT individuals allowed exposure to a unique combination of gender and sexuality within the city.

New York boasts accessibility for its citizens, but extends an international accessibility that draws people in for a plethora of reasons, including a need to find queer culture. This accessibility was emphasized by the people we met: in the Bronx, a bearded, military-booted individual in a skirt introduced us to a community garden space, in Manhattan, a young, bespectacled lesbian from Toronto explained that she was interning as a librarian, a group of drag queens in Brooklyn's city hall and a Montreal-based choreographer expressed sexuality, gender and identity through interpretive dance. We discovered organizations focused on issues as specific as women-based filmmaking at Women Make Movies, supporting international women's rights at Madre and Unifem, and collecting and archiving all things lesbian at the Lesbian Herstory Archives. Amongst such diversity, to exist in the public space in New York was much different than in the Prairies.

What were similar, perhaps, were the constant patriarchal attitudes of a lot of the men in the area. Encouraged by the number of freely moving women, men constantly preyed on them in the public spaces. I often thought twice about some of my smaller outfits and, repeatedly, deflected comments about my legs, hair and body. We spoke firsthand to women at NYU about their detours to and from their homes. They often avoided the subway because of preying men, and this reduced their accessibility of the city. It was clear that New York's "freedom" depended on a specific movement through the accessible concrete jungle. While people in public are often tolerant and integrate with such different people in one space, sexuality ran rampant and, more often than not, followed a heteronormative patriarchal framework.

This was emphasized by the New York police officers who man almost every street corner, at all hours of the day. Despite the freedom of cultures, the police shadow everyone's movements, emphasizing that New York's "freedom" is strictly controlled.

Large public demonstrations were corralled by fences if the demonstrators weren't moving; otherwise they were constantly flanked by the police. Public buildings were guarded by scanners, detectors and guards. The constant surveillance seemed to be intended to enforce tolerance, but presented itself as heteronormative, patriarchal and classist through the interactions of police with distinct groups of civilians. There has been consistent mistreatment of sex workers, transgendered individuals and drug users, and while the police seemed to tolerate queer individuals while we were there, they also seemed to expect adherence to their authority. More than once, a member of my group felt pressured by the patriarchal attitudes of the men with badges around us. This authoritarian presence restricted free movement for many queer individuals we met, particularly because the LGBT demographic is often opposed to authoritarian ideals and is therefore at risk of harassment by those who enforce them.

**THUNDER BAY**

In almost complete contrast, northern Ontario's landscape influenced a more private display of sexuality. In a unique area that belongs to the latitudes of the Canadian border, Thunder Bay is surrounded by an isolated northern landscape due to the dip of Hudson Bay. The combination of the landscape with the proximity to Lake Superior results in a myriad of waterways shallowly cascading by the city, allowing for a large collection of private camps and properties. The towns and camps have strong gendered expressions and heterosexual expectations, carrying a traditional viewpoint from rural influences. Family camps have a strong gendered presence and segregation; women tend to be in the kitchen and men outside with boats and tools. Even temporary camps insert a human gender into the space that was previously occupied only by plants and animals. The pockets of permanent habitation in Northern Ontario are concentrations of gendered culture in a space that remains neutral: the sprawling northern wilderness.

These isolated outdoor areas surrounding the city allow for a certain amount of freedom, which seemed to change the presence of public sexuality within the city limits. Along the urban waterfront of Lake Superior, exposure of skin was much less prevalent than in Saskatoon. Even with landscaping that creates compartments of privacy within the city, which differ from the flat open parks on the Prairies, the people in Thunder Bay refrained from bringing their sexuality into the public spaces. The size and shape of the city allow a close relationship with the wilderness, leaving the city itself free of unnecessary bathing attire.

The shape of the city is due to the fact that Thunder Bay is an amal-gamation of two cities, which has formed a third centre between the two older neighbourhoods, supporting a central city system. Built to streamline consumerism for access to the suburbs by car, the newer systems of movement encourage a social hierarchy for the people in the space. The newer inter-city centre contradicts pedestrian movement and prevents accessibility unless you are moving by vehicle between the looming buildings and shopping centres similar to those in Saska-toon. The fast-paced construction of new buildings in the area mimics that of Saskatchewan's shopping centres, where fast-paced consumerist demand draws businesses away from the pedestrian areas that still exist.

Thunder Bay's older neighbourhoods show the results of the shop-ping centre construction. Boarded and abandoned buildings are left behind, as businesses have joined the trend of car access and moved into the inter-city area. While pedestrian consumer culture is inhibited, the spaces that are abandoned are taken over by identities that use or pass by the space regularly. Thunder Bay's citizens continually insert themselves into these urban spaces, similar to the community gardens in New York. Supported by the spaces they are able to inhabit, cultures that lack a permanent space, including the transient queer culture, are able to sustain visibility.

**BANFF**

Nestled in the wilderness, Banff is similar to Thunder Bay in its rela-tionship to nature. But it has an additional urban factor in that it is an international hub like New York. Banff is surrounded by nature, with quick and easy access to socially-neutral wilderness spaces. The lack of culture within the wooded mountains resists masculine and feminine signifiers, and invites gender only with human intervention. In the spaces exterior to the town of Banff, gender is noticed only in hikers' gear, interactions at popular meeting areas or cabins, and occasionally permanent markers in nearby settlements. Those who occupy the space transiently, or even those who live in an undefined location, bring with them their own context, inserting a temporary gender upon the space.

The Banff Centre emphasized humans' influence on nature due to the intimate relationship many Banff artists have had with the space. Throughout the grounds of the Banff Centre, artists have placed many works of art, all of which read as insertions of gendered sexual-ity. Adan Parades Vera's *Untitled* (2001) consists of long, phallic forms constructed from ceramic discs, stacked erect in the Institute's garden, emphasizing gender and sexuality by juxtaposing culture with nature. Most notable is Mark Clintberg's 2010 commission for the Banff Centre, *Meet Me in the Woods,* which, perhaps unintentionally, suggests a sexual liaison or rendezvous. With an accompanying sign, *Meet Me in the Town*, Clintberg implies that nature is a space that we occupy with our cultured sexuality, in the same way that we occupy the town.

The identity of Banff as an international hub directly results in a highly sexualized atmosphere in a gender-neutral surrounding. Individuals are drawn to the area because it is easy to participate in the urban night life, daily wilderness activities, and gathering on the main strip, which is built for pedestrian movement through the town. As in New York, shops are located in basements, on main floors and second levels, allowing for a comfortable pedestrian accessibility to a large amount of social and commercial space. Bars open on the top floor in the evening, allowing for overlapping demographics to share the small space.

The town of Banff seemed to ooze sexuality, the transient and tourist populations creating an environment for sexual conquest. A strong sexual agenda is promoted throughout the town, activated by a large rotating demographic of international young adults. However, the size of the city resulted in mostly heterosexuality, while the small active queer scene seemed hidden from the public space. In my pursuit of queer culture, I could find hardly more than a poster for one queer event, in a consumer culture saturated in heteronormativity. Perhaps the size or density of the city contributed to queer invisibility, but despite many queer-friendly visitors, Banff remained heteronormative. I was not there long enough to find any reason for this heteronormativity within the public spaces of the city, except for a lack of a permanent queer space.

## URBAN LIMINAL

Each of my experiences tells a story about the gendered and sexual identity of each city. Using my time in Banff to summarize my experiences, I created two works, shown alongside Niknaz Tavakolian's videos in the exhibition *Urban Liminal* at the Banff Centre. Bringing together my experiences as a visual exploration for the viewer, *Sex, Sexuality, Gender and Place* exposed through visual imagery the gender and sexuality of the physical spaces I visited. Alongside this, *A Necessary Room for Gentlemen* emphasized a cultural construction of place and the resulting human interaction, represented through the obvious restricted movement into gendered washroom spaces.

Creating an environment that could facilitate the viewers' movement through the space as representative of my travels to each city, *Sex, Sexuality, Gender and Place* embraced interactivity. The wall to the left depicted the Saskatoon landscape, using the prairie sky as the iconic imagery of the area, above a minimal urban silhouette. Below the horizon, luggage tags mimicked the grain growing on the land, constructed like the prairie fields. Hung on tacks, each tag could be removed to lead the participants around to an image, providing them with more information about where the image came from, and how it contributed to my exploration. Moving back and forth in the restricted area of the gallery, viewers could search for Vera's phallic forms, Banff's breast-like mountains and New York's voyeuristic security cameras. A number of the tags referenced places, others contained printed quotations gathered from each space, for their charged sexuality or blatant gendered expressions. Emphasizing the public interaction in each space, these were expressions I had heard in the space—like "Let's do it in Brooklyn it will be easier for everyone to come" and "Hey girls, We're the oil boys service ... if you need any suntan lotion or anything, we're here

*Sex, Sexuality, Gender and Place*—Saskatchewan wall.

for you"—and they allowed sexuality to be inferred through more than visual signifiers.

Above the fields and the sparse city skyline, the sky mimicked a bathroom stall with graffiti scrawled across, mirroring the smaller text tags below. "You are going to fucking LOVE me," found in one of "Divas'" bathrooms, presented a desire to express a public sexuality. Emphasized as separate from the tags below, the quote displayed the queer desire which is currently hidden behind the prevalent heteronormative sexuality. Further creating an obvious separation between the queer community and the heteronormative public, the work activated the architecture in the gallery space by placing a drag queen from "Divas" on top of a step in the wall, separating it from the image of Saskatchewan's horizon. Instead, the large figure seemed to exist closer to the New York imagery, drawing a visual connection between queer culture and New York City.

The right-hand mural boasted breast-like mountains from the Banff skyline, to counterbalance the Prairies on the opposing wall. Below the swollen horizon, Banff's connection with nature was emphasized through the sparse human presence and strong animal representation. Depicting a deer threesome, image courtesy of the Museum of

*Sex, Sexuality, Gender and Place*—Banff wall.

Sex in New York, and a fourth deer showing us his tail, looking like a flaccid penis when rendered in a simple black-and-white outline, the work acknowledged animal sexuality while emphasizing the need for our cultural perspective to interpret each image as sexual. Between the deer was the text from Clintberg's *Meet Me in the Woods,* and an outline of Vera's phallic forms, both of which represented the human insertion of sexuality into nature's space.

Between Saskatchewan and Banff, the focal wall representing New York utilized projection to combine sexualized imagery with animated motion. Emphasizing the privacy of anonymity with the public spaces, the image consisted of a single ink drawing of me in my Pride parade outfit, arm raised to grab the subway rail/security cameras with my armpit hair exposed. Illustrating my identity through a singular image, the overlapping projection animated some of my experiences of the city. Three animations interacted with the drawn figure, creating scenarios for the viewer to watch. The longest animation consisted of a male and female: the female sat on the subway as the male approached and took the seat next to hers. His legs spread wide, emphasizing his "sex" through a gendered performance of claiming space, his legs interrupting her personal space. She attempted to hold her ground, but soon

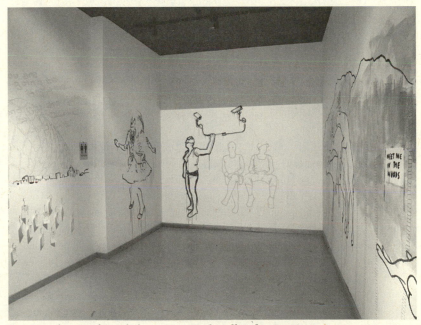

*Sex, Sexuality, Gender and Place*—New York wall and animation.

crossed her legs, allowing the male more space than he required. This subconscious attitude that "the balls need more room" is an action that places the masculine as dominant through assertion of space. Emphasizing the close proximity of bodies and the tolerant nature of the people in public, the animation defined the patriarchal but tolerant interactions of those who share the space. The next animation consisted of armpit hair growing out of the ink figure's pit, reaching the floor before falling out. The ink figure remains static in the space, confident and undisturbed by others in the public who may be revolted by her public queer display. The final animation focussed on the surveillance in the city by depicting two figures oozing out of the security cameras to run away. Upon seeing the other, each ditched its gendered clothing, donning the other, emancipated from the boundaries of gendered authority. Escaping from the intensely monitored gender binary system that prevails in North American centres, the figures proudly show their non-conforming identities.

Finally, *A Necessary Room for Gentlemen* questions the necessity of segregating toilets by sex in public spaces, summarizing North America's relationship with gender and space. Urinals or not, each bathroom space was split into male and female bathrooms, denying a space for others. This unified each of the spaces I visited, representing a North

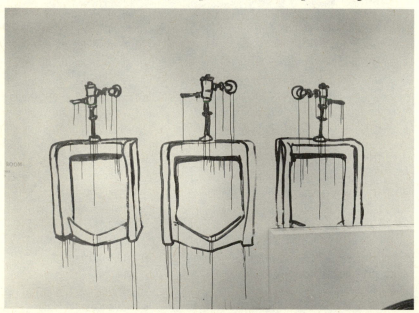

*A Necessary Room for Gentlemen.*

American controlling of gendered movement. Emphasized by the bathroom signs I documented through my trip, the only gender-free bathrooms I encountered were in New York City's largest LGBT center. Visualizing the difference between a room for men and a room for women, *A Necessary Room for Gentlemen* depicts three urinals, drawn in acrylic; representing the only architecture that defines the space as gendered. Bringing the urinals into public space defied gendered boundaries and the placement of the third urinal over a heat vent labelled the gendered architecture as dangerous to individuals who don't fit within the gender binary.

**CONCLUSION**

In my exploration of space I found that some factors seemed to have more influence than others. Attempting to label each space as gendered, sexual, heteronormative or queer, I found that population, size, accessibility to public spaces, proximity to nature, and pedestrian versus car culture all seemed to be major influences in my reading of each space. Adding unique geography, weather, political influences and historical background, each city is far more complex than I could speculate here.

What I did notice however, was that culture-wide divisions of male and female washrooms seemed to strengthen gendered bonds across all of the cities I visited. Additionally, each city contributed its own unique gendered and sexual identity. Saskatoon boasts a strong sense of heteronormative gender roles and sexuality in its public spaces, encouraged by a water-starved landscape and rural influence. New York's population seems to affect the visibility of the variety of people, supporting a stronger understanding for othered individuals, despite the security that controls movement through space. Thunder Bay has a large amount of accessible water and nature, which seemed to result in a muted display of sexuality, while sustaining a transient queer culture using available urban space. Finally, Banff possesses a unique combination of landscape, social culture, and low permanent population which results in an intense sexuality within the city, but lack of space for queers to gather. Each city expresses its own identity through its unique combinations of geographical, environmental and political positions, which in turn affect the people who use the space.

While each observation was made with the bias of my female lesbian identity, it was obvious that there were differences in the experiences each city could provide. Looking at how each public space is

constructed to facilitate movement, I attempted to gender and sexual-
ize each space. This led to my conclusion that these cities maintain a
strong heteronormative structure, formed by the specific movement of
social bodies in their public spaces; the lack of queer spaces available
further emphasizes the need for permanent, public queering of space
to gain prominence. However, because of the complex factors that
form the relationship between public interaction and space in each city,
there is no one effort that could facilitate culture-wide change toward
queer visibility. I look to each city to assess its own structure of gender
and sexuality to decide how to facilitate a change towards queering
its space.

**NOTE**

1    Doreen Massey, *Space, Place and Gender* (Minneapolis, MN: University of Minne-
     sota Press, 1994), 186.

# Gay, Straight and In-Between:
# John Money on Homosexuality

TERRY GOLDIE

n 1993, Camille Paglia said, "Dr. John Money was one of my principal intellectual influences when I was writing *Sexual Personae*. He is the leading sexologist in the world today."[1] Whereas Paglia is certainly given to overstatement, she is not overstating the case here. In the 1970s and 1980s Money was ubiquitous, from interviews in many mainstream magazines to numerous appearances on television and constant quotations in newspapers. His pleas for sexual liberation made him hot copy for journalists and also a frequent target for the many conservatives who feared the idea of sexual freedom. His theories were at the cutting edge of changes in views of intersex, of transsexuals, of homosexuality and of all aspects of sex and gender.

Today John Money is a name that is often vilified, predominantly for what has become known as the Reimer case. The Reimer case has had a variety of other names, such as "John/Joan." It became a *cause célèbre* as a result of John Colapinto's book, *As Nature Made Him: The Boy Who Was Raised as a Girl* (2006). I explore the nuances of the case in my forthcoming book *The Man Who Invented Gender*, but the quick summary is that an identical twin in Winnipeg had his penis burned off in a circumcision accident and was raised as a girl, until he rejected the gender reassignment and lived the rest of his life as a male.

*As Nature Made Him* demonizes Money as the sole cause of what is presented as a maniacal attempt to prove a boy could be made into a girl. At the time many specialists believed it to be an appropriate treatment in response to such mutilation. The fact that this later became regarded as an error does not change the way it was viewed then: an unusual but reasonable course of action. While that summary presumably shows why the case became a scandal, it says little about why a psychologist at Johns Hopkins in Baltimore became involved in a case that began with a surgical decision made in Winnipeg. The simple answer is that, at the time, John Money was becoming the most famous sexologist in the world.

Richard Green, probably Money's most important student, refers to John Money as a "libertine" (Green, 2008: 613). In his early years Money seems to have considered himself heterosexual but after his brief marriage failed, he was very much a part of gay culture and referred in his diary to a few individuals as "the boyfriend." One of his colleagues told me that Money had "come out" to the administration at Johns Hopkins in the late 1960s and the reaction was so negative that he became much less open about his sexual orientation. Green recalls Money's advice that continuing to research on homosexual topics would be career suicide for Green. Yet there is little to suggest that Money's personal relationships with women reflected some attempt at staying in the closet. Later in life Money had relationships with women that were romantic and sexual but never led to cohabitation. Throughout his career, he had casual sex with women and participated in different types of sex parties. He often served as an expert witness in trials on issues concerning homosexuality and in one, the prosecution asked him if he was homosexual and he replied, "No." One of his post-doctoral fellows asked him how he could say that and he replied, "Because I am bisexual."

So his concerns about homosexuality were a personal matter but his writings never reflected that personal investment. All his books maintained a detached tone, with a decided air of the objective scientist. Money was ardent to be published and he decided what would fit in any publication, at times producing books that seem somewhat arbitrarily assembled. Thus *Gay, Straight, and In-Between: The Sexology of Erotic Orientation* (1988), with the, excuse the expression, rather straightforward title, includes many parts that seem at best vaguely related to the topic. He was a pediatric psycho-endocrinologist, and therefore his concerns for the possible relevance of intersex conditions might seem appropriate but he also strayed in a variety of other directions, including transgender and all of the possible paraphilias. Perhaps he was attempting to overcome the simplicity of the gay/straight divide, to present sexual orientation as one more of the many aspects of gender and sexuality.

Money had long realized that society's division of the world into male and female did not reflect the expansive continuum of either gender or biological sex. In 1963 he published an article titled "Factors in the Genesis of Homosexuality," which began "Hermaphroditism and related disorders are anomalies that, because of the incongruences inherent in them, raise some puzzling semantic technicalities as to the very definition of homosexuality" (19). This had an inevitable effect on assumptions of sexual orientation. Money noted that societal concern for the medical needs of intersex persons can change very quickly when those needs seem to lead to homosexuality:

> No infringement has aroused more fanatical vindictiveness than that which pertains to the morphologic sex of the partner in sexuoerotical practices, namely, when the partner of a male is transposed from female to male so that two males are together, and similarly for two females together. This is the transposition for which the modern term "homosexuality" was coined by K.M. Benkert, also known as Kertbeny, in 1869 (Kennedy 1988; Herzer 1986), although the phenomenon had been on record since antiquity. (Money, *Unspeakable*, 1999: 191)

A similar effect is found in the treatment of transsexuals, who have often been regarded as unfit for surgery if they intend to continue with the same sexual object, in effect turning from a heterosexual into a homosexual. Money recognized that many negative responses to sexual diversities could reflect society's deep-seated fear of homosexuality. Thus the recent tendency in some cultures, such as Iran, to accept transsexuals as diseased persons in need of surgery and yet to reject homosexuals as criminals in need of punishment would not surprise him.

Some of the spots on the intersex continuum might provide insights about what controls the choice of sex objects by all humans. In 1970 Money published a paper entitled "Sexual Dimorphism and Homosexual Gender Identity." There he stated, "Errors of differentiation, notably in both clinical and experimentally induced hermaphroditism, are important to the theory of homosexuality. In some instances these errors result in what is, in effect, homosexuality by experiment or by experiment of nature" (428). In other words, someone who has Complete Androgen Insensitivity Syndrome and is thus a woman who is XY, is chromosomally homosexual if she is in a heterosexual relationship with a man. For Money, as for many later theorists, the intersex individual provided a biological problem that might offer a biological answer to sexual diversity.

Not that it would ever be a simple answer. He noted in an article he wrote with Green in 1961 that "Effeminate boys (and men) have normal hormone functioning. It is also known that effeminate boys have normal sex chromosomes" ("Tomboys," 2). In a later article co-authored with Anthony Russo in 1979 he observed that "each boy had developed a conviction that he should change into a girl, and that he should be able to do so by somehow or other losing his penis" ("Homosexual," 38), and yet they turned out not to be transgendered, as one might have expected, but rather homosexuals with no cross-dressing and no "inadequacy of genital functioning" ("Homosexual," 39). In other words, while there seemed a clear relationship between childhood "discordant gender identity/role" and adult sexual orientation, it was not a simple continuity from a discordant gender identity in childhood to a discordant gender identity in adulthood. In the 1970 paper he stated,

> Clinically, it is true that some homosexuals have a history of chromosomal error, sexual birth deformity, undescended testes, small penis, delayed puberty, gonadal insufficiency, poorly developed or contradictionary sexual dimorphism of body build, gynecomastia (in boys) and hirsutism (in girls). But the frequency of any one of these disorders among homosexuals is so sporadic as to not create special hormonal research vigilance at the present time. Conversely, the incidence of homosexuality in the clinical population of

each one of the listed disorders is so sporadic that one
cannot seriously entertain the hypotheses of a primary hormonal cause-effect link between the physical
symptoms, on the one hand, and homosexuality on
the other. If there is any link, it is more likely to be
secondary. There is far and away more homosexuality
among organists, hairdressers, actors, or antique deal-
ers than among patients with endocrine diagnosis!
("Sexual," 434)

Money here was moving in two directions. First, he suggested that
endocrine disorders are not causes of sexual disorders—or to put it a
less pejorative way, sexual diversities. Second, he suggested that those
who inhabit the sexual diversities cannot be defined by some endocrinological deviance. In the 1961 article he found consistencies in both
family structure and morphology in the effeminate boys:

In our study, the most consistently recurring findings
were the infrequency of fatherly domination in the
household, the lack of preference by the child for the
father as the favorite parent, the relatively fragile body
build of some of the boys, and as previously stated, the
frequency with which the mother viewed the son's
behaviour in a more serious light than did the father.
However, no simple point-for-point association of
cause and effect of sissyishness or tomboyishness was
revealed. ("Tomboys," 3)

While none of these possibilities, from hormones to parenting, satisfied
any scientific standards for causality, causality remained the goal. Perhaps this was the reason he returned again and again to intersex. The
possibility of a person who is not wholly male or female, a possibility
that seems to deny the simplicity of homosexuality or heterosexuality,
might provide an insight into the key to sexual orientation.

Money began *Gay, Straight, and In-Between* with a chapter on "Prenatal Hormones and Brain Dimorphism." His primary concern was
the various animal studies of dimorphism. There are many elements
to such studies but they tend to follow one basic model: something is

modified on an animal of one sex in order to move it towards the behaviour of the other sex. Almost invariably, the success of this change is judged according to sexual behaviour. A male animal becomes female if it acts receptive to mounting and a female becomes male if it tries to mount. Regardless of the accuracy of this assessment among animals, it seems obviously simplistic if applied to human gender identity. Gender for humans is much more complex than mounting or not mounting. It seems to me self-evident that we have many important markers of gender that are equally evident in persons of different sexual orientation.

Money's opening chapter might come close to the arguments of his opponents, such as Milton Diamond, who seem to believe that biology is destiny: by their chromosomes you shall know them. This view, that the sexual subject and gender subject are more accurately defined by the scientific observer than by the subject him- or herself, continues throughout many supposedly scientific studies. A good example of this attitude is Diamond's view of the plethysmograph, which judges sexual orientation by erectile response:

> While pupillary and genital responses are probably a valid reflection of erotic interest, the responses might also be to novelty, shock, or something else. Nevertheless, practiced test givers can most usually differentiate the responses of erotic interest from other causes. Many studies have documented the heuristic and practical value of such measures. (Diamond, 63–64)

This faith in the "practiced test givers" seems less than scientific. Many other studies have suggested that the best way of defining homosexual is just to ask the subject. Strangely enough, the testimony of a human voice is better than that of a penis.

Money, like earlier students of sexuality such as Havelock Ellis and Kinsey, was much more willing to accept the subject's autobiography. Still, autobiographies are of little value in the search for an explanation that at least suggests causality. Money made statements such as this, about an intersex woman:

> In the human species, the site where hormonally responsive brain cells are prenatally masculinized so as

to induce a predisposition toward subsequent bisexuality or homosexuality has not yet been demonstrated. One must infer, on the basis of laboratory animals, that the site of masculinization is not in the neocortex of the brain, but in the old brain, the paleocortex, also known as the limbic system, which is intimately connected with the hypothalamus. (*Gay*, 37)

Even with the advanced GPS systems of twenty-first 21$^{st}$ - century science we remain unable to find that "site of masculinization." For a fascinating, entertaining and very critical examination of this search for brain dimorphism look at Cordelia Fine's *Delusions of Gender*. Fine says, "when we follow the trail of contemporary science we discover a surprising number of gaps, assumptions, inconsistencies, poor methodologies, and leaps of faith—as well as more than one echo of the insalubrious past" (Fine, xxvii). In a freewheeling interview with *Cosmopolitan* magazine Money summed up his view:

> Before we're born, while we're under the control of sex hormones, certain things happen to our brains. If a girl baby is forming and nature adds some male hormone—testosterone—then what would have been an exclusively feminized brain is going to have a masculinized predisposition, and the chance of the girl's being bisexual or lesbian is greatly increased. With a male, the exact opposite is true. If *not enough* testosterone is added, the chance of bisexuality or homosexuality is increased. Of course the social experiences of the child may override those predispositions. But remember, while this is a very good hypothesis, it can be demonstrated one hundred percent only in animals. ("Cosmo," 111)

I was quite delighted recently when one of the central purveyors of what might be called gay science, Simon LeVay, published a new book titled *Gay, Straight, and the Reason Why: The Science of Sexual Orientation* (2011). LeVay is likely to know Money's book of the similar title but he makes no mention of it. LeVay's one reference to Money in *Gay,*

*Straight, and the Reason Why* is the usual attack on Money's involvement in the Reimer case. But it amuses me that Money in 1988 offered only "and in-between," whereas in 2011, LeVay is ready to assert "the reason why." Well, no. As LeVay admits in his comments on Dean Hamer's famous study of the "gay gene": "Unfortunately, Hamer's report has not been robustly confirmed" (171). As every student of science knows, "robustly" is a standard modifier to assert that some study exceeds the possibilities of chance, but I still love the butch tone it produces. It seems to offer the hope of a macho recognition that all is as it must be. If sexual orientation had either a biological cause or a clear biological marker, then it would seem logical that some studies would have proven this by now. Instead, after almost 300 pages of discussions of everything from chromosomes to finger length, LeVay is only able to conclude with that "biological factors may be closely involved" ( 290). It is difficult to think of any aspect of human life to which this phrase would not apply.

Money's own work some thirty years before clearly had hopes for scientific answers. Going back to 1961, in an article entitled "Components of Eroticism in Man," Money asserted the importance of hormones in the sex drive and yet the failure to differentiate either between male and female or between gay and straight:

> Failure to detect an hormonal anomaly in homosexuals has been paralleled by a failure to effect a cure with hormonal treatment. Androgen does not masculinize the erotic inclination of a male homosexual. It either leaves his eroticism unchanged or else intensifies it in the homosexual direction.
>
> The obverse of a lack of abnormal hormonal findings in homosexuality is the lack of increased incidence of homosexuality in sex-endocrine dysfunction. Estrogen levels are elevated in males with gynecomastia sufficiently to cause prominent breast feminization. There is no corresponding feminization of the personality. Androgen levels are elevated in females with hyperactive adrenals or, more rarely, a virilizing tumor. There is no corresponding lesbian virilization of the personality. (246)

His belief in science was something wider, however, that included experience and society. Money always recognized the eagerness we all have to find a cause and yet the rarity of finding a cause that clearly produces an effect. If one of his post-docs suggested a simple cause for something they were studying, Money would say, "Do you have a crystal ball? Why don't I have a crystal ball?" Yet he had experience of both biological and social causes. For the former, increased knowledge of endocrinological deviations from the norm gave him the suggestion of strident work by biology against biology. Complete Androgen Insensitivity Syndrome had shown him that it was possible for someone with completely male chromosomes to seem completely female in almost every other way. His studies of abuse dwarfism showed that it was not simply a response to physical conditions, such as lack of nourishment and physical abuse, but rather physiological effects of psychological treatment.

In a 1964 review of a book that claimed "familial psychodynamics" to be the cause of homosexuality, Money showed how strongly he believed that science needed to recognize the larger picture:

> The authors' bias in favour of this inference shows up clearly in their handling of the heredity issue in their last chapter. Alas! They risk disgracing the professions of psychiatry and psychology in the eyes of other scientists when they show themselves still in the Nature-Nurture age of Herbert Spencer, unacquainted with the advances and concepts of modern genetics. Heredity is not a synonym for a blind kind of predeterminism, a fatalism against which all therapeutic effort is futile. ("*Homosexuality*," 199)

Money's central argument about nature and nurture was this:

> It is counterproductive to characterize prenatal determinants of sexual orientation as biological, and postnatal determinants as not biological. The postnatal determinants that enter the brain through the senses by way of social communication and learning also are biological, for there is a biology of learning and remembering. That which is not biological is occult,

> mystical or, to coin a term, spookological. Homosexol-
> ogy, the science of orientation or status as homosexual
> or bisexual rather than heterosexual, is not a science of
> spooks. Nor is the science of heterosexology. (*Gay*, 50)

Money wanted scientific answers and the most convincing answers about the body are those that can be linked to biology. Thus he began with the animal studies and the hopes that they might offer. He stated in the epilogue to his first chapter:

> Human sexological syndromes in the clinic represent
> experiments of nature that are the counterpart of
> animal sexological syndromes induced experiment-
> ally in the laboratory. Despite species differences and
> variations, data from these two sources are mutually
> compatible. (*Gay*, 49)

But as all these studies of homosexuality seem to miss sometimes, the human mind is very complex. The digestive systems of mice and humans are "compatible" but that does not explain why humans like French restaurants. What the narrator in Herman Melville's "Billy Budd" says of Claggart could be said of the human mind in general: "a nut not to be cracked by the tap of a lady's fan."

From the animal studies Money moved on to "Gender Coding." A good part of this section discusses transsexuals. This might seem a strange direction for a book ostensibly about homosexuality but once again Money used his expertise in other areas of sexology to address sexual orientation. Thus he stressed the importance of the subtleties of gender identity and gender role for the trans woman, who needs to find all aspects of her life in the world to be understandable as gender coded. Money saw the definitions of gender as invariably based on identification and complementation, or the process of saying "I am this thing because I am the same as X" and "I am this thing because I am not the same as Y." In this process, Money included sexual orientation and thus reinforced the idea that in our society a major part of gender coding is compulsory heterosexuality. Reminiscent of Monique Wittig's claim that the lesbian is not a woman, Money suggested that the sexual other is a clear part of the idea of the sexual self. Money based this on a rather doctrinaire view of the world:

> In the theology of natural law, there is decreed an absolute standard of what is normal in sex, and that standard is procreation. If we were a species in which all the sexual acts of all males were exact replications of one another, and the same for females, then there would be an absolute standard by which to measure masculinity and femininity. That being not the case, we as a species must live with two standards of normality, the statistical and the ideological. (*Gay*, 76)

So Money descended from the doctrinaire, in which nature offers an absolute, with all of gender defined by sexual acts, through the scientific response, which is primarily statistical, to his, which is the ideological, in opposition to other ideologies.

Whenever there was an agenda in Money, it was usually towards sexual liberation. In *Gay, Straight and In-Between,* he referred, as he so often did, to the importance of "sexual rehearsal play" in children. This became a key aspect of his theories of sexual dysfunction. Money claimed that cultures that allowed overt sexual play among children had no sexual perversions, and no homosexuality. But if Money was not some self-hating homophobe, why did he make such a claim? One of Money's constant examples was Aboriginal Australia. He claimed that his anthropological excursion to a mission in Arnhem Land was the source of his information. In one of his appearances as an expert witness he testified, ""I think one of the reasons why they had no sexual problems in a homosexuality [*sic*] was they have an ancient and very long tradition of being extremely open-minded about sexual play in infancy"("Expert," 7–123). I have read his notes from the expedition and his observations seem to have been an act of will: in interviews he made sure he heard what he already knew to be the case. The likelihood is that there was less sexual rehearsal play than he claimed and that there was more homosexuality than anyone in that very Christian environment would tell him about. But Money needed evidence for the causality that would justify his pleas for the sexual liberation of children. It is tempting to look to biography and Money's own repressive fundamentalist Christian upbringing as a reason for this belief. He had examples from clinical experience of the negative, men whose unusual sexual needs seemed a product of childhood trauma, but he needed something positive, such as the absence of homosexuality in a world with children merrily exploring their sexuality.

If Money's claims about sexual rehearsal play and sex education for children seem somewhat homophobic this could be simply polemicism, as he tried to convince his perhaps homophobic audience of the need for freedom. Among Money's many discontinued projects to be found in his papers is one from 1970 called "Significant Aspects of Erotica." There he asked,

> Is it better for a growing boy, walking in the park, to be greeted by a pleasant and friendly homosexual before or after having been advised of homosexuality and its implications for his future? Is the boy to wonder for the rest of his life what a homosexual encounter entails? Is he apt to try a homosexual experience in an effort to satisfy whatever curiosity he may have about sex with his own sex? Which is to be preferred: a physical encounter or a dialog leading to an understanding of the homosexual's way of life, a dialog inspired by the knowledgeable use of candid pornography depicting two men making love to each other. It is a good question, and worth pondering. ("Significant," 10)

One of the central concerns in *Gay, Straight and In-Between* that reflected sexual liberation but perhaps went beyond it is the statement that homosexuality is not a pathology but rather a parallel state to heterosexuality. The *Diagnostic and Statistical Manual of Mental Disorders* (DSM) had removed homosexuality in 1986 but this did not mean that many outside the North American gay community treated it as just part of the norm. Besides the homophobia of society in general and the anxiety of the world of the justice system, many psychologists continued to perceive it as a pathology. The ideas of earlier theorists such as Edmund Bergler were still prominent and there were many contemporaries, such as Charles Socarides, who continued to state that homosexuality was a disease. There were many instances when Money felt the need to confront Socarides in print. The primary justification for what might be called homophobic psychoanalysis was that so many homosexuals were troubled by their sexual orientation. Money's response was that the problems were easily explained by social oppression, as in his analogy of left-handedness to point to something formerly pathologized and a focus of medical and psychological intervention but now generally accepted.

Money's opposition to homophobia was based on a number of factors. One was simply the error inherent in the views of people such as Socarides that the distress of the homosexual about his sexuality made it necessary for medicine to find a cure. In 1965 Money told an interviewer:

> I become quite incensed about this criterion of "wanting to be cured." I don't think medical people have any right to lay the blame on the patient as to whether he will be cured or not. It is their responsibility. Our basic job eventually, I will admit, is that we should know how to change a person's wants on an issue like this. Just to sit there and say we can cure you, if you want to be cured, I think is really malpractice. ("Interview," 17)

The definition of the sickness cannot simply be that a person is convinced that he is sick. Medicine might see that the more appropriate cure would be to change the person's understanding rather than his condition.

In *Gay, Straight, and In-Between,* Money devoted a great deal of space to the paraphilias, what used to be called perversions. This once again might be seen to be questionable given his topic but his central point was to exclude homosexuality from the paraphilias. He stated that "Its classification as a paraphilia is scientifically untenable, insofar as all of the forty-odd paraphilias may occur in association with homosexual, heterosexual, or bisexual mating" (*Gay*, 84). For Money one of the central problems of sexuality is the lust-love split, in which the paraphilia is considered by the subject to be an evil lust that must be separated from the love experienced in the subject's primary relationship. Money's position was that this has nothing to do with sexual orientation. The lust-love dichotomy is created for some homosexuals by society's condemnation. Money enjoyed presenting this opinion in many courts as an expert witness, including two of the classic cases in the United States military, Leonard Matlovich and Vernon Berg, which led to this comment in 1993: "it is conceivable in the national interest that the quack of the ugly duckling will be listened to, lest the United States military ban on homosexuals become the Achilles heel of national defense" ("Parable," 23).

One particularly interesting example of Money as expert witness was his testimony in 1979 at the trial of the Toronto magazine, *The Body Politic*. The publishers had been accused of obscenity for publishing a supportive portrait of the National Association for Man Boy Love. The author, Gerald Hannon, suggested that the men he described were "the heirs of Mr Atkinson, 'Leader in Boys' Work,' community workers who deserve our praise, our admiration and our support" (Hannon, 11). To call pedophiles "community workers" no doubt irritated many but they probably also were not happy that Hannon used the term "pedophile" to describe C.J. Atkinson, founder of the Broadview Boys' Institute, later part of the YMCA. Money's testimony went on at great length about masturbation, degeneracy and even witchcraft to suggest that *The Body Politic* was the victim of societal prejudices: "There is always a temptation and a tendency to fall back on these antiquated worn out concepts simply because science hasn't entered into, filled the vacuum yet" ("In the Provincial," 252). Part of Money's agenda to remove legal restrictions on homosexuality was sexual liberation but also what might be called medical liberation, from the assumption that doctors must treat "sicknesses" such as left-handedness, something that had proved to be neither damaging nor curable. He said in 1977,

> with sexuality, it is malpractice to enforce treatment on homosexuals and bisexuals ostensibly to make them heterosexual. If such treatment were enforced by law, the suffering of stigmatized people on the waiting list would be enormous, for the ratio of therapists to patients would be forever inadequate—to say nothing of the failure of outcome. ("Cytogenetics," 232)

When the defense at *The Body Politic* trial asked about "a normal homosexual," Money responded with "the two correct definitions of normal ... at the midpoint of the normal curve of distribution ... [and] the ideological definition and ideologically society, or a family, or a group of people, have the norm of that which they themselves and their membership to behave by [*sic*]" ("In the Provincial," 252). He said of the latter, "that way of thinking about homosexuality does not tell us anything about either the somatic health or the mental health of the homosexual who is just as likely to be healthy as the heterosexual person is, in that sense" ("In the Provincial," 253).

The problem of "normal" is an ongoing one. In one of his comments on intersex, Kenneth Zucker was very careful to avoid the view of "abnormal" as "a monster," and yet he asserted that intersex is abnormal and that "it is hard to argue that such conditions are simply variants from the norm" (1). But in simple fact, all "abnormal" represents is variants from the norm. It is up to society to decide what variants are so extreme as to inspire either medical or judicial action. Thus while the article in *The Body Politic* represented abnormal behaviour, Mr. Atkinson's speech on "The Boy Problem" to the very establishment Canadian Club in 1909 was presumably the quintessence of normal. There he referred to "a red-headed, freckled boy, not much in appearance but who had a twinkling little eye which suggested much" (54). Suggested much what? The innuendo is avoided on the simple assumption that Atkinson could not have been suggesting what the men in Hannon's article were suggesting. I make this tangent to support the importance of Money's combination of the tenor of objective science and the assertion that homosexuality could be an acceptable variant from the norm. Money believed that there had been an inevitable progress as society came to be less frightened by homosexuality, yet the law kept treating it as a crime. In an interview with the American Psychological Association he asserted, "It really does turn the clock back when in a quiet sort of way society was finding its way out of the morass it has been in since the era of the Inquisition on this topic" ("Sex," 10).

Money's attempt to be dispassionate and scientific causes some confusion. Thus, in *Gay, Straight and In-Between* he provided a chart of "gender crosscoding" (*Gay*, 85), which he divided into "continuous" and "episodic." In "continuous," "total" is "transexualism," "partial unlimited" is "gynemimesis" (appearing as a woman), and "partial limited" is "homophilia." In episodic, "total" is "fetishistic transvestism," "partial unlimited" is "nonfetishistic transvestism" and "partial limited" is "bisexualism." The chart itself represents a belief in taxonomy that overreaches the possibility. It seems akin to the anecdote about the zoologist Cuvier, noted by Donald Rogers in "The Philosophy of Taxonomy": "One day the devil appeared in his laboratory, complete with horns, hoof, and tail, and threatened to eat him up. Cuvier said, 'Quit bothering me. You're obviously strictly herbivorous. Go on outside and eat grass. You can't eat me'" (Rogers, 332). The question that should be posed to any taxonomy is the relevance of the claimed distinctions. Besides the obvious problem of just figuring out Money's chart, many would question his continuum because they doubt that any kind of cross-dressing is intrinsically related to homosexuality. In his 1963 article, Money had seen some degree of cross-gender identity in even the most male homosexual: "a more masculine homosexual's feminism of imagery may be limited to the erotic arousal-power of a body with the same sexual morphology as his own" ("Factors," 34).

In rather typically pugilistic style, Money attributed any disagreement with his analysis to "gay polemicists." He attacked them for "censoring basic homosexological science" (*Gay*, 153). But, as so often in Money's work, some basic observations and a rather freewheeling application of common sense took matters too far. Many have attacked Money for any reference to gender cross-coding and homosexuality. To them variant sexual orientation does not suggest any variance in gender identity or gender role, and therefore including sexual orientation in the assessment of gender identity in intersex is just homophobic. But to return to Monique Wittig, one need not be an extremist of either the gay or straight variety to see that our ideas of gender are largely based on heterosexual assumptions, Cordelia Fine's "insalubrious past." Thus gender identity and sexual orientation are not the same but neither are they separate. Yet Money accepts some degree of separation when he comments on the ease of identifying homosexuality according not to biological sex but to gender identity. In 1963 he suggested that while the term "homosexual" would generally be thought of as relatively simple, it actually had multiple components: "In its ordinary usage, homosexuality implies that a couple are chromosomally, gonadally, hormonally, and morphologically homosexual and are assigned to the same sex" ("Factors," 30). But in many cases, often invisible to the public at large, some of those components are not homosexual. Homosexuality must be based only on gender identity and gender role. Thus a trans man with a female partner is clearly heterosexual and a trans man with a trans man partner is clearly homosexual. The only quibble would be with someone who does not have a secure gender identity.

But regardless of Money's constant assertions that gender identity is larger than sex, he also constantly asserted that sex is central to gender identity . While his concept of gender identity is a major part of the reason why we now believe sex is not a property proven by simple observation, this does not mean that gender identity is a somewhat arbitrary matter shaped primarily by the needs of the culture. Instead, Money viewed gender identity as a base human attribute that can eventually be understood through careful scientific analysis. Yet there are various examples in Money's work, not of careful science but rather of a leap of faith based on his analysis. Thus as an expert witness in the case of L.M. Smith, who was fired from the United States state department for homosexuality, Money stated, "My evaluation of him, I may say in passing, he is not a very convincing homosexual. He is really a bisexual" ("Expert," 7–25). This is not because of the subject's identity claims or the subject's sexual history but rather Money's own observations of his gender presentation: "I told him my evaluation of him was he was one of the many people who falls into the trap in our society of calling himself a homosexual when his mental potentiality is to be bisexual and I thought as time went on, he could explore and find out more about this other dimension in himself" ("Expert," 7–66).

This view of bisexuality as manifested in gender contrasts with bisexual experience which, as Kinsey showed, is quite wide-ranging. Those most convinced of the biological truth of homosexual and heterosexual orientation tend to be least convinced of bisexuality. Diamond states, "When it exists, while it is much less common than heterosexuality or homosexuality, it is nevertheless, no doubt, the result of the same biological biases which determine either distinct androphilic or gynephilic arousal" (23). Those such as Diamond who see sexual orientation as a biological fact are uncomfortable with an idea that bisexual potential might be part of many more people than those few who identify as bisexual. Those such as Money, who see a true homosexual as someone who is also deviant from the gender norm, see bisexuality as something like a homosexuality that is not deviant from the gender norm. Then there are those such as Wittig, who are able to see sexual orientation as an almost completely political choice. One need not wholly agree

# Terry Goldie

with Wittig to see that sexual desire could be ultimately much more dependent on complex intersections of behavior, in which the human ability to choose figures very strongly.

Many of Money's concepts do seem commonsensical. One aspect that was given an unusual applicability in the context of Money's treatment of homosexuality is the trajectory of "limerence," or intense romantic attachment. He suggested that "[t]he natural history of a love affair is that the duration of the leaping-flame stage is around two years, after which the molten glow takes over. For the reproduction of the species, this is time enough for the pairbonding of the love affair to have progressed to sexual intercourse, pregnancy, and delivery of the baby" (*Gay*, 151). He noted that this was the same for childless couples, but also for gay couples. He presented the latter primarily to oppose the "shibboleth of promiscuity" (*Gay*, 151), but is it accurate? Money seemed to claim that the two-year cycle represented just a general human condition. Perhaps a more apt suggestion would be that the long existence of the nuclear family has created a pattern that permeates the whole of society. According to Money, it is not just compulsory heterosexuality but compulsory reproduction that shapes our sexualities.

While Money's overall view of homosexuality was that of a sexual liberationist, the parts to the whole were much more diffuse. Back in 1963 he had referred to genetic male hermaphrodites who "cannot be masculinized and so are assigned as girls. Then they grow up very well with the gender role and identity of girls, and are, if you will permit, experimental homosexuals of a sort, on the criterion of either chromosomal or gonadal sex" ("Factors," 31). He would have been unlikely to use the term twenty-five years later, but the idea of the "experimental homosexual" suggests the temptation to seek an analysis beyond the claims of self-identified gay men and lesbians.

In 1963, Money presented a careful assessment of the possible process of becoming homosexual:

> In the genesis of homosexuality, it is an open question which is the stage in development from zygote to adult when the die is cast in favour of subsequent psychosexual differentiation along homosexual lines, whatever the degree of severity. There may be no one specific stage, but a variance in timing, upon

176

which might depend the ultimate severity of the condition—whether chronic and pervasive (essential homosexuality), alternating and bisexual, or transient and circumstantial (opportunistic homosexuality). ("Factors," 37)

I can quibble with the pejorative tone of some of the words but this remains the best encapsulation I have read of the scientific approach to homosexuality. And yet its complete lack of a speculation of cause is what makes it the best.

Regardless of his comments elsewhere about causality, Money was as drawn to speculation as any of us. In the 1963 study he provided an emphasis that was gone by the time of his 1988 book, but that remains interesting in its angling towards a potential:

Virtually nothing is known of the functioning of the special senses in relation to the formation of gender identity. From studies of imprinting in animals, it is known that some behavioral traits and activities are set in motion by the release of a neuromuscular mechanism that is phylogenetically preset to be released by a suitable perceptual stimulus…. It is conceivable that some analogue of imprinting takes place in the establishment of human gender role and identity. If so, then the possibility exists that boys and girls may be differentially equipped phylogenetically to distinguish male and female stimuli and to respond to them as objects of identification. ("Factors," 37)

Money elsewhere seemed still more convinced of the validity of understanding human behaviour as imprinting. Money's word "conceivable" suggests an extreme hesitation, one for which conception is not perhaps the best representation, but the idea of imprinting is a useful one for sexual orientation. If the many vagaries of human agency are added, this seems a possible explanation of what might be called preset homosexuality, a preset that in some cases might never receive sufficient imprinting and in others might be imprinted by the slightest encounter.

Yet while this might be the case, it could be that this phylogenetic response is not gender specific. It is possible that this unidentifiable mechanism, that cause so yearned for by scholars such as LeVay, is the same for all humans, male, female or intersex:

> A still more likely possibility is that boys and girls are phylogenetically the same in their preparedness to establish a gender role and identity, being equipped only to impersonate an identity with a stimulus object. The decision whether this object will be male or female is not phylogenetic at all, but a product of ontogenetic opportunities and rewards. ("Factors," 38)

While "ontogenetic opportunities and rewards" might seem to suggest scientific specificity, they might be translated as "Someone is homosexual because he is homosexual." We all have ontogenetic opportunities and rewards, some of which are quite similar for all humans, but different humans respond differently. Money's final words in the 1963 article were:

> One arrives at the conclusion that the final common pathway for the establishment of a gender identity and, hence, his erotic arousal pattern, whatever the secondary and antecedent determinants, is in the brain. There it is established as a neurocognitional function. The process takes place primarily after birth, and the basic fundamentals are completed before puberty. The principles whereby all this happens await elucidation. ("Factors," 41)

Today, we continue to await elucidation. As Fine might suggest, the search for sexual orientation as a "neurocognitional function" might give rather too much credit to the brain over the amorphous philosophical construct known as the mind. As Helena says in *A Midsummer Night's Dream*, "Love looks not with the eyes but the mind." Yes, but how does the mind look?

**NOTE**

1    This phrase was quoted often in references to Money but there never was a precise attribution. It is most likely from her introductory remarks to her lecture "A Question of Sex," given at Johns Hopkins University on September 28, 1993.

**REFERENCES**

Atkinson, C.J. "The Boy Problem." *Canadian Club* (December 20, 1909): 52–60.

Bergler, Edmund. *Homosexuality: Disease or Way of Life?* New York: Collier, 1962.

Colapinto, John. *As Nature Made Him: The Boy Who Was Raised as a Girl.* New York: Harper, 2006.

Diamond, Milton. "Bisexuality: A Biological Perspective." In Erwin J. Haeberle and Rolf Gindorf (eds.), *Bisexualities: The Ideology and Practice of Sexual Contact with Both Men and Women.* New York: Continuum, 1998: 53–80.

Fine, Cordelia. *Delusions of Gender: How Our Minds, Society, and Neurosexism Create Difference.* New York: W.W. Norton, 2010.

Goldie, Terry. *The Man Who Invented Gender: John Money.* Vancouver: University of British Columbia Press, forthcoming.

Green, Richard. "The Three Kings: Harry Benjamin, John Money, Robert Stoller." *Archives of Sexual Behavior* 38, no. 4 (June 21, 2008): 610–13.

Hannon, Gerald. "Men Loving Boys Loving Men," *The Body Politic* 39 (December 1977/January 1978).

Herzer, Manfred. "Kertbeny and the Nameless Love." *Journal of Homosexuality* 12, 1 (Fall 1986): 1-25.

Kennedy, Hubert. *Ulrichs: The Life and Works of Karl Heinrich Ulrichs, Pioneer of the Modern Gay Movement.* Boston: Alyson, 1988.

LeVay, Simon. *Gay, Straight, and the Reason Why: The Science of Sexual Orientation.* New York: Oxford University Press, 2011.

Money, John. "Components of Eroticism in Man: I. The Hormones in Relation to Sexual Morphology and Sexual Desire." *The Journal of Nervous and Mental Disease* 132, no. 3 (March 1961): 239–48.

———. "Cosmo Talks to John Money Pioneer Sex Researcher." *Cosmopolitan* 209, no. 6 (December 1990): 108–11.

———. "Cytogenetics, Behaviour and Informed Consent." *Modern Medicine of Canada* 32, no. 2 (February 1977): 127–30.

———. "Expert Witness Testimony on Homosexuality, in the Case of L.M. Smith v. Kissinger, U.S. Department of State Agency for International Development, Washington, D.C. 3.25.1975." John Money Collection Hocken Library, University of Otago, Dunedin, New Zealand.

———. "Factors in the Genesis of Homosexuality." In George Winokur et al. (eds.), *Determinants of Human Sexual Behavior.* Springfield, IL: Charles C. Thomas, 1963: 19–43.

——. *Gay, Straight, and In-Between: The Sexology of Erotic Orientation*. New York: Oxford University Press, 1988.

——. "*Homosexuality*." [Book Review] *Journal of Nervous and Mental Disease* 138 (1964): 197–200.

——. "Interview with Maxine Davis. 9.04.1965." John Money Collection, Kinsey Institute, University of Indiana, Bloomington.

——. "In the Provincial Courts (Criminal Division) Judicial District of York" "Her Majesty the Queen *vs.* Kenneth David Popert, Edward Arthur Jackson, Gerald Campbell Hannon, Pink Triangle Press." Toronto, January 4, 5, 8 ,1979. Canadian Lesbian and Gay Archives, Toronto.

——. "Parable, Principle, and Military Ban." *Society* 31, no. 1 (November–December 1993): 22–23.

——. "Sex and Money." APA *Monitor* 7, no. 6 (June 1976): 10–11.

——. "Sexual Dimorphism and Homosexual Gender Identity." *Psychological Bulletin* 74, no. 6 (1970): 425–40.

——. "Significant Aspects of Erotica." Unpublished typescript marked "1970." John Money Collection Hocken Library University of Otago, Dunedin, New Zealand.

——. *Unspeakable Monsters in All Our Lives*. Amherst, NY: Prometheus Books, 1999.

Money, John and Richard Green. "'Tomboys' and 'Sissies'." *Sexology* 28, no. 5 (December 1961): 2–5.

Money, John and Anthony J. Russo. "Homosexual Outcome of Discordant Gender Identity/Role in Childhood: Longitudinal Follow-up." *Journal of Pediatric Psychology* 4, no. 1 (1979): 29–41.

Rogers, Donald P. "The Philosophy of Taxonomy." *Mycologia* 50, no. 3 (May–June 1958): 326–32.

Socarides, Charles W. *Homosexuality*. New York: J. Aronson, 1978.

Wittig, Monique. *The Straight Mind and Other Essays*. Boston: Beacon, 1992.

Zucker, Kenneth J. "Intersexuality and Gender Identity Differentiation." *Annual Review of Sex Research* 10 (1999): 1–69.

# Thinking through Blood in Post-9/11 Visual Culture: *The Passion of the Christ* and *Bobby*

RANDAL ROGERS

In her book *Seeing Ghosts* (2009) Karen Engle writes the following:

> The haunting that has arisen since 9/11 to trouble our minds and borders is not the (simple) recognition of remains—of absence intertwined with presence—of which Derrida writes in so many books on mourning. Coming from the future, this haunting "resists even the grammar of the future anterior" and indicates that we are not in a position to articulate what will have happened from all this. (18)

Engle is writing about artist Eric Fischl's controversial memorial sculpture titled *Tumbling Woman* when she states that, "She has not yet finished dying, and the future between her impact and death remains open. This is a history we cannot yet begin to imagine" (18). This essay looks back at the haunting generated by the events of 9/11/01 and considers the manners in which the ghosts of 9/11 have appeared in popular culture during this time. By arguing that *Tumbling Woman* "has not yet finished dying," Engle further suggests that the destruction of the World Trade Center in New York City by hijacked planes on September 11, 2001, now referred to as "9/11," itself is also a history we cannot yet begin to imagine.

Here I argue that, despite the perceived unrepresentability of 9/11, popular culture has offered audiences multiple ghosted versions of the events to ponder, mourn and become aroused by. In the face of the failure to recover, name, and account for the affective politics of 9/11, a compulsive repetition has marked popular culture in the years since then as it attempts to come to terms with the "materialization of invisibility" (Engle, 78), which is a primary signifier of 9/11. Echoing Friedrich Nietzsche, Jacques Derrida reminds us that "our entire world is the cinder of innumerable *living* beings" (Derrida, 4), the cinder understood as "the trace here of a non-present there" (6), or "what remains without remaining" (43). 9/11 provides cinders both literal and figurative, ghosts of bodies not found and left unmourned, melancholic repetitions in multiple media forms, and ashen traces which return to presence as spectres of this impossible history. In words that could be about the World Trade Center, Derrida writes:

> If a place is itself surrounded by fire (falls finally into ash, into a cinder tomb), it no longer is. Cinder remains, cinder there is, which we can translate: the cinder is not, is not what is. It remains from what is not, in order to recall at the delicate charred bottom of itself only non-being, or non-presence. Being without presence has not been and will no longer be there where there is cinder and where this other memory would speak. (39)

To "remain from what is not" is a very useful notion for questioning the manners in which 9/11 as an event has also remained as a ghostly presence haunting contemporary media.

This essay examines two films in an effort to demonstrate how cinders of 9/11 remain and inform a surprisingly broad range of film genres today. In particular it focuses upon the representation of blood, trauma and bodily disintegration as tropes that define such ghostly returns. Blood holds a certain representational power that 9/11 both tapped into and generated in multiple ways. Retracing a line through the event that is less well-known and certainly less examined than the predominant public images, a blood line—a cinder—this paper frames several "red events"¹ in the years that followed which are significant, not only to the themes of this paper but to history and cultural studies as well.

## 9/11'S BLOOD

Before discussing the films it is important to define two contexts that set the trajectory for this study: 9/11's blood, and bloodletting in the contemporary period. Immediately following the terrorist attacks at the World Trade Center in New York City, the search dogs were in a state of frenzy as they attempted to locate survivors, their task made so difficult by the incredible abundance of forensic evidence—human tissue, bone fragments, DNA and the traces of blood from the bodies of the 2,819 people that died there on September 11, 2001 (9/11 by the Numbers). Of these, only 289 bodies were recovered and the task of finding the 19,858 fragments of human bodies and related DNA samples from these (9/11 by the Numbers)—an enormous task taking years to finalize and never able to be completed—was attended by a sense of enormous loss and the will to memorialize victims as the United States set a new course in history. How to react to and assist with the crisis was the immediate impulse for citizens, in the US and elsewhere. "What can I do?" was the question asked as citizens watched the towers crumble over and over again on television. The response was univocal. "Give blood," they were told, an appeal that immediately transformed into a call for a demonstration of responsible citizenship.

In fact, the call to give blood came early. By 12 p.m. on September 11, the Red Cross had requested donations of blood, and media outlets at the local, national, and international level responded to the call. Later that day, at 7 p.m., in the first group address by the government to the nation, White House Secretary of Health and Human Services, Tommy Thompson, stated:

> Every single American lost something today. And every one of us at this time expresses our deepest sympathy to the victims of today's tragedies, and their families. It is our mission to begin healing from this tragedy. From the moment we learned of these attacks, the Department of Health and Human Services has begun readying teams and resources to be sent to New York City and the Washington area to meet any needs

of state and local officials... Americans all over are calling up and asking what they can do. The best thing they can do is respond to this great call by volunteering to give blood. We need Americans to continue to answer that call. No matter where you are, please, *do your civic duty and assist by donating blood* (emphasis added). (White House, Thompson)

The response was overwhelming and accounts of it pervaded media coverage in the days following. Indeed, by the end of the day on September 12, President George W. Bush said from the Pentagon:

We're here to say thanks to not only the workers on this site, but the workers who are doing the same work in New York City. I want to say thanks to the folks who have given blood to the Red Cross. I want to say thanks for the hundreds of thousands of Americans who pray for the victims and their families. (White House Press Release, Bush)

The following day, September 13, *New York Times* columnist Mirta Ojito reported how volunteers came by the thousands from across New York City, only to learn that they were not needed: "They lined up for hours at Red Cross headquarters on the West Side, at the Jacob K. Javits Convention Center, at hospitals, blood banks, and police command posts, offering themselves for whatever was needed." She then added: "We have had such an overwhelming response that we are actually asking people ... to postpone making a donation" [Ojito A11]. Of course, the "overwhelming response" was also attended by the slow realization that few, if any, survivors would be found. Thus a moment arrives and then disappears. Although the call to give blood vanished on September 13 as quickly as it had arrived on September 11, its force must not be underestimated, especially its articulation in the discourses of citizenship, the body and the nation in the days, months and years that followed.

Only 258 units of donated blood were actually used after the attacks of September 11, 2001, according to a *New York Times Magazine* article titled "9/11 by the Numbers," but the rhetoric of blood donation and its

material ties to citizenship at this moment is undeniable. Blood donation became a means by which to demonstrate civic responsibility—to
be a national subject in its most fundamental form—and to collectively
heal the wounds of a nation in crisis. And, importantly, while the era-
sure of actual citizens was slowly being recognized, a symbolic national
body arose in their place with Washington described as the "head" and
"brain," and the World Trade Center itself as the "economic heart" of
America.[2] In addition, through blood donation, an enormous circulatory system was produced within this symbolic body, taking literal
material form as blood flowed from the nation's extremities to New
York and Washington.

Blood donation, however, is not a benign activity. The tainted blood
scandals in the US, the UK and Canada, as elsewhere, remind one of the
connection to citizenship that has been entrenched in the system since
the mid-1980s when HIV was first discovered. Since then, IV drug users,
gay men, entire African nations and anyone who has had sex with persons on the Red Cross list of interdictions since 1977 have been refused
the privilege of donating.[3]

Through such interdiction, one's relation to the body politic is
unsettled. With regard to the events of 9/11, when citizenship was being
materially mapped through the volunteerism of blood donation, and
the contours and boundaries of the national body were being reformu-
lated, people on this list were excluded from political participation at
precisely the moment in which they wished to participate most. As the
symbolic wound began the process of scarring, suturing the body into
a totality once again, the nature of a new body emerged with (at times)
dire consequences for certain populations, firstly Islamic but slowly,
through ever-widening circles, for anyone who was considered to have
been not "with us," according to President Bush's new dictum (White
House, State of the Union, Bush).

This new body contained physical attributes (head, brain, heart,
circulatory system) but, importantly, it also came to possess affective
states. Words such as strength, resolve, good, evil, and anger were
pervasive in media coverage in the days following September 11, and
quickly gained momentum in President Bush's speeches. For example,
on September 20, in an "Address to a Joint Session of Congress and the
American People," he stated:

> My fellow citizens—for the last nine days, the entire
> world has seen for itself the state of our Union—and
> it is strong... Tonight we are a country awakened to
> danger and called to defend freedom. Our grief has
> turned to anger and our anger to resolution. Whether
> we bring our enemies to justice, or bring justice to our
> enemies, justice will be done... I will not forget this
> wound to our country or those who inflicted it. I will
> not yield; I will not rest; I will not relent in waging this
> struggle for freedom and security for the American
> people. The course of the conflict is not known, yet
> its outcome is certain. Freedom and fear, justice and
> cruelty, have always been at war, and we know that
> God is not neutral between them. Fellow citizens,
> we'll meet violence with patient justice—assured of
> the rightness of our cause, and confident of the victor-
> ies to come. In all that lies before us, may God grant
> us wisdom, and may He watch over the United States
> of America. (White House State of the Union, Bush).

Through such rhetorical mobilization, the national body obtained both
physical and affective states of being. The physical wound symbol-
ized its material presence, while references to grief, anger and resolve
described its emotional state, as that of a material body that feels.

While the affective elements of the nation-body turned from loss,
mourning and grief to resolve, determination, anger and a desire for
vengeance, a concomitant hardening of the body took hold, with strictly
policed borders that were quickly established in American culture
at every level. According to President Bush, it was time for America
to act in response to the attack on its body, and the War in Iraq is but
one example of the response to this breach, if the most literal. As "red"
events, these responses tapped into a long history of representation
related to the spilling of blood from the body, which are taken up in the
next section.

### BLOODLETTING IN HISTORY AND POPULAR CULTURE

Bloodletting was a custom practiced by the Mesopotamians, ancient
Egyptians, Greeks, Mayans and Aztecs. It began to fade in the

seventeenth century, as modern medical ideas about health were established and interdictions against human dissection disappeared. By the middle of the nineteenth century, bloodletting had receded in mainstream medicine, although it still occurs today in alternative and marginal non-Western practices.

For the ancient Greeks, bloodletting was connected to bodily health through the presence of the four humours responsible for animating human life and maintaining bodily balance: phlegm, yellow bile, black bile and blood (Conrad et al., 23–25). While the great early medical practitioner and theorist Galen of Pergamon discovered in the second century CE that veins and arteries were filled with blood rather than air, it was long believed that the humours simply ebbed and flowed in the body, a point finally contested by William Harvey's proof in the seventeenth century that blood circulated (Conrad et al., 325–27). Restoration of balance to the ill body was achieved, or at least attempted, through diuretics, emetics, induced sweating, bloodletting and various other actions undergone by patients at the hands of early medical practitioners. Releasing the dominating humor was thought to restore bodily health.

Here I posit that bloodletting continues in the contemporary period but with important distinctions from its historical precedents. Bloodletting has always included two important forms: the medical intervention in which a practitioner let blood from the physical body of the patient; and the more symbolic letting of blood associated with social bodies, such as in carnival and war. This second type is particularly important to the concerns of this essay. For example, the symbolic social order associated with carnival festivals in early modern Europe functioned to negotiate and redefine social tensions by inverting the social order through topsy-turvy refashioning, as Natalie Zemon Davis has argued. Public processions, performances, plays, etc., focused on the theme of "the world turned upside down" through forms of topsy-turvy inversion that were widely varied: "low" imitated "high" through the parodic imitation of kings and bishops as well as cross-dressing, inversions of pious rites, mocking satires, etc. Symbolic violence toward the monarch, local government and religious officials or social groups who were seen to embody forms of power was commonplace during carnival festivals. For example, pigs in Venice were tried and executed in the place of local, regional and later proto-national figures of power, to name one example among many (Davis, 97–123).

Throughout the calendar year there were several carnival seasons, such as May Day, Midsummer and Feast of Fools, but perhaps the most significant was the celebration that occurred just prior to Lent in the Catholic traditions of Europe, in which the ritual scarcity and control of forty days of abstinence, fasting and prayer was preceded by a period of consumptive frenzy. As a symbolic ritual of the body for Holy Week, Lent prepares the believer for the sacrament of Eucharist, in which the body and blood of Jesus Christ is ritually consumed to mark "The Passion" of his death and resurrection. Through symbolic consumption of body and blood, believers are brought into the realm of ritual performativity which is historically associated with the letting of blood and sacrifice of life represented by Jesus Christ.

Natalie Zemon Davis, historian of early modern France, has argued that carnival is more than merely a safety valve: it can reinforce the existing order, but it can also critique it and even underpin rebellion (Davis, 152–88). Furthermore, carnivalesque events were not always easily contained; imagery, ritual language and actions could migrate beyond set festive occasions to be engaged in multiple ways. While Carnival allowed taboo-breaking and created liminal spaces in which new or alternative ideas could be expressed, symbolic violence could turn into real violence, particularly against authorities or minority social groups.

In this way a direct link can be made between symbolic and real bodies through the related figures of carnival and war. War is bloodletting's ultimate social form, redefining the boundaries of the (national) body as impenetrable to foreign transgression at the same time as bodily penetration and the resultant spilling of blood of the enemy is marked as normative. Yet, because of war's differential relation to citizenship and democracy today, it is negotiated and renegotiated at the cultural level in multiple and competing manners. For example, since 2001 a sub-genre of war film, the terror genre, has expanded dramatically to become a popular and tightly codified form.

The relation between the rapid expansion of such a genre, 9/11 and recent forms of governmentality need not be argued. One need only witness the spate of films centred on torture since 2004 to understand the relation between film and ideology, as Mark Anderson notes for the earlier Western film genre (Anderson, 125–26). It is important to analyze such films as comprising a field of their own. For the purposes of this essay, however, a narrow sample focused upon two films demonstrates the relation between film and ideology. These films show how bloodletting continues today in popular culture forms as well as showing the necessity of investigating examples in their singularity as blood is let from the body in different manners and to differentiated effect. This last point is critical.

The spilling of blood is most commonly associated with the horror and war genres of film where spectacle is the objective. Such a generalized framing of blood is insufficient, and the examples chosen here demonstrate the necessity of defining an approach capable of addressing the multiplicity inherent to blood's appearance in popular media forms. The choices here are also significant because of the historical context of the films and their relation to 9/11; they are bracketed by the moments when the Bush administration, arguably, located its *raison d'être* and when it was entering the final stages of its political life.

In early 2004 the United States was at war in Iraq and the torture crisis of Abu Ghraib unfolded. In 2006 the Bush administration had been elected for a second term (in late 2004) but was then unable to act upon its promise of providing stability in Iraq at the same time as the political tensions related to the US prison in Guantanamo Bay began to appear. Both films examined here point back to 9/11 and respond to the context of terrorism, war, violence and American political ideology in this period, but in very different ways, as will be made clear through an examination of blood.

**CHRIST'S BLOOD**

In 2004 Mel Gibson's blockbuster *The Passion of the Christ* dramatically extended the filmic depiction of Christ by means of a singular dwelling on blood as it hemorrhages from his tortured and martyred body. Gibson's film, without paying close attention to established Christology (Holderness, 384), follows Jesus Christ through the last twelve hours of his life, from the Garden of Gethsemane to his crucifixion, retracing his steps and teachings through flashbacks in which viewers are reminded of his message and life. *The Passion of the Christ* follows the processes by which Christ came to be crucified, with his suffering being the primary focus of the film. In scene after scene, this is represented with extreme attention through classical cinematic techniques such as close-up and slow motion.

The scourging of Jesus Christ by the Romans is an excellent example among many in the film. In it, Jesus has been captured, taken before the Roman Prefect Pontius Pilate and sentenced to scourging in an effort to satisfy the Jewish priests who have called for his death. In a problematic but not unexpected framing of the scene by Gibson (whose racism and anti-Semitism are widely known), Roman soldiers take Jesus away with instructions to beat severely but not kill him. It is an incredible scene. The scourging itself is over twelve minutes in length, an eternity in filmic time, and it bears only a partial relation to scriptural texts. In this scene, Jesus Christ is tied to a post and two Roman soldiers are instructed to whip him with a variety of instruments, each more sadistic than the previous one, as the camera lingers on Christ's body from this tortuous beating. From simple lashing to the use of instruments with hooks and spikes that penetrate, rip and shred his body, Jesus Christ undergoes the punishment and repeatedly steadies his body while onlookers, including the Roman soldier in charge, turn from relative fascination to disgust as the scourging goes on and on and on in a frenzy of violence. The scene turns on blood, which oozes and sprays from Christ's body to stain the stones of the courtyard as the camera lingers on his violated body, and it ends as Jesus Christ is dragged away. His body, no longer able to support itself, leaves a long streak of blood on the stones of the courtyard. Mary, with the assistance of Mary Magdalene, begins to clean the bloody stones left behind with white cloth given to them by the wife of Pontius Pilate.

Gibson has taken up a particular version of this narrative, which he inherited from a nineteenth-century book, Anna Catherine Emmerich's *The Dolorous Passion of Our Lord Christ*. Thus the film is situated within a mystical tradition of "The Passion" which focuses upon vision and demonstration, on the image rather than the word (Holderness, 397). This is the martyrdom to end all martyrdoms, and audiences responded with profound emotion.

The book (and DVD) *Changed Lives: Miracles of Passion* "documents" eye-witness accounts of supposed miracles derived from having seen the film: "80,000,000 changed lives" it states at the beginning, and the DVD recounts five. It is about "How lives are changed by God through *The Passion of the Christ*," a convert states in the film. This theme is central. In *Changed Lives, The Passion of the Christ* is perceived to function simultaneously as both a medium and as direct experience. God uses the film to reach people; the filmic medium itself, on the other hand, is erased: "It is not like I am in a theatre. It is like watching the real thing" (Eldred, DVD). Viewers participate in the event of the film as if it were real, as blood shifts its status from a presence that invokes horror to one that produces extreme identification, as will be argued below.

This essay suggests that there has been a shift in blood's articulation in recent years, in quantitative and especially qualitative terms. *The Passion of the Christ* demonstrates both elements through the incredible abundance of blood in the film as well as through the manners in which Gibson focuses viewer attention upon it. For example, blood sprays in slow motion from Jesus Christ's body during the scourging, and it leaves a dark trail as he is dragged from the square; again, when Jesus is nailed to the cross at Golgotha, a close-up of his hand shows blood draining from it in a crimson stream. This is blood mobilized for purposes beyond spectacle.

In Gibson's film, blood is articulated to the film's core meanings in ways not seen in the primary spaces of bloodletting in mainstream Hollywood film, the horror and war genres, where spectacle renders the body as image, thus breaking viewer identification with the victim. Conversely, the bloodletting in Gibson's film is meant to bring viewers closer to Christ's body in order to identify with his suffering. This shift is accomplished through the deployment of what film theorist Laura Marks refers to as haptic visuality, which is marked from the conventional cinematic gaze, or optical visuality, through its ability to engage optical, tactile, kinesthetic and proprioceptive functions simultaneously:

> Because haptic visuality draws on other senses, the viewer's body is more obviously involved in the process of seeing than is the case with optical visuality... Haptic images do not invite identification with a figure so much as they encourage a bodily relationship between the viewer and the image. Thus it is less appropriate to speak of the object of a haptic look than to speak of a dynamic subjectivity between looker and image. (Marks, 2–3)

*The Passion of the Christ* exploits precisely such dynamic subjectivity through its use of cinematic techniques that bring viewers so close to Jesus Christ's body as to eliminate the distance required for affective separation. The two bodies are brought into such proximate contiguity as to render them nearly indistinguishable.

The scourging is only one scene among many in *The Passion of the Christ* in which blood is deployed at the affective level in scenes that are extended in time, bringing the film closer to real time. That the film depicts only the last twelve hours of Christ's life brings it even more near, just as the extension of scenes like the scourging, the carrying of the cross to Golgotha and the crucifixion itself—each of which focuses incredible attention not only on Christ's suffering but directly on his blood as it leaks, flows and sprays from his body—forces viewers to participate in this bloodletting that is also a mass.

As Holderness argues, *The Passion of the Christ* operates as something more than, or at least other than, a film. It is also a votive offering, a memorial of the Christian Redemption, and a celebration of the Eucharist. The audience is not invited passively to gaze, nor even actively to watch; but rather voluntarily to participate in a ritual of shared suffering (Holderness, 395). Embodying Matthew chapter 26, verses 26–28, where Jesus tells his disciples to "Take this and eat. This is my body... Take this and drink. This is my blood," viewers are conveyed into the narrative with its foretold death as Jesus offers his body for sacrifice. Aided by sacramental traditions that figuratively consume Christ's body and blood, Gibson closes the space between viewer and figure such that Christ's body and blood become the viewer's own, his suffering ours, seemingly without a medium and in close to real time (i.e., twelve hours in three).

In the years immediately following 9/11, such representation of suffering, loss, mourning and martyrdom, not to mention the suggestion of resurrection, was a powerful trope, especially for American audiences. If 9/11 had stolen actual bodies at the site of mourning, then *The Passion of the Christ* returned the body through the figure of Jesus Christ himself. When translated through sacrifice, these two "red events" could finally meet, with the body and blood of Christ standing in for those "martyred" at the World Trade Center. When it was released at Easter in 2004, *The Passion of the Christ* delivered on the memorial promise of the body. The film provided a site on which to enact memory and encouraged a return to faith at the moment after faith had been turned against America. The original "passio"—from which the passion is taken—means to suffer, to endure, to bear the burden. The filmic Jesus Christ could suffer, endure and bear the burden while viewers could believe that "by his stripes we are healed," thereby bridging the gap between filmic and real event, between the absence and presence of bodies and between the stalled process of mourning and healing of the national body so central to 9/11.

### BOBBY'S BLOOD

Emilio Esteves' film *Bobby* (2006) is a fictional account of the last day of Senator Robert Kennedy's life, June 5, 1968, which focuses upon the narratives of people that were also shot that day at the Ambassador Hotel in Los Angeles, and includes historical footage from the campaign and assassination by disaffected Palestinian-Jordanian immigrant Sirhan Sirhan. Although the film had mixed reviews, its final scene—the point at which the characters' separate narratives intersect—has great relevance to the arguments here. Over five minutes in length, the scene portrays Kennedy's assassination in the kitchen of the hotel, including prolonged representation of the other people that were shot, as well as historical footage from the day and the murder itself.

Estevez has also voiced over the scene, using Robert Kennedy's own speech given at the City Club of Cleveland on April 5, 1968, only two months before. "The Mindless Menace of Violence" was the speech RFK delivered on the day after the assassination of Martin Luther King in Memphis. In many ways, this speech captures the moment, hinging as it did on the civil rights movement and the Vietnam War, while offering a path out of the crisis that was the basis of Kennedy's campaign. It is the coincidence of the assassination and shootings with "The Mindless Menace of Violence" that delivers such, some say melodramatic, impact to the film.

This speech is arguably the best in American history. Delivered at a time of great hope dashed by the assassinations of John F. Kennedy and Martin Luther King, it has resonances that are once again poignant and pointed. It begins: "This is not a day for politics," and continues to describe how violence is destroying America, the foundations upon which the nation is built and the lives of all Americans. With a final verse that implores American citizens to find once again a "common fate" and "common bond" and "to work a little harder to bind up the wounds among us and become in our hearts brothers and countrymen once again" (*Bobby*), the speech stands as a document of possibility in a moment of collective uncertainty and fear. These words, delivered over the scene of Kennedy's own assassination, have a stunning impact. And the scene turns on blood.

As Kennedy and his crush of supporters move from the ballroom to the kitchen of the hotel, the camera follows into the *melée* as he shakes hands with people in the crowd and workers in the kitchen. As this happens, Sirhan Sirhan is seen approaching Kennedy before shooting him, then being overwhelmed by security guards who wrestle the gun from his hands as he continues to fire rounds into the crowd, hitting each of the main characters from the film. The scene takes place in slow motion as each person is being shot and the mayhem continues, seemingly without end, around them. Switching between historical and contemporary film shots and techniques, the scene retains the look and palette of handheld Super 8 film. However, within the muted, faded and overexposed tones of the film, blood returns viewers to the body and its affective layers as the film shifts from optical to haptic visuality.

Through a subtle economy of representation, Estevez demonstrates how the violence of this single act touches people as individuals and citizens. Viewers witness each of the characters being struck by Sirhan's bullets and we hear the scene at times amplified in the din of the kitchen, at other times muted as though in the head of the dying individual. The scene stretches time in slow motion as Robert Kennedy's words from "The Mindless Menace of Violence" ring profoundly. Viewers stand witness as the characters upon which the film is based fall from their injuries, some lives taken and others shattered. The camera lingers on the stunned look in the eyes of victims as each person tries to rationalize what is happening to and around them, as they lie dying quietly, alone, in the chaos that was the historical scene.

And yet, so little actual blood is present that its crimson hues stand out deeply and thickly against the muted palette of the remainder of the scene. Blood is not horror here. Its deep red tones push out from the film and demand singular address and it is in this singularity that the film's blood touches history and the present, our humanity and the violence that shreds it. Viewers do not react by distancing themselves from it. Rather, blood draws them into the scene, emphatically connecting them as witnesses to the violence.

At the same time, the crimson spill of blood connects the filmic event to contemporary events and themes. RFK states in "The Mindless Menace of Violence": "Some look for scapegoats, others look for conspiracies, but this much is clear: violence breeds violence, repression brings retaliation, and only a cleansing of our whole society can remove this sickness from our soul" (*Bobby*). Recent history, and not just for the USA, demonstrates this with too many examples to list, even as Estevez himself takes a political shot at then President Bush and his administration with the words: "Too often we honor swagger and bluster and the wielders of force. Too often we excuse those that are willing to build their own lives on the shattered dreams of other human beings" (*Bobby*). Just as the Kennedys and Martin Luther King represented hope for the future of the nation (and humanity), Estevez calls for a return to hope in a time of cynicism, paranoia, securitization, militarization, war and bloodshed, with RFK reminding contemporary viewers of the potential for political hope and change in difficult times.

As viewers, we are brought from the past into the present through blood as it is articulated to violence and equally to contemporary American politics. We are also returned to the events of 9/11, and not just through references to violence and memory, but to the career of George W. Bush and the search for a presidential signature to mark his legacy. The tagline on the poster for the film is explicit: "He saw wrong and tried to right it. He saw suffering and tried to heal it. He saw war and tried to stop it." This begs to be read as an indictment of the Bush political regime as much as a nostalgic return to history and memory of a simpler time, just as these words seem to suspend the very question they ask as discourse bleeds from one era to another. A final still taken from *Bobby* makes this point explicitly, asking who will lead America out of the morass of the mindless menace of violence. Written on the kitchen wall of the Ambassador hotel because of an act of generosity (involving baseball tickets) from a kitchen worker to a chef, the words "The Once and Future King" are seen in close-up in stark black on white, spattered in blood after the shooting. If hope for the future has been dashed in the film, then the words ask who will be the future king when the present one is responsible for the violence. Where will America turn?

Of course, after the election of Barack Obama as President of the United States in 2008, many believed that a return to the Kennedy era had occurred and that hope had been restored; this hope seems less prevalent today. Yet in 2006, *Bobby* held a prescience of better times to come. As political and economic crises remain the landmarks of American politics at the end of the first term of the Obama presidency, hope remains—and it remains uncertain.

## CONCLUSION

If the "red events" that have been considered here establish ground for bleeding discourse, to suggest that blood's encoding is differentially mobilized in visual culture, then this research only touches upon a complex network of blood relations. Blood cultures such as the one here articulated to the "red event" of 9/11, when a material and symbolic body was discursively and materially constructed, and then tortured, martyred, killed and sacrificed in popular culture forms in the years since, appear at moments of cultural tension. As a recurrent trope of crisis, blood is inscribed and re-inscribed at such moments. Blood pressures build and are released as a matter of survival for social bodies as for individual bodies. In this way "red events" mark life, everyday. In Arturo Aldama's words:

> The violent act, the violent event, is a bodily occurrence. It is the sharp flash against flesh, and it is the blood-colored response... The spilling of human blood is the fact of violence, and in those instances where it is not spilled, it nevertheless remains as the flow of life barely kept from the blows or beating by the thinness of human skin. Because our lives are metered in the flow of blood at every moment, its appearance, its color, accompany attacks on our lives. Violence, act and event, is red... Violence is not apart from blood, but rather the hot articulation of it. It is a blood act; it is a red event. (Aldama and Arteaga, vii)

Thinking blood evokes the body and the senses. What is seen is the bloody cinematic spectacle, the stain of violence, the gentle rocking of clear plastic bags being filled for donation, the needle's sting and the shooting of crimson into a vacuum receptacle, its microscopic separations beneath the lens of forensics and crime detection. Blood is affective, producing a visceral response that is physiological, social and cultural simultaneously, the point at which the biological and the social intersect. Red seizes the body and commands response, evoking what Lauren Berlant refers to as a "feeling politics" (Berlant, 133) where blood returns the subject to a sensory system and affect propels it toward sociality.

As blood flows from one media discourse to the next, it invokes familiar and wide-ranging tropes: life, family, citizenship, nation, sacrifice, bodily cycles, kinship, courage, death, etc. If the body is data, then blood is code that is written and rewritten through an informational economy (Poster, 2006) that contains multiple and, at times, competing nodes. Being at the nexus of important theoretical, historical and cultural debates, blood cultures engage the body in a new social contract. The term used here, bleeding discourse, attempts to capture the manners in which blood's qualities of leaking, flowing and transfusing permeate or stain discourse, refusing to remain disciplined or contained within the body.

Of course, the spilling of blood through violence is not new; however, the manners in which blood today enters visual culture mark a transformation that significantly differentiates it from pre-millennial concepts. We are today saturated by the blood of recent "red events": wars in Iraq and Afghanistan; in video games like Bioshock; ubiquitously in films; through deepening and rigidifying notions of family structure; in violence against women and queers; through security measures associated with "tainted" blood; in television's disciplinary dramas such as *Law and Order*, CSI, and more recently, *Dexter* and *True Blood*; even when advertising meets social consciousness in the recent "Red" AIDS campaign. But if bleeding discourse has reached a saturation point in recent years, and this is doubtful, then it is not simply a quantitative measure that will reveal its significance; rather, it is blood's qualitative allusions and denotations that propel further investigation.

To this end the current essay attempts to locate and position blood's articulation to discourse in the contemporary period through readings of several representations drawn from visual culture. By examining blood through the methods outlined here, a useful approach to academic study emerges. Readers will have noted that this essay does not examine the events of 9/11, *The Passion of the Christ* or *Bobby* as objects in their totality. Neither is it claimed that academic study can "know" a film, a text, or any other type of object in this way. The challenge is to locate methodologies capable of accounting for any object's resistance to analysis, for its incompleteness and its excess, for its refusal to finally be sensible and known. Here, a blood line has been identified and drawn through these "red events", without making claims to knowledge about the much broader fields evoked by these objects.

This is not to state, however, that "sense" cannot be made of objects of study. In this instance, blood has been positioned as a singularity running through several forms and moments. In its singularity (Agamben, 1993), that is, in its "moment-ness"—correct in this moment but perhaps not in the next, able to be sensible, for now—a powerful methodological trope is revealed. Through such a focus on singularity, an approach that captures the actually existing ontological status of objects in their incompleteness and excess, their status as fragmented and transitory—that is, in their singularity—is emphasized. From this point, the relations of singularities can be drawn to reveal significant fields of investigation, and potential new objects, as well as approaches suitable to them.

Blood is interesting for precisely the manners in which it traverses—bleeds, if you will—across forms, genres, boundaries and limits. *The Passion of the Christ* and *Bobby* are interesting in this sense as well. Each of these films articulates blood to differentiated effect when compared to other forms of blood representation to reveal a field, defined by blood relations, that traverses and inflects conventional thinking about blood in multiple media discourses and forms. This framing of blood, therefore, encourages research that challenges the taken-for-granted status of many objects of academic study and approaches used to understand them, a challenge that must be met by academic approaches today.

**NOTES**

1    See Arturo Aldama and Alfred Arteaga (eds.), *Violence and the Body: Race, Gender, and the State* for the idea of the "red event." It is used here to refer to any moment in which the spilling of blood occurs to representational/ discursive effect. A red event may include single elements, such as when a person documents a bleeding nose with a photograph or blog entry, or, as is the case here, when a field of single events accumulates into a larger discursive field.

2    In the period immediately following 9/11 these terms were pervasive in media coverage of the events across news organizations.

3    For a full listing of the interdictions of the American Red Cross see their web site at http://redcross.org.

**REFERENCES**

"9/11 by the Numbers." *New York Magazine.* http://nymag.com/news/articles/wtc/1year/numbers (February 2009).

Agamben, Giorgio. 1998. *Homo Sacer: Sovereign Power and Bare Life,* trans. Daniel Heller-Roazen. Stanford: Stanford University Press.

——. 1993. *The Coming Community.* Minneapolis: University of Minnesota Press.

Aldama, Arturo and Alfred Arteaga (eds.). 2003. *Violence and the Body: Race, Gender, and the State.* Bloomington and Indianapolis: Indiana University Press.

Anderson, Mark. 2007. *Cowboy Imperialism and Hollywood Film.* New York: Peter Lang.

Berlant, Lauren. 2001. "Love: A Queer Feeling." Pp. 432–51 in Tim Dean and Christopher Lane (eds.), *Homosexuality and Psychoanalysis.* Chicago: University of Chicago Press.

*Bobby.* 2006. Directed by Emilio Estevez. MGM.

Conrad, Lawrence, Michael Neve, Vivian Nutton, Roy Porter and Andrew Wear. 1995. *The Western Medical Tradition, 800 BC to AD 1800.* Cambridge: Cambridge University Press.

Davis, Natalie Zemon. 1975. *Society and Culture in Early Modern France: Eight Essays.* Stanford: Stanford University Press.

Eldred, Jody. 2004. *Changed Lives: Miracles of the Passion.* Wilmington, CA: Harvest Press.

Holderness, Graham. 2005. "Animated Icons: Narrative and Liturgy in *The Passion of the Christ.*" *Literature and Theology* 19, no. 4: 384–401.

Marks, Laura. 2000. *The Skin of the Film: Intercultural Cinema, Embodiment, and the Senses.* Durham and London: Duke University Press.

Ojito, Mirta. "Untitled," *New York Times* (September 13, 2001): A11.

White House. 2001. "Press Release" (President George W. Bush). http://www.whitehouse.gov/news/releases/2001/20010912-12.html

**PART IV**

# NEGOTIATING
# PRIVATE REALM(S)

Is life not a hundred times too short
for us to stifle ourselves?
—FRIEDRICH NIETZSCHE,
FROM *Beyond Good and Evil* (1886)

# "Hours Continuing Long" as Whitman's Rewriting of Shakespeare's Sonnet 29[1]

NILS CLAUSSON

"Poetry is made out of other poems." —NORTHROP FRYE

"Any poem is an inter-poem, and any reading of a poem is an inter-reading. A poem is not writing, but *rewriting*, and though a strong poem is a fresh start, such a start is a starting again."—HAROLD BLOOM

When Horace Traubel asked Walt Whitman if Keats' poetry "suggest[ed] the Greek" to him, Whitman replied:

> Oh, no; Shakespeare's sonnets, not the Greek. You know, the sonnets are Keats and more—all Keats was, then a vast sum added. For superb finish, style, beauty, I know of nothing in all literature to come up to [Shakespeare's] sonnets. They have been a great worry to the fellows, and to me, too—a puzzle, the sonnets being of one character, the plays of another.[2]

This odd preference for Shakespeare's sonnets rather than the plays at first seems inconsistent with Whitman's poetics. Indeed, as the bardic voice of American individuality, expansiveness and freedom, Whitman surely embodies everything in poetry that is antithetical to the tight, restrictive form of the sonnet. Although he did write "O Captain! My Captain!"— the most popular of his poems during his lifetime—in the ballad measure common in many folk songs of his day, Whitman rejected most traditional metrical forms, and of all poetic forms the sonnet is the least likely to be mentioned in the same breath as the name Whitman. It seems impossible to imagine him saying, with Wordsworth, that "'twas pastime to be bound/Within the Sonnet's scanty plot of ground."³ Indeed, it is almost as difficult to imagine Whitman writing a sonnet as to imagine him composing *Leaves of Grass* in heroic couplets.

And yet write sonnets he did, at least of a sort. On the back of a separate sheet of the title poem of the "Live Oak with Moss" series, he referred to this sequence of twelve poems, which were later incorporated into the "Calamus" poems in *Leaves of Grass*, as "A Cluster of Poems, Sonnets, expressing the thoughts, pictures, aspirations."⁴ Since they obviously are not sonnets in the strict definition of that term, why did Whitman call them sonnets? What attractions did the sonnet form hold for him?

Critics have been almost unanimously silent on these questions. Alan Helms detects an echo of Shakespeare's Sonnet 121 ("'Tis better to be vile than vile esteemed") in the eighth poem in the series, "Hours Continuing Long." And in his biography of Whitman, Justin Kaplan describes the series of "Calamus" poems as "a narrative sequence, like Shakespeare's [sonnets], that dramatizes—not necessarily *recounts*— a passionate attachment to a younger man."⁵ But for both Helms and Kaplan, the similarities between Shakespeare's sonnets and the "Calamus" poems are confined to the similar subject matter (the male speakers' relationships with younger men) rather than to similarities in form.

I am convinced that, at least in "Hours Continuing Long," Whitman was doing more than echoing Sonnet 121 or drawing a general parallel between his sequence of poems about male relationships and Shakespeare's sonnets addressed to a beautiful youth. There is substantial textual evidence to suggest that in composing "Hours Continuing Long," Whitman clearly modeled both the form and the content of his "sonnet" on Shakespeare's Sonnet 29 ("When in disgrace with fortune and men's eyes"). While it is obviously not a prototypical sonnet whose form has been inexplicably overlooked by critics, "Hours Continuing

Long" is certainly a reply to Shakespeare's sonnet and a transformation of the traditional sonnet into a new form.

Whitman wrote his poem as a deliberate response to Shakespeare's antecedent poem, and he expected his readers to be aware not only of the similarities between the two poems (enforced by numerous verbal echoes and structural parallels) but also—and more importantly—of the significant differences. But, of course, we cannot be aware of the deliberately deviant form of Whitman's "sonnet" unless we read it in the context of conventional sonnets, and specifically of Shakespeare's Sonnet 29. The intertextual relationships between Whitman's "sonnet" and Shakespeare's Sonnet 29 suggest that Whitman is a more "traditional" poet than is usually acknowledged, though certainly not in the pejorative sense of that term.

In an anonymous interview in 1879, Whitman said, "As we are a new nation with almost a new geography, and a new spirit, the expression of them will have to be new. In form, in combination we shall take the same old font of type, but what we set up will never have been set up before. It will be in the same old font that Homer and Shakespeare used, but our use will be new."[6] Although this remark can, and usually is, taken as a manifesto of the new American poetic that Whitman advocated and embodied, it certainly does not imply a complete break with tradition. Whitman's claim that the expression of the American spirit will be new but the form will be "the same old font that Homer and Shakespeare used" could be read as an anticipation of T.S. Eliot's doctrine of the relationship between tradition and the individual talent. That relationship, or at least Whitman's idea of it, is illustrated by the complex relationship between "Hours Continuing Long" and the Shakespearean poem it both imitates and re-forms.[7]

Whitman does more than echo Sonnet 29; he models his own poem on its structure. Sonnet 29 is, in one important way, closer to the structure of the Italian than the English sonnet: it consists of two parts, an octave in which the speaker describes an "outcast state" of mind very similar to that of Whitman's and a sestet in which he is rescued from "these thoughts" by "remember[ing]" the "sweet love" of the beautiful young man to whom the sonnet is addressed. "Hours Continuing Long" consists of twelve lines, divided into two parts of six lines each: the first six and a half lines, which describe Whitman's forsaken state occasioned by a failed relationship, resemble the octave of a traditional sonnet; and the next five and a half lines, consisting of a series of questions in which Whitman wonders whether there are "other men" like him, or even "one other like him," are the counterpart of the sestet. Note that the "turn" comes not at the end of the sixth line but in the seventh, after the dash.

Thus the division between the two parts retains the same imbalance—six and a half lines vs. five and a half—characteristic of the Petrarchan sonnet. Whitman's "sonnet," then, follows the bi-partite structure of the Italian sonnet, and it is that structure that Whitman is borrowing, not such external markers of the form as a specific number of lines or a particular rhyme scheme. Even unconventional sonnets, whatever their rhyme scheme or number of lines, retain this essential structural feature of the form, which is why an unrhymed sonnet is conceivable but an unrhymed 14-line poem with no equivalent of the sonnet's "turn" is just a 14-line poem and calling it a sonnet would serve no critical purpose.

But it is not just the bi-partite sonnet form (two asymmetrical parts) and the situation of a male speaker expressing his love for a man that "Hours Continuing Long" shares with Sonnet 29. Whitman's "sonnet" contains numerous verbal echoes of Shakespeare's: so many, in fact, that they cannot be accidental. Here are the two poems:

### XXIX

When in disgrace with fortune and men's eyes,
I all alone beweep my outcast state,
And trouble deaf heav'n with my bootless cries,
And look upon myself and curse my fate,
Wishing me like to one more rich in hope,
Featured like him, like him with friends possessed,
Desiring this man's art, and that man's scope,
With what I most enjoy contented least;
Yet in these thoughts myself almost despising,
Haply I think on thee, and then my state,
Like to the lark at break of day arising
From sullen earth, sings hymns at heaven's gate;
    For thy sweet love rememb'red such wealth brings
    That then I scorn to change my state with kings.[8]

**HOURS CONTINUING LONG**

Hours continuing long, sore and heavy-hearted,
Hours of the dusk, when I withdraw to a lonesome
    and unfrequented spot, seating myself, leaning
    my face in my hands;
Hours sleepless, deep in the night, when I go forth,
    speeding swiftly the country roads, or through
    the city streets, or pacing miles and miles, stifling
    plaintive cries;
Hours discouraged, distracted—for the one I cannot
    content myself without, soon I saw him content
    himself without me;
Hours when I am forgotten, (O weeks and months are
    passing, but I believe I am never to forget!)
Sullen and suffering hours! (I am ashamed—but it is
    useless—I am what I am;)
Hours of my torment—I wonder if other men ever
    have the like, out of the like feelings?
Is there even one other like me—distracted—his
    friend, his lover, lost to him?
Is he too as I am now? Does he still rise in the
    morning, dejected, thinking who is lost to him?
    and at night, awaking, think who is lost?
Does he too harbor his friendship silent and endless?
    harbor his anguish and passion?
Does some stray reminder, or the casual mention of a
    name, bring the fit back upon him, taciturn and
    deprest?
Does he see himself reflected in me? In these hours,
    does he see the face of his hours reflected?[9]

The parallels are striking. The long "when" clause that governs Shakespeare's octave is paralleled by Whitman's two "when" clauses: "when I withdraw..." and "when I go forth... ." Whitman's "plaintive cries" echo "Shakespeare's "bootless cries," with the word "cries" appearing at the end of line three of both poems. In the second line of his poem, Whitman "withdraw[s]" to a "*lonesome* and unfrequented spot," and Shakespeare's speaker (also in the second line) "all *alone* beweep[s]" his "outcast fate." Whitman says that he is "discouraged, distracted," for the man that he "cannot *content* [him]self without" can now "*content* himself without" Whitman; Shakespeare's speaker says that with what he does "most enjoy" he is "*contented* least." Whitman refers to the "Sullen and suffering hours" when he is "*forgotten*"; Shakespeare's speaker concludes the poem with a description of the joy arising from his friend's "sweet love *remembered*." In addition, Whitman echoes Shakespeare's choice of the world "sullen." Shakespeare's lark "arising/From *sullen* earth sings hymns at heaven's gate"; the "discouraged" Whitman describes himself as "*Sullen* and suffering." There is also the parallel use of the words "thinking" and "think." Shakespeare's speaker says, "Haply I *think* on thee," and Whitman wonders if there is a double of himself, suffering similarly: "Does he still rise in the morning, dejected, *thinking* who is lost to him? and at night, awaking, *think* who is lost?" Whitman's choice of the words "rise," "morning," and "awaking" were likely suggested by Shakespeare's line, "Like to the lark at break of day arising." And finally, Shakespeare's speaker confesses that he has reached the point of "almost despising" himself, while Whitman says he is "ashamed" of himself—not a verbal echo but a synonym used to describe a similar psychological state.

When these numerous verbal echoes are considered along with the similar situations of the two speakers and the bi-partite structure of the two poems, the only reasonable conclusion to draw is that Whitman is not simply alluding to Shakespeare's Sonnet 29 but is quite deliberately modeling his poem on one of Shakespeare's most popular and frequently reprinted sonnets—one that he can safely assume many of his readers would be familiar with.

An obvious reason for Whitman's imitation of Sonnet 29 is that Shakespeare's famous poem about a man addressing a beautiful youth provides a literary precedent, and hence a justification, for the subject matter of his later poem. But in calling attention to these echoes and parallels, it is important to recognize that Whitman is not merely imitating Shakespeare's poem to legitimize his own: he is responding to it and rewriting it by setting up a contrast between his new "sonnet" and Shakespeare's old one. Whitman's deliberate echoes of Sonnet 29 create expectations in the reader about the direction the poem will take—expectations that the poem then significantly fails to fulfill.

The first thing to notice is that Whitman, in contrast to Shakespeare, reverses the usual structure of the Renaissance Italian sonnet and the English sonnets written in imitation of it. A frequent pattern of the form is to pose in the octave a problem or a question (or questions), which the sestet then resolves or answers. This pattern provides a resolution to the speaker's thoughts, and thus tends towards a formal closure that offers assurance and hope. Sonnet 29 clearly follows this well-established pattern. In contrast, Whitman moves from a description of his suffering to a series of questions that he cannot answer and thus his "sonnet" lacks the closure that the traditional form leads the reader to expect. (In Robert Frost's sonnet "Design," the famous last line—"If design govern in a thing so small"—similarly deviates from the form's expected closure, leaving the reader in a state of unresolved uncertainty.)

According to Paul Fussell:

> The standard way of constructing a Petrarchan sonnet is to project the subject in the first quatrain; to develop or complicate it in the second; then to execute, at the beginning of the sestet, the turn which will open up for solution the problem advanced by the octave, or which will ease the load of idea or emotion borne by the octave, or which will release the pressure accumulated in the octave. The octave and the sestet conduct actions which are analogous to the actions of inhaling and exhaling, or of contraction and release in the muscular system. The one builds up the pressure, the other releases it; and the turn is the dramatic and climactic center of the poem, the place where the intellectual or emotional method of release first becomes clear and possible. From line 9 it is usually plain sailing down to the end of the sestet and the resolution of the experience.[10]

The first half of "Hours Continuing Long" certainly builds up the pressure, but the second half, far from providing a resolution or release, as happens in Sonnet 29, continues the same repetitive structure as the first half, building up even more pressure. The "octave" contains six lines that begin with "Hours"; the sestet is similarly repetitive in its syntactic structure:

Is there even one other like me… ?
Is he too as I am now?
Does he too harbor his friendship silent and restless?
Does some stray reminder… ?
Does he see himself reflected in me? (ll. 8–12)

The most common pattern of the Petrarchan sonnet follows an emotional arc from problem to solution, or from question to answer, or (as in Shakespeare) from dejection to hope. The key image in Sonnet 29 is the lark rising from the sullen earth, soaring towards heaven's gate, an image that is the objective correlative of the speaker's soaring spirit when he remembers the young man. The movement of the poem is linear, in an ascending line from earth to the skies, the soaring flight of the lark figuring the emotional movement of the poem. In contrast, the repetitive pattern of Whitman's poem, as the title implies, suggests that the speaker is trapped in a static state of mind that he cannot break out of. The repetition of "hours" in the last two lines, echoing the first six lines, implies that Whitman—unlike Shakespeare's speaker—has not progressed beyond the state of "sullenness and suffering" described in the first six and a half lines. All he can do is imagine someone suffering like himself, repeating his sullen thoughts.

The reason that Whitman deviates from the conventional, expected pattern of the sonnet is that his poem, as the series of unanswered questions shows, does not express the confidence, assurance and hope that we find in Shakespeare's Sonnet 29.[11] The seven questions that make up the "sestet" of this re-formed sonnet are all questions for which Whitman has no answers. The hopelessness he expresses in the first half of the poem recalls a famous Renaissance sonnet that is part of the intertextual grid against which Whitman invites us to read his re-formed sonnet, namely Michael Drayton's "Since there's no help, come let us kiss and part." The octave of Drayton's famous poem suggests that the love affair is irretrievably over, and that there is no hope of the lovers reviving their former feelings for one another. But the sestet holds out the hope that the woman addressed by the speaker, "when all have given [Love] over,/From death to life … mightst him yet recover."[12] A similar possibility in Whitman's poem is strongly suggested by the depth of despair and hopelessness described in the first six and a half lines, paralleling the feelings of Drayton's speaker, but Whitman's sestet takes a different, unexpected "turn." Instead of imagining a "recovery" of his relationship with his beloved, as Drayton does, taking comfort from a remembrance of the beloved (as Shakespeare's speaker does), Whitman wonders, as the last six lines shift the focus from the beloved to an imagined other, if there is any other man in his "outcast state," a double of Whitman. Consolation, if there is to be any, will come not from remembering the lover described in the octave, but from imagining the possibility of there being another man as dejected as himself, a brother in sullenness and suffering.

Biographical criticism of the poem identifies the young man as a young Irish stage driver named Fred Vaughan, with whom it is believed Whitman had an intense relationship in the late 1850s. It is also speculated that Vaughn may have been the inspiration for the sequence of twelve homoerotic love poems that Whitman called "Live Oak, with Moss," poems that would later become part of the "Calamus" cluster in *Leaves of Grass*.[13] If read biographically, these twelve "sonnet-like love poems"[14] record Whitman's dejection and despair over his failed relationship with Vaughn, who married and thereafter kept at best a tenuous relationship with Whitman. The failure of the relationship with Vaughn was doubtless a traumatic event for Whitman and may very well have occasioned the "Live Oak, with Moss" series. But there is no need to assume that "Hours Continuing Long" reflects Whitman's biography. It is, after all, a poem, not a journal entry. And its poetic status is in part conferred by its relationship to the sonnet form and specifically to Shakespeare's Sonnet 29.

If the poem is read in terms of the conventions of the sonnet, its biographical elements take on a new significance. One reason that Whitman "turns" in the sestet to an imagined double of himself instead of anticipating a reunion with the beloved is that he realizes that there is little likelihood that his love for this man will be requited. The most likely reason is not that the man has broken off the relationship and chosen someone else (as Vaughn did), but that the man does not even know of the speaker's love for him, since the speaker has not declared it to him. Once the poem is taken out of the original "Live Oak with Moss" series and placed in the "Calamus" cluster, there is nothing in the first six lines to definitively indicate that the speaker's love for the man was ever reciprocated.

Indeed, the echoes of Sonnet 29 suggest that his feelings are *not* reciprocated. A more likely scenario is that the beloved man knows nothing of the speaker's feelings for him. This does not mean, of course, that there is no biographical element in the poem at all—only that Whitman has reconstructed his biography to suit the rhetorical needs of the poem. It is the speaker's shame (and Whitman's), specifically mentioned in the poem ("I am ashamed"), which has prevented him from declaring his love, and so he wonders if there are countless other men in the same situation as him: men who, like him, are ashamed and lack the courage to declare, "I am what I am" (as Shakespeare's speaker does in Sonnet 121). He is not imagining men who have loved and lost, but men who have never had the courage to declare, "I am what I am."

My proposal to read "Hours Continuing Long" as a modified sonnet that responds to Shakespeare's Sonnet 29 gains additional support when we realize that this is not the only Whitman poem that both borrows the conventions of the sonnet form and echoes a particular sonnet. "When I Heard the Learn'd Astronomer," like a conventional sonnet, sets up in the first four lines (all of which begin with "When") a contrast between the analytic, mathematical study of the heavens and (in the last four lines) an alternative way of viewing and experiencing the awe of the cosmos.

Not only does this poem borrow the bipartite form of the conventional sonnet, it specifically echoes the form and language of Keats' famous sonnet "On First Looking into Chapman's Homer," which sets up a contrast between Keats before he read Chapman's translation of Homer and Keats after that transforming experience. Just as Keats goes from the octave's imagery of familiar real-estate, worldly principalities and travel around the Mediterranean to images of discovery—a new planet and a new ocean—Whitman takes us from the astronomer's analytic world of "proofs," "figures," "charts and diagrams," and precise mathematical measurement to a world that cannot be added, divided or measured. Not only does an astronomer appear in both poems, but Whitman's response to the starry heavens parallels the response of Balboa's men to the sight of the Pacific Ocean, even down to the repetition of the words "looked" and "silent" in the last two lines of both poems:

> —and all his men
> *Look'd* at each other with a wild surmise—
> *Silent*, upon a peak in Darien.[15]

Whitman's poem ends:

> In the mystical moist night-air and from time to time,
> *Look'd* up in perfect *silence* at the stars.[16]

Although "When I Heard the Learn'd Astronomer" is not a sonnet, the parallels with Keats' famous sonnet are, I would argue, relevant to our appreciation of the poem's form and meaning. Reading it *as* a re-formed sonnet makes us realize just how unexpectedly conventional and traditional Whitman's poem in fact is, as well as how much its originality depends on its deliberate deviance from a well-established generic form.

"[A] text is at its most informative," says Terry Eagleton, "when it deviates unpredictably from one of its codes, creating effects which stand out against this uniform background."[17] It is certainly significant that the experience Whitman records in the last line is expressed, unexpectedly, in a deviant line of regular iambic pentameter: "Look'd up in perfect silence at the stars." Paul Fussell anticipated Eagleton's point in *Poetic Meter and Poetic Form*: "Many free-verse poems," he observes, "establish a non- or anti-metrical verbal continuum as a grid against which occasional metrical moments are perceived as especially forceful."[18] As an example of this poetic practice, he cites "When I Heard the Learn'd Astronomer," which, he says, "devotes seven lines to establishing a loose 'sincere' quasi-prosaic grid as a field against which the final line of iambic pentameter emerges with special emphasis reinforcing the irony."[19] But it is not just the free-verse of the poem that provides an irregular metrical grid against which the final line of regular iambic pentameter emerges with special emphasis; it is also the regularity of the traditional sonnet, familiar to poet and reader alike, that provides a formal grid against which Whitman's deviations from the expected pattern, and particularly the contrast with Shakespeare's Sonnet 29, emerge with special emphasis.

The relationship of "Hours Continuing Long" to the sonnet form and to Shakespeare's Sonnet 29 is complex. Modifying the form of the traditional sonnet enabled Whitman to participate in a major literary tradition, but by alluding specifically to Shakespeare's Sonnet 29, he could also contrast his own "silence" with Shakespeare's explicit representation of a positive relationship between men. And while the sonnet form provided Whitman with a precedent for writing about his own experience, it also enabled him, to some extent, to depersonalize it and hence to move from the personal to the social and the political.

The shift from the friend who has forsaken him to the imagined double of himself suggests that this poem is not only an expression of Whitman's personal situation—the usual subject matter of a love sonnet—but also a political meditation on the absence of a community of similar men who experience the same feelings as Whitman does. This shift from the psychological to the social is the main way in which Whitman's poem deviates from the subject matter of both the Petrarchan love sonnet and Shakespeare's Sonnet 29. Whereas the traditional love sonnet is personal and psychological, Whitman's reformed sonnet has a social dimension absent from the conventional love sonnet. In order to make his "Sullen and suffering hours" bearable, Whitman tries to imagine another "outcast" man who is also "Sullen and suffering" like himself—and suffering for the same reason.

The contrast between the sestet of Shakespeare's sonnet and the last · five and a half lines of Whitman's poem now becomes clear: For Shakespeare's speaker the remembered love of the youth is sufficient to lift his spirits, like the lark arising from sullen earth. But for Whitman, the remembered love of his friend—"I believe I am never to forget!"—can provide no such benefit. What ultimately troubles Whitman, however, is not that he has lost his friend but that he has to "harbor his friendship *silent*," just as he imagines his double doing. The unacceptability of that silence, rather than the taboo on writing about a same-sex relationship, likely explains his decision to exclude the poem from later editions of *Leaves of Grass*.

Whitman's confession of silence and shame, an acknowledgement of political impotence, later became inconsistent with the political aims he wanted the "Calamus" poems to serve. "Hours Continuing Long" was simply too autobiographical and confessional. In the mid-nineteenth century, it was widely believed that Shakespeare's sonnets, like Petrarch's and Dante's, were autobiographical, and that the sonnet (despite the political sonnets of Milton and Shelley) was primarily a form of self-expression. Wordsworth, in his famous sonnet beginning

"Scorn not the sonnet," defends the form on the grounds that "with this Key/Shakespeare unlocked his heart."[20]

But Whitman wanted to do more than unlock his heart. By 1876, Whitman explicitly saw the "Calamus" poems as political poems:

> [I]mportant as they are in my purpose as emotional expressions for humanity, the special meaning of the *Calamus* cluster of Leaves of Grass ... mainly resides in its Political significance. In my opinion it is by a fervent, accepted development of comradeship, the beautiful and sane affection of man for man, latent in all the young fellows, North and South, East and West—it is by this, I say, and by what goes directly and indirectly along with it, that the United States of the future, (I cannot too often repeat,) are to be most effec-tually welded together, anneal'd into a Living Union.[21]

In writing about a same-sex relationship in "Hours Continuing Long," Whitman was writing about a subject for which there was no precedent or model in American literature. And since he lacked an American precedent, it is hardly surprising that he should have turned to a European one. Nor is it surprising that he should turn to one of the few literary models that he could count on many of his readers being familiar with, Shakespeare's Sonnet 29. The Shakespearean model of a sonnet addressed to a beautiful youth might to some extent provide a literary precedent that would legitimize the taboo subject matter of Whitman's poem, but Whitman did not just want to write about his own private experience, and thus the conventional love sonnet, as he inherited it, was unsuitable for his purpose.

The inadequacy of the form for his purpose is reflected in his deci-sion to re-form it from a predominantly autobiographical form into a vehicle through which he could express not only his own sullenness and suffering, but also—and more importantly—his political pro-test against having to suffer, like countless others, in silence. But that protest was, at best, tepid in "Hours Continuing Long"—most of the poetry is in the sullen suffering. So when he eventually came to value the "Calamus" poems primarily for their "Political significance," it is understandable why he removed "Hours Continuing Long" from later editions of *Leaves of Grass*: the reason was not so much that its autobiographical content was too explicitly sexual but that its merely personal "plaintive cries," too reminiscent of Shakespeare's "bootless cries," were insufficiently political.

**NOTES**

1 This chapter was originally published in the *Walt Whitman Quarterly Review*, Vol. 26, No. 3 (Winter 2009), 131–142. Reprinted with permission.

2 Joel Myerson (ed.), *Whitman in His Own Time: A Biographical Chronicle of His Life, Drawn from Recollections, Memoirs, and Interviews by Friends and Associates* (Iowa City: University of Iowa Press, 1991), 234.

3 William Wordsworth, "Nuns Fret Not." In Jonathan and Jessica Wordsworth (eds.), *The New Penguin Book of Romantic Poetry* (London: Penguin Books, 2003).

4 Quoted in Alan Helms, "Whitman's 'Live Oak with Moss.'" In Robert K. Martin (ed.), *The Continuing Presence of Walt Whitman: The Life after the Life* (Iowa City: University of Iowa Press, 1992), 186.

5 Justin Kaplan, *Walt Whitman: A Life* (New York: Simon and Schuster, 1980), 236.

6 Myerson, *Whitman in His Own Time*, 15.

7 Our too-rigid definition of the sonnet form has also contributed to our failure to read "Hours Continuing Long" in the context of the sonnet form and specifically Shakespeare's sonnets. In spite of what we were taught in high-school English classes, and notwithstanding the definitions of it in countless glossaries of literary terms, the sonnet is not as restrictive a form as is usually supposed, which partly explains its power to endure. Although the prototypical form of the sonnet consists of fourteen lines arranged in a predetermined pattern of rhyme schemes and groupings of lines (octave and sestet, four quatrains and a concluding couplet), not all sonnets contain fourteen lines (including some of Shakespeare's) and there are many examples of modern unrhymed sonnets. Hopkins experimented with a shortened form of the sonnet he called "curtal sonnets," as well as with 18- and 20-line "sonnets." Robert Hayden's great unrhymed sonnet "Frederick Douglass," composed in the tradition of the political sonnets of Milton and Shelley, reverses the division of the traditional sonnet, devoting only six lines to the "octave" and eight to what in a conventional sonnet would be the sestet, the turn coming at the end of line six. And in Sandra Gilbert's satirical, anti-Petrarchan "Sonnet: The Ladies' Home Journal," there are just two rhymes (including a Shakespearean couplet at the end), and a "turn" that comes unconventionally in the middle of line 11. Genres survive through adaptation, and the sonnet has proved to be perennially adaptive.

8   William Shakespeare, "Sonnet 29." Pp. 27–28 in Stephen Booth (ed.), *Shakespeare's Sonnets* (New Haven: Yale University Press, 1977.

9   Walt Whitman, "Hours Continuing Long." In *Leaves of Grass: Authoritative Texts, Prefaces, Whitman on His Art, Criticism* (New York: W.W. Norton, 1973), 596–97.

10  Paul Fussell, *Poetic Meter and Poetic Form*, rev. ed. (New York: Random House: 1979), 116.

11  Helms sees a similar contrast between "Hours Continuing Long" and Sonnet 121: "At the heart of this poem, Shakespeare echoes Sonnet 121 ("I am that I am") in which Shakespeare is "vile esteemed" by those who "count bad what I think good." But Shakespeare's self-definition is affirmative and defiant in the face of such judgment, whereas in Whitman the judgment combines with his pain at being abandoned in a way that defeats him" (190).

12  Michael Drayton, "Since There's No Help, Come Let Us Kiss and Part." In M.H. Abrams et al. (eds.), *The Norton Anthology of English Literature*, vol. 1, 5th ed. (New York: W.W. Norton, 1979), 993.

13  See Charley Shivley, *Calamus Lovers: Walt Whitman's Working Class Camerados* (San Francisco: Gay Sunshine Press, 1989).

14  Ed Folsom and Kenneth M. Price, *Re-Scripting Walt Whitman: An Introduction to His Life and Work* (Oxford: Blackwell, 2005), 62.

15  John Keats, "On First Looking into Chapman's Homer." In John Stillinger (ed.), *Complete Poems* (Cambridge, MA: Harvard University Press, 1982), 34.

16  Walt Whitman, "When I Heard the Learn'd Astronomer." In *Leaves of Grass: Authoritative Texts, Prefaces, Whitman on His Art, Criticism* (New York: W.W. Norton, 1973), 271.

17  Terry Eagleton, *How to Read a Poem* (Oxford: Blackwell, 2007), 55.

18  Fussell, *Poetic Meter and Poetic Form*, 84.

19  Ibid.

20  William Wordsworth, "Scorn Not the Sonnet." In Jared Curtis (ed.), *Last Poems, 1821–1850* (Ithaca, NY: Cornell University Press, 1999), 82.

21  Walt Whitman, "Preface," *Leaves of Grass* [1876]. In Sculley Bradley and Harold W. Blodgett (eds.), *Leaves of Grass: Authoritative Texts, Prefaces, Whitman on His Art, Criticism* (New York: W.W. Norton, 1973), 747.

# *Red Rover* Revisited: The Making of a Lesbian Mystery Novel

LIZ BUGG

Standing at the front of this classroom feels very strange. In September of 1967 I was in this space for the first time, but I was sitting somewhere out there, an apprehensive 17-year-old, attending her first English 100 class. It was in that course where I was introduced to the escapades of Joseph Andrews, and it was during that course that I fell in love with *King Lear*. In fact, I still have the *Lear* essay I wrote. At the time, I was naive enough and pretentious enough to end the paper by butchering The Bard and his metre. Here is what I said. Imagine for a moment that I'm Kent:

> [H]e hates him much
> That would upon the rack of this tough essay
> Stretch him out longer.

Despite the ending, I managed to get a decent mark on the paper. I probably wouldn't have kept it all this time otherwise.

Now, almost forty-five years later, I'm here to talk to you and share with you something I wrote, which is a bit more original: my first mystery novel, *Red Rover*. When Jean Hillabold told me that this event would be more than just a reading, I explained to her that I am not an academic, nor am I an expert on the mystery genre. So what I'm going to share with you is information on how this book came to be; more specifically, what my major influences were, literary and otherwise, why I made certain decisions about the book, and what sort of process I followed in order to reach the final draft.

I haven't always been a fan of mystery novels. I read a few Nancy Drew books when I was young, but over the years my interests were elsewhere. Until the last ten or fifteen years, TV was where I had the most exposure to crime stories. That started in the late 1950s with shows like *Dragnet* and *Perry Mason*. Like other viewers, I watched for the entertainment value, for the fun of following the clues along with whichever detective was hot on the trail, secure in the knowledge that justice would prevail in the end. I still enjoy nothing better than curling up in front of the TV to watch my favourite detectives save the day, although now you can't count on a happy ending as in the past.

It's quite a leap, however, from watching TV mysteries to writing a mystery novel, and I ended up covering the space with many short steps, some of them seeming to go off in totally different directions. From about the age of 20, I had a vague interest in writing. That resulted in a handful of bad poems during my student days, and later some songs and a couple of plays and short stories. These all ended up packed away in a box, possibly the same one that contains the *Lear* essay. The only thing I have ever had a burning desire to write is my grandmother's story. She immigrated to Saskatchewan from England in 1904, and in her old age she wrote down her memories of that move using dime store writing pads and scraps of paper. I'm the lucky custodian of that material, along with hundreds of her poems. I have always intended to do something with it, but because of the depth and scope of the story, I knew that in order to do it justice, I would first have to experience something of life myself. I am now finally getting down to work on it. I think I've lived enough to qualify.

After receiving my B.A., and with my writing plans on hold, I attended Theatre School in England. As one might expect, I was immersed in things like character development, relationships and dialogue, but I learned some things I hadn't anticipated. I was fortunate to study literature with a brilliant woman and Thomas Hardy scholar named Jean Brooks. She guided us through *The Iliad, The Odyssey, The Aeneid*, and on through the ages. Eventually she introduced us to two writers who have become my favourites: Thomas Hardy, of course, and Virginia Woolf. Jean Brooks taught me to appreciate the cinematographic nature of Hardy's novels and to marvel at Woolf's amazing skill with language, as I grew to know her characters and their stories through her compelling use of stream of consciousness. Those things have remained with me, sometimes buried deep in my subconscious, other times surfacing to provide practical applications.

To give you a specific example of this, I refer to the beginning of *Red Rover*. When I received notes from my editor, one of the things she wanted me to work on was the first chapter. I had written it very chronologically, with Calli, the main character, getting up in the morning and eventually ending up at her office, where the case is introduced. My editor explained that it would be perfect for the opening of a film, when the credits are running, but in a book, it just took too long to get to the point. Of course she was right.

My revisions of that section would have been much more challenging had she not said, "Think of Mrs. Dalloway going to buy flowers." That was the key (apologies to Virginia). I took all of Chapter One and part of Chapter Two, chopped them up, reorganized them, and put them back together. The resulting Chapter One begins with Calli entering her office. There is a brief introduction to the case followed by a trip through the neighbourhood to pick up coffee. During that short journey the reader learns not only about the setting, but also about Calli and her perception of her new client.

The question still remains: how did I end up writing a mystery novel? Not only that, but how did the novel end up having a lesbian protagonist? My little steps continued. When I came out in the late 1990s, as is common with most people in that situation, I was looking for reflections of my new reality, not only in daily life, but also in the arts; in fact, wherever I could find validation. As it turned out, during the 1980s and 1990s there had been a boom in gay and lesbian mystery novels, and somehow I caught wind of it.

I visited This Ain't the Rosedale Library, the bookstore that was on the main drag in Toronto's "gaybourhood." Unfortunately it has since gone the way of many independent bookstores. On that first visit the owner recommended two writers: Sandra Scoppettone and Ellen Hart. Scoppetone soon after stopped writing her Lauren Laurano series, saying that she was finding the first person point of view too restricting.

Ellen Hart is still going strong, and I recently got a kick out of becoming one of her Facebook friends.

Reading those books made me feel as if I'd found a literary home, and within a couple of years I'd read every novel in their respective series. The characters had become my friends, and although the books were obviously fiction, I had found something to which I could relate, in the middle of a very straight world. I remember feeling a great sense of loss, when I finished the last books by those writers then available.

Fortunately by that time the Internet was a part of my life, so of course I did some research. I discovered a large number of novels— mysteries and other genres—that were the result of gay and lesbian publishing houses having been established in the 1970s. There were some great books, and lots that weren't, but I didn't care as long as there was a lesbian in sight. As time went on, however, my reading of queer writing became more discerning. It was about then that I began questioning whether or not it would be possible for me to write something that could also reach publication.

Years passed, and I continued to read, mostly mysteries, some mainstream, some lesbian and gay. I found new favourite mystery writers such as Patricia Cornwell, her dense novels full of her first-hand knowledge of forensic pathology, and my favourite Canadian writer of lesbian mysteries, Alex Brett. Unfortunately she's written only two novels in the scientifically-based Morgan O'Brien Series. Joseph Hansen's Dave Brandstetter Series gave me insight into how effective the description of setting can be, and Anthony Bidulka's Russell Quant Series assured me that humour is still alive and well in the genre. It was also due to Bidulka that I chose my publisher.

While I was doing all of this reading, crime series were taking over prime time spots on TV: the *Law and Order*s and *CSI*s, and in recent years those with a humorous spin like *Bones* and *Castle*.

Everything I read or saw was seeping into the dark, unused recesses of my brain, but I still had no plans to actually write a mystery. I was busy, too busy, most of the time. The high school where I taught is very academic, and my life revolved around marking. Thanksgiving weekend was always devoted to marking short stories. Every Christmas holiday was *Romeo and Juliet* essays. March Break was more short stories and sometimes *Macbeth* essays, and on it went.

Then in the second semester of the 2003–04 school year there was a change in my timetable. I was asked to teach Grade 12 Writers Craft for the first time. As I took those eager students through the various reading and writing exercises, that little voice in my head started nagging me. This time it sounded much more positive. Maybe I could actually write something. The big question at that point was, what would I write? I didn't have the time or the resources to get started on a project as big as my grandmother's story. But what else did I have to say?

Then I asked myself the pivotal question: what do I like to read? The answer was simple: mysteries. Being a bit of a procrastinator, however, I didn't dive right into the challenge. Instead, I set about researching the structure and content of novels that fell within the parameters of the mystery genre. Much of what I encountered was familiar to me, based on the novels I'd read. Even so, what was being said about red herrings, following the clues, being honest with your reader, character types, sub-genres, point of view and so on had my full attention. Not only did I read everything I could find on the subject, I made copious notes. When I'd finished, I put them all away. Yes, possibly they're in that box with *Lear* and all my other writing attempts.

Research done, it was time to start writing. I had no outline, no idea where I would go with a plot. The only things I did know at that time were that it would be set in Toronto, since it was easy for me to be authentic with the setting, and that my main character would be a woman, who just happened to be a lesbian. Once again, I chose what I knew.

I would like to stress that my writing process is not necessarily one I would recommend. I admire people who can make a detailed outline, but I rarely know from one scene to the next what my main character will encounter in her daily life or in relation to the mystery. If I were writing in third person, perhaps that more omniscient perspective would allow me a more expansive view of the plot. I did, in fact, start writing *Red Rover* in third person, but it wasn't working for me, or for my characters. Once I'd settled on first person, I was able to move forward, short-sighted as that movement was.

I don't even have an idea of the crime, until it presents itself, and about three quarters of the way through, the end of the novel starts to take shape in my mind. I sometimes have an idea of issues I might want to explore, but the themes, symbols and overall structure develop as the book grows. Although this process—or lack of process—is often unnerving, it is also very exciting, because every page is full of surprises for me. There is nothing better than reaching a point where out of the blue a connection to something a hundred pages prior appears. Or hitting a brick wall and then having an "Of course!" or an "Ah ha!" moment. I try not to edit myself as I write early drafts. My motto is, "I can always change it later."

When I began to write *Red Rover*, I didn't have a computer with a decent word processing program, and so I wrote the entire first draft by hand. I still prefer to work that way; it feels like I have a more direct connection with the words. If you've been keeping track of some of the dates I've been mentioning, you'll realize that it took me a long time to write the novel, slightly over five years. That was because I only wrote during my summer holidays, and never for the full two months. The only thing that really bothered me about this long process was my bad memory. Each summer I had to go back to the beginning of the book, because I couldn't remember the details. And every time I did this, I felt compelled to revise. Huge portions of the book were changed beyond recognition, which was good.

The positive aspects of my extended process far outweighed the negative, however. Each year I approached the work with fresh eyes, each year I came to the manuscript with new ideas, and for some reason, each year my writing skills seemed to be better. It was during the later years that a few sections of the book appeared fully formed on the page. These sections immediately felt right, which is unusual. My editor didn't even suggest revisions. Chapter Fifteen is the best example of this. Calli has had a rough day, and she has the sudden urge to visit her mother. The chapter doesn't move the plot forward, but it does reveal some very important details about Calli's background, specifically referring to her father and their relationship. This information is new not only to the reader, but also to the character. The chapter is a moment of calm insight before all hell breaks loose in the plot.

Something else that was developing during those later years was a clarification in my mind of what I wanted the novel to be. Yes I had my lesbian PI, she had her colourful sidekick, she had at least one major flaw, a hobby, a pet, and humour was thrown in for good measure. Although I had chosen to include those aspects of "the formula," I wanted to go beyond that. I pushed the humour into the realm of camp on occasion, which traditionally has been more associated with gay mystery writers and their male protagonists. I did things structurally that I knew were chancy, but because for me the mystery was just a vehicle for exploring people and relationships, I felt it was worth the risk.

At least one book that I had read on mystery writing had warned against beginning with a prologue. Not only did I choose to have a prologue, but I put the prologue in the third person, and I linked it to several of Calli's dreams, which are scattered throughout the book. Not stopping there, I chose to change verb tense for the dreams and put them in the present. None of these short sections are needed for the mystery plot, but they are useful in uncovering Calli's demons.

Another thing I did was experiment with tone. About halfway through the book the humour fades into the background as the conflicts become not only more serious, but also more sinister.

I didn't have the final title for the book until about a year before it was finished, and it popped into my head because of one of the dream sequences. Although I'd always wanted *Red Rover* to be the first book in a series, it wasn't until I had the title that a unifying idea for the series appeared to me. Red is the colour of the first stripe on the rainbow flag, and it stands for courage. This is appropriate since throughout the novel Calli is not only testing her courage, but also seeking it. The second book in the series, *Oranges and Lemons*, is based on orange, which in the flag and in the novel represents possibilities.

I'm sure that almost everything I have said so far about the book makes it sound as if my goal is to write queer novels. Ultimately, I would like *Red Rover* and other books in the series to be known as mystery novels that just happen to have a lesbian detective. Yes, I do deal with issues like homophobia in this novel and same-sex marriage in the next, but those are just aspects of broader, more universal concerns. Relationships between parents and children, friends and lovers, transcend the boundaries of orientation, as do the rights of individuals or minorities within society.

Keeping in mind my desire not to be pigeonholed, I took another risk, this one with characters. I purposely used some stereotypes, particularly with Calli's sidekick, Dewey, and in the butch-femme dynamic between Calli and Jess, but as with all stereotypes, they are founded on truth. Since I was not appropriating voice, I had a broad palette from which to choose the colouring of my characters. Hopefully that enabled me to go beyond the stereotypes and end up with well-rounded and individualized human beings.

I not only wanted to make Calli human, I wanted her to be a reluctant heroine. In addition to her wandering eye and a love for caffeine, her baggage includes a fear of conflict tied to an anxiety disorder, which developed due to problematic relationships with her parents. Hence the main sub-plot is Calli's personal journey through an emotional minefield, which is planted when she feels compelled to take the Spencer case, a search for a missing teenage lesbian.

For me, Calli's journey is much more important than the solving of the case, and although by the end of the novel, Calli has made progress in her psychological marathon, she has, due to the events in the novel, developed new personal challenges.

As you can tell, I had many things I was sorting through during the gestation period of the novel. I'm glad that there was no pressure, and there were no expectations on me. It was an enjoyable challenge that I had set myself. By the summer of 2009, however, I felt I'd spent enough of my time on the project, so I created a deadline: the manuscript would either be ready to send to a publisher by the time I went back to school in September, or I would put it away in my box of late, great writing efforts. I'm glad to say I managed to meet my deadline, and *Red Rover* didn't end up in the box.

# The University of Regina Queer Initiative (URQI) In and Out Speakers Series: 2007–2012

JANUARY 19, 2007
*Jean Hillabold (Faculty of Arts, English)*
The Christian Martyr and the Pagan Witness
in *The Well of Loneliness*

MARCH 2, 2007
James McNinch (Faculty of Education)
"Que(e)rying" the University Classroom

MARCH 23, 2007
*Randal Rogers (Faculty of Fine Arts, Interdisciplinary Studies)*
Of Bodies and Blood: Queer Citizenship Between
9/11 and *The Passion of the Christ*

SEPTEMBER 28, 2007
*Carla Blakley (pastor at Christ Lutheran Church, Regina)*
Que(e)r(y)ing the Image of God

OCTOBER 19, 2007
*Darci Anderson (Faculty of Graduate Studies
and Research, Political Science)*
The Search for Form: Testimony and Fiction
on the Settler Colonial Landscape

FEBRUARY 27, 2008
*Don Cochrane, professor emeritus (Faculty of
Education, University of Saskatchewan)*
Chinese University Students' Perceptions on Gay and Lesbian Issues

MARCH 7, 2008
*Charity Marsh (Faculty of Fine Arts, Interdisciplinary Studies)*
Lez Girls Part One: Representations of Desire on
*The L Word* or Why All the Girls Love Shane

MARCH 28, 2008
*James McNinch (Faculty of Education)*
Queering Seduction: Reflections on the
Construction of a Gay Teaching Identity

OCTOBER 3, 2008
*Charity Marsh (Faculty of Fine Arts, Interdisciplinary Studies)*
What It Feels Like for a Girl: The Transgressions and
Triumphs of Madonna's Imaginary Cyborgs

OCTOBER 17, 2008
*Kelly Handerek (Faculty of Fine Arts, Theatre)*
"akimbo of thoughts"

NOVEMBER 14, 2008
*Wes D. Pearce (Faculty of Fine Arts, Theatre)*
"I Won't Discuss Who I'm Dating": Same Sex Gossip as Social Control

JANUARY 30, 2009
*Nils Clausson (Faculty of Arts, English)*
"Hours Continuing Long" as Walt Whitman's
Rewriting of Shakespeare's Sonnet 29

FEBRUARY 13, 2009
*Troni Grande (Faculty of Arts, English)*
She-Tragedy, He-Comedy, and the Very
Queer Problem of (the) Woman

APPENDIX

MARCH 27, 2009
*James McNinch (Faculty of Education) and Krista*
*Baliko (Faculty of Graduate Studies, IDS)*
Race, Space and the Two Spirit Place

OCTOBER 23, 2009
*Wes D. Pearce (Faculty of Fine Arts, Theatre)*
Bridging Pedagogy and Practice: *The Laramie Project,*
Lord Byng Secondary School, and Community

NOVEMBER 6, 2009
*André Grace (Faculty of Education, University of Alberta)*
Camp fYrefly: Linking Research to Advocacy in Com-
munity Work with Sexual-Minority Youth

NOVEMBER 27, 2009
*Jes Battis (Faculty of Arts, English)*
No Sex in the Made-Up City: Queer Adolescence
in David Levithan's *Boy Meets Boy*

OCTOBER 22, 2010
A reading of Harvey Fierstein's *On Tidy Endings* (with excerpts
from *The Normal Heart, The Hope Slide,* and *Angels in America*)
Organized by Nils Clausson (Faculty of Arts, English)
and Wes D. Pearce (Faculty of Fine Arts, Theatre)
*This event was to commemorate the 25th Anniversary*
*of the founding of AIDS Regina*

FEBRUARY 18, 2011
*Jes Battis (Faculty of Arts, English)*
Queering the Siglo de Oro: Cosmo Pérez and
Comic Theatre in Renaissance Madrid

MARCH 4, 2011
*Caitlyn Jean McMillan (M.F.A. candidate, Faculty of*
*Graduate Studies and Research, Visual Arts)*
Repressed Identities: A Travelling Exploration
of Sexuality, Gender and Place

APPENDIX

## MARCH 18, 2011
*Terry Goldie (Faculty of Arts, English, York University)*
Gay, Straight and In-Between:
John Money and Homosexuality

## SEPTEMBER 30, 2011
*Jean Hillabold (Faculty of Arts, English)*
Blood on the Page: First Menstruation in
Two Coming-of-Age Narratives

## OCTOBER 20, 2011
*Gary Varro (artistic director of Queer City Cinema)*
WideOpenWide

## NOVEMBER 17, 2011
*Kelly Handerek (Faculty of Fine Arts, Theatre)*
*and Byrna Barclay (award-winning author)*
Selections from *The Music of Swans* (a play in progress)

## MARCH 9, 2012
*Laurie Sykes Tottenham (Faculty of Arts, Psychology)*
Sexual Orientation and Prenatal Sex Hormone Exposure:
Current Understanding and Future Directions

## APRIL 5, 2012
*Randal Rogers (Faculty of Fine Arts, Interdisciplinary Studies)*
Birth Rights (and Wrongs): the Queer Biopolitics of a
Very Straight Story (or Being, Born in Blood)

# Contributors

**JES BATTIS** is an assistant professor in the Department of English at the University of Regina. He teaches in the areas of speculative fiction, Restoration literature, and queer studies. He is also the author of the Occult Special Investigator series with Ace Books.

**LIZ BUGG** was born and raised in Regina. After being one of the first graduates from the University of Regina Drama Department she continued her studies at the Rose Bruford College of Speech and Drama in England where she received a three-year diploma in acting and teaching. She later earned an M.Ed. in Arts Education from the University of Toronto (OISE). In 2010 after many years of acting professionally and over twenty years of teaching high school English, Drama and Music, Liz's first novel, *Red Rover*, was published by Insomniac Press and won a Goldie Award in the Debut Author category from the Golden Crown Literary Society. *Red Rover* was followed by two more novels in the Calli Barnow Series, *Oranges and Lemons* (2012) and *Yellow Vengeance* (2013). Liz currently lives in Toronto where she continues to write, teach, and act.

**DONALD COCHRANE** is professor emeritus in the College of Education, University of Saskatchewan. His research interests centre on the intersection of ethics and education. His fourth-year elective course "Gay and Lesbian Issues in Education," taught initially in 1998, was the first course approved in the university to be devoted exclusively to sexual minority issues. For fifteen years, he has been the chief organizer of the university's Breaking the Silence conference (http://www.usask.ca/education/breaking-the-silence/). He has co-edited four books in philosophy of education and co-authored *Ethics in School Counseling* (1995). With his colleague Melanie Morrison, he has completed a research study that assessed Saskatchewan high school students' perceptions of how homophobic they believe their schools are for their GLBQ peers. He has made over forty presentations in schools, universities, and youth groups based on this study.

**NILS CLAUSSON** received his Ph.D. from Dalhousie University and, after spending two years as a research associate at the Disraeli Project at Queen's University and teaching English at several universities, he arrived at the University of Regina in 1984. His main research interests are Victorian and early twentieth-century English literature, with a particular interest in Arthur Conan Doyle. Nils teaches drama and has been active in Regina's theatre community since 1989, both producing and directing plays. He has served as the theatre coordinator of the Cathedral Village Arts Festival for many years and was chair of the Festival in 2008 and 2009. He has a long history in the gay rights movement and was an original member of the Gay Alliance for Equality in Halifax when it formed in 1972.

**TERRY GOLDIE** teaches gender and sexuality studies at York University. He is the author of *Fear and Temptation: The Image of the Indigene in Canadian, Australian and New Zealand Literatures* (1989); *Pink Snow: Homotextual Possibilities in Canadian Fiction* (2003); and *Queersexlife: Autobiographical Thoughts on Sexuality, Gender and Identity* (2008); and the editor of *In a Queer Country: Gay and Lesbian Studies in the Canadian Context* (2001). His next book will be *The Man Who Invented Gender: John Money*.

**ANDRÉ P. GRACE** is a Killam professor and director of the Institute for Sexual Minority Studies and Services in the Faculty of Education, University of Alberta. In SSHRC-funded research over the past decade, André has examined the positionalities and needs of sexual and gender minority (SGM) students and teachers. He has also studied educational interest groups and their political and sociocultural impacts on inclusion and accommodation of sexual and gender minorities in education and culture. He is co-founder of Camp fYrefly, a summer leadership camp for SGM youth, and national consultant on SGM issues for the Canadian Teachers' Federation. André has also served as an external reviewer for the 2011 and 2012 Chief Public Health Officer's Reports on the State of Public Health in Canada.

**KELLY HANDEREK** has recently returned from a sabbatical that included teaching in London, England, at the Rose Bruford College. While in Los Angeles he was Dramaturge on Garth McLean's play *Looking For Lightning*. Kelly has recently completed a three year term as National Councillor for Canadian Actors' Equity, also serving as co-chair of the Directors committee and a member of the Honours committee. He holds a B.F.A., B.Ed., and M.F.A. from the University of Alberta and is currently a professor in the Faculty of Fine Arts, Theatre Department, at the University of Regina. He is past artistic director of London Ontario's Grand Theatre. His acting and directing work spans the Stratford Festival, Citadel Theatre, A.T.P., National Arts Centre, Neptune Theatre, and the Banff Centre, to name a few. He was one of Uta Hagen's last students attending the H.B. Studio in New York. Kelly grew up in Medicine Hat, Alberta.

**JEAN HILLABOLD** is an instructor in the Department of English, where she has taught first-year courses for over twenty years and will begin teaching Creative Writing in September 2013. She is also one of the consulting editors for the literary journal

*Wascana Review.* Since 1999, her diverse erotic stories have appeared under her pen name, "Jean Roberta," in approximately one hundred print anthologies, two single-author collections and a novella. In 2009, Jean gave a talk on censorship which was televised as part of the Coffeehouse Controversies series at Chapters bookstore. Her former on-line columns include "Sex Is All Metaphors" (based on a line in a poem by Dylan Thomas) for the Erotic Readers and Writers Association. Her twenty-five essays for that site are now available as an e-book from Coming Together, a project that sells erotic fiction to raise funds for charity organizations.

**CAITLYN JEAN MCMILLAN** has now completed her Master of Fine Arts degree, based in large part on the content she included in her presentation for the University of Regina Queer Initiative Speakers Series. She is looking forward to beginning her academic practice looking at sex, gender and sexuality studies alongside her multi-media-based art practice.

**JAMES MCNINCH** is professor and dean of the Faculty of Education at the University of Regina. In 2003 he pioneered the first Canadian undergraduate education course on Schooling and Sexual and Gender Identities. His research includes constructs of masculinity, two-spiritness, queer pedagogy and gay privilege.

**MADELEINE MORRIS** is an author of erotic fiction. She holds an M.A. in Writing from Swinburne University, Australia, and has embarked on a Ph.D. in Creative Writing at a Roehampton University, UK. She lives in Ho Minh City, Vietnam, where she has been teaching and writing for the last twelve years. Her areas of academic study are the metanarrative functions of the "happily ever after" ending and the death of transgression in modern literature.

**WES D. PEARCE** is currently associate dean (undergraduate) for the Faculty of Fine Arts at the University of Regina, where he also teaches design and courses in Canadian Drama and LGBTQ Drama. Since its inception in the fall of 2006 he has coordinated the URQI Speakers series and has thoroughly enjoyed the depth, breadth and range of speakers and topics that have been presented at the series. An active costume and set designer in Canada, he has, over the past fifteen years, designed for a variety of companies across Canada, including Alberta Theatre Projects, Perseph-one Theatre, Western Canada Theatre, Prairie Theatre Exchange and nearly twenty productions for Regina's Globe Theatre. He presently sits on the executives of the Canadian Association for Theatre Research and the Associated Designers of Canada and is a frequent contributor at theatre (and theatre-related) conferences around North America.

**RANDAL ROGERS** is associate dean (graduate and research) in the Faculty of Fine Arts at the University of Regina. He teaches in the areas of media studies, critical theory and art history. While continuing with research on world fairs, increasingly Randal has turned toward media theory and investigating issues in popular culture studies, television, film and media broadly conceived. Developing research on "blood cultures", he is part of an international group of researchers working on multiple aspects of blood in the contemporary period. He is currently working on a monograph of the king of blood—Dexter Morgan.

**JINJIE WANG** completed her masters in the College of Education, University of Saskatchewan, with a thesis entitled "Chinese University Students' Perspectives Toward Their Gay and Lesbian Peers" (2007). She is currently studying for a Master of Arts degree in the Department of International Education and Transcultural Studies, Teachers College, Columbia University. Her thesis topic is training Chinese exchange teachers for "cultural intelligence" through peer coaching.